TOBACCO ROAD

TOBACCO ROAD

**DUKE, NORTH CAROLINA, N.C. STATE, WAKE FOREST
and the History of the Most Intense
BACKYARD RIVALRIES IN SPORTS**

ALWYN FEATHERSTON

THE LYONS PRESS
Guilford, Connecticut
An imprint of The Globe Pequot Press

The Lyons Press is an imprint of The Globe Pequot Press.

10   9   8   7   6   5   4   3   2   1

Printed in The United States of America

ISBN 1-59228-915-0

Library of Congress Cataloging-in-Publication Data

Featherston, Alwyn, 1949-
   Tobacco Road : Duke, North Carolina, N.C. State, Wake Forest, and the history of
the most intense backyard rivalries in sports / Alwyn Featherston.
      p. cm.
      ISBN 1-59228-915-0
Basketball teams—North Carolina—History. 2. Sports rivalries—North Carolina—
History. 3. Duke University—Basketball—History. 4. University of North Carolina at Chapel
Hill—Basketball—History. 5. North Carolina State University—Basketball—History. 6. Wake
Forest University Basketball—History. I. Title.
   GV885.72.N8F43 2006
   796.323'6309756—dc22
                                                        2005028849

TABLE OF CONTENTS

PROLOGUE

Sunday, March 6, 2005 was a special day on Tobacco Road.

Across the South, people were enjoying the first warm hints of spring after a long, cold winter. While it was still a bit early for the beach or the swimming pool, the golf courses were crowded and it was warm enough for tennis, biking, or cranking up the backyard barbeque. In the football bastions of Tennessee, Georgia, and Alabama, the talk was all about the start of spring practice. In the big cities of the North and West, the big sports story was baseball's spring training, which was just getting under way in Florida and Arizona.

But in that crescent of North Carolina's Piedmont region, where college basketball is king, all the attention, all the interest, all the excitement that Sunday was focused on the final day of the 2005 Atlantic Coast Conference regular season and two basketball games that were to be played four hours and twenty-five miles apart. The pair of nationally televised contests would match four collegiate neighbors—three of them ranked in the top six in the most recent Associated Press poll—in a renewal of four-way rivalry that has made Tobacco Road famous far beyond the bounds of North Carolina or the ACC.

The CBS crews were at work soon after dawn, setting up in Chapel Hill's Smith Center for the 4 p.m. matchup between No. 2 North Carolina and No. 6 Duke. The network's A-team—consisting of Jim Nantz and Billy Packer—was prepping for a renewal of college basketball's premier rivalry. However, it's likely that Packer, a star guard at Wake Forest in the early 1960s, had a few stray thoughts about his alma mater and the game the No. 4 Deacons would play at 8 p.m. that night against unranked, but dangerous, N.C. State in Raleigh's RBC Center.

The two games were intertwined—and not just by history. North Carolina, emerging from a three-year slump that was its worst stretch in more than fifty years, was on the verge of clinching its fifteenth outright ACC regular season championship. But the Deacons, headed for the winningest season in the school's history, could tie for the title with a Duke win and a victory of its own over the Wolfpack. And the Blue Devils, the ACC's dominant program for almost a decade, could still tie for second in the standings with a win in Chapel Hill and a Wake Forest loss in Raleigh.

Far more important to the North Carolina faithful—by far the largest fan base in the state—was regaining parity with the hated Blue Devils. Duke made the ten-mile bus ride from Durham to Chapel Hill having won fifteen of the previous seventeen games from its old rival. Second-year Tar Heel coach Roy Williams was 0–3 against Mike Krzyzewski since succeeding Matt Doherty on the UNC bench, including a heart-breaking one-point loss in Duke's Cameron Indoor Stadium a month earlier.

Never before in the long history of the rivalry had Duke been so dominant for so long.

"It's definitely something in the back of our minds and it's been a taste that's been sitting in our mouth for a long time," UNC junior David Noel, who grew up in Durham in the shadow of the Duke campus, said. "We're definitely ready to get it out."

By tipoff, the Smith Center was packed with almost 1,000 fans more than its listed capacity of 21,572. As the Duke coach walked through the tunnel from the visiting locker room to the court, a fan above him dangled a plastic bag of cheese in his face (because of his prominent nose, Tar Heel fans have labeled their hated nemesis "Ratface"). Ironically, legendary North Carolina coach Dean Smith was also blessed with a big nose. So was N.C. State's brilliant coach Jim Valvano. Could the relationship between a prominent proboscis and great coaching acumen be more than a coincidence?

Krzyzewski was certainly doing one of his greatest coaching jobs, guiding a team stripped of two prospective starters by the NBA draft and crippled by injuries into a team of national prominence as the 2005 season wound toward its conclusion. And even with injured point guard Sean Dockery beside him on the bench, Coach K kept the Blue Devils close to the powerful Tar Heels through the first half in Chapel Hill.

Late in the half, the Duke coach exploded when he thought the officials at the scorer's table were slow to buzz in a substitute. His tantrum evoked memories of Dean Smith's similar tirade twenty-one years earlier, when he thought the Duke scorers were slow to buzz in one of his subs. Taking matters into his own hands, Smith reached across the scorer's table and tried to push the buzzer. Instead, he hit another button and gave his team a quick twenty-point boost on the scoreboard.

On this occasion, veteran official Larry Rose stopped by the scorer's table to see what was going on and was taunted by a fan in the second row. Rose ordered a UNC security guard to eject the heckler, not knowing that it was Scott Williams, the son of the Tar Heel coach and a former walk-on at UNC under Smith.

The elder Williams had problems of his own. The game UNC had to win seemed to be spinning out of control for the Tar Heels. Three straight inside baskets by Duke's Shelden Williams—a player Williams recruited hard when at Kansas and Doherty tried to recruit at UNC—pushed the Blue Devil lead to six with four minutes to play. A three-pointer by Lee Melchionni (the son of a Duke point guard who engineered three straight homecourt victories over the Tar Heels more than thirty years earlier) put the visitors on top 73–64 with just three minutes left.

"I thought we played beautiful basketball for about thirty-seven minutes," Melchionni said. "But the game is forty minutes and we just couldn't close it out."

Memories of past Duke-UNC comebacks appeared to echo through the Smith Center as junior center Sean May brought the Tar Heels back. It was thirty-one years ago that Walter Davis banked in his buzzer-beater to cap a UNC rally that made up eight points in seventeen seconds. Eleven years later, Duke erased exactly the same eight-point deficit in exactly the same seventeen-second span when Jeff Capel threw in a midcourt shot in Cameron.

This comeback was not nearly so dramatic. But as Duke went scoreless over the last three minutes, UNC began to chip at the nine-point lead. A three-point play by May cut the margin to two points with ninety seconds to play. The Tar Heels missed a chance to tie when Williams blocked away a shot by UNC point guard Ray Felton, but with less than fifty seconds left, Noel knocked the ball away from Duke senior Daniel Ewing and for several agonizing seconds, players from both teams scrambled on the floor to claim it.

It's amazing how many times in the last decade that a Duke-Carolina matchup would come down to a scramble for a loose ball. In 1996 in the Smith Center, a mediocre Duke team was on the verge of a monumental upset when Chris Collins—now an assistant coach to Krzyzewski—got to a loose ball first, but could not call time-out before he was tied up by UNC's Dante Calabria. The possession arrow favored UNC and Calabria scored the game-winning basket on a follow shot. A year later in Durham, almost exactly the same thing happened, only this time the arrow favored Duke and Trajan Langdon hit the game-clinching three-pointer. The two most recent games in Cameron also turned on loose balls: Duke's J.J. Redick beating Rashad McCants to the ball to protect a narrow Blue Devil lead in 2004, and Noel kicking a loose ball out of bounds in February as the Tar Heels tried to set up the game-winning shot.

This time the possession arrow favored Duke, but UNC's Felton got there first and, unlike Collins in 1996, he got the time-out called. The ensuing possession would turn into a four-point play for the Tar Heels as Felton hit the first of two free throws, missed the second, and saw freshman Marvin Williams rebound the miss and convert it into a three-point play. Duke, suddenly down two, got the sharp-shooting Redick a three-point look at the other end—but the ball clanked off the rim, and after a desperation follow shot by Daniel Ewing also missed, the Tar Heel fans were able to rush the court to celebrate the long-awaited victory over the Blue Devils.

Williams wanted to celebrate something else. He fought to clear the court.

"Folks, I like the fact that you're out here, but please get off the floor," Williams pleaded over a courtside microphone. "We're going to have a party. We're going to cut down the nets."

The net-cutting ceremony was brought to Tobacco Road more than a half-century earlier by N.C. State coach Everett Case, but was usually reserved for celebrating tournament titles.

There was considerable outrage in the bowels of the RBC Center, where the Fox TV crews and early arriving media for the N.C. State–Wake Forest game had paused in their pregame preparations to watch the finish of the Duke-UNC classic. The TV working groups were loaded with Tar Heel fans who cheered UNC's triumph, but the tradition-bound reporters were a bit taken aback by Williams's twisting of Tobacco Road tradition. They didn't realize that Williams's action was an eerie echo of a similar celebration fifty-two years earlier, when first-year UNC coach Frank McGuire cut down the nets in Reynolds Coliseum to mark a monumental regular-season victory over N.C. State.

Still, the net-cutting controversy was a minor issue in Raleigh. The big question was whether or not the N.C. State–Wake Forest game would seem like an anticlimax after the thriller in Chapel Hill. The game now meant little to the Deacons, locked into second place in the ACC standings no matter the outcome. For N.C. State, scrambling to bolster its credentials for the NCAA selection committee, the game could be postseason life-or-death.

The Wolfpack season, which began with such high hopes and peaked at No. 12 in the AP rankings in December, was tarnished by a parade of injuries and illnesses as the New Year opened. The Pack lost nine of twelve games during one nightmarish stretch but had recovered to win four of its last five heading into the finale against the Deacs.

The nearly 20,000 fans who packed the six-year-old RBC Center—a plush public facility that N.C. State shares with the NHL Carolina Hurricanes—all knew that an upset of Wake Forest would go a long way toward securing a fourth straight NCAA Tournament bid. That was important at a school acutely conscious of its basketball heritage. Banners hanging from the RBC ceiling honored N.C. State's two national championship teams, its ten ACC title teams, and such great players as David Thompson, Ronnie Shavlik, and Tommy Burleson.

Those reminders of the Pack's heritage seemed a silent rebuke of Fox commentator Mike Gminski, who had denigrated N.C. State's basketball history during a broadcast a year earlier. It was typical for Tobacco Road that Wake Forest grad Packer would be broadcasting the Duke-UNC game, while Gminski, a star center at Duke in the late 1970s, would be the analyst at the N.C. State–Wake Forest game.

Very early in the game, Gminski would have something shocking to analyze. Wake Forest was leading 16–12 after eight minutes, when Wolfpack star Julius Hodge dropped to the floor, withering in agony. It wasn't clear what had happened until Fox reran the sequence in slow motion. The cameras revealed Deacon star Chris Paul delivering a vicious and unprovoked punch to Hodge's groin.

None of the three officials saw the blow. Even though NCAA rules allow the refs to use replays to determine if a punch was thrown, no check was made and no action was taken against Paul as Hodge was helped from the floor. Not many fans at the RBC Center saw what happened—but one who did was Hodge's older brother, Steve, who rushed the court and physically confronted Paul. Two police officers grabbed the irate Wolfpack fan. As they escorted him out of the arena, N.C. State Athletics Director Lee Fowler intervened, directing Hodge's brother and the rest of his family to his own private box. Fowler, who had seen a replay of the blow, wasn't ready to let the matter rest. The tall, normally placid Wolfpack athletic boss stormed into the Deacon locker room at halftime and screamed at Wake Forest coach Skip Prosser.

In the media room at the break, reporters watched the punch replayed over and over, wondering where it fit in the long pantheon of Tobacco Road pugilism. As a cheap shot, it may have been worse than the sucker punch future NBA exec Donnie Walsh threw in the middle of the historic Art Heyman–Larry Brown fight in 1961. It was definitely more significant than the confrontation between UNC's Tony Radovich and N.C. State's Davey Gotkin in the first ACC Tournament, but not quite as bloody as the showdown between Wake Forest's Dave Budd and N.C. State's Anton Muehlbauer in the 1960 ACC Tournament.

Paul's blow would take on tremendous significance in the next few days. But as the second half started in Raleigh, the sophomore point guard was still on the court and very much in control as the Deacons and the fired-up Pack dueled with the same intensity the Duke-UNC game showed earlier in the day. In fact, some Wolfpack fans let their intensity carry them too far; a handful of students behind the Wake Forest bench, angered by Paul's low blow, began to taunt the Wake Forest star with cracks about his grandfather, who was tragically murdered when Paul was in high school.

The majority of the Wolfpack faithful were content to boo their latest villain every time he touched the ball. And with the clock winding down, it appeared that their passion would be rewarded. N.C. State built a three-point lead with twenty-two seconds left before Justin Gray, one of the best clutch shooters in modern ACC history, tied the game with a remarkable three-pointer from just in front of the Deacon bench.

N.C. State attempted to play for the last shot. With 5 seconds left, Turkish guard Engin Atsur launched a three-point try from the top of the key. Replays clearly showed that he was hit on the wrist as he launched the shot—an eerie echo of a controversial foul that helped the University of Connecticut edge N.C. State in the 2002 NCAA Tournament. This time no foul was called and the air ball went out of bounds to the Deacons with 4.2 seconds left.

Eight years earlier, N.C. State's C.C. Harrison hit a controversial buzzer beater to upset Wake Forest in Winston-Salem and cost the Deacons an ACC regular season championship. There wasn't as much at stake on this occasion, but it's impossible to measure the pain Paul caused the Wolfpack nation as he took an inbounds pass from Lithuanian forward Vytas Danelius and streaked the length of the court. He threw in an off-balance ten-footer at the buzzer and raced off the court to the crescendo of boos from 20,000 angry fans.

"I can't explain it," a tearful Hodge told reporters after the game. "I got punched in the groin by Chris Paul. I would never do anything dirty like that."

Paul arrogantly denied the accusation.

"The little mishap between me and Julius Hodge?" Paul laughed. "I don't believe I popped him. It was just a part of the game."

Indeed, such moments are very much a part of the game of basketball on Tobacco Road. In the next week after that remarkable Sunday, N.C. State and Wake Forest would meet again with dramatically different results. Seven days after watching UNC cut down the nets in Chapel Hill, Duke would cut down a different set of twine at the ACC Tournament in Washington, D.C.

That's the beauty of basketball on Tobacco Road. Past, present, future: they are all are connected by what Abraham Lincoln called "the mystic chords of memory." From Everett Case to Bones McKinney to Dean Smith to Mike Krzyzewski, all four schools on Tobacco Road intertwined their hopes and dreams to build a tradition that's unmatched in college basketball.

Sunday, March 6, 2005 was indeed a remarkable day—but just one of many, many remarkable days on Tobacco Road.

TOBACCO ROAD

1

THE FOUNDING FATHERS

YOU WON'T FIND TOBACCO ROAD ON ANY MAP. IT'S NOT EVEN clear where it starts and where it ends. Would you include Wilmington, where Michael Jordan played high school ball and grew up dreaming of playing for N.C. State? If so, then you need to stretch the road across the state to tiny Newland in the Appalachian Mountains, where a young Tommy Burleson was more interested in 4-H than the Big Four. Curve the road back around to Shelby in the southwestern corner of the state to pick up the home of the incomparable David Thompson at the end of a long dirt road, run east through Gastonia, where James Worthy learned the game, and be sure to keep going past Laurinburg near the South Carolina border, where Charlie, pardon me, Charles Scott first attracted Dean Smith's interest. Only then can you turn north and head past Fayetteville—home of Rusty Clark, Van Williford, and Robert Brickey—for the Raleigh-Durham-Chapel Hill Triangle, the heart and soul of Tobacco Road.

In this place, the remarkably compact region of North Carolina's populous Piedmont, college basketball was born in the South and grew to mythic proportions. Four schools, originally all located within a thirty-mile radius, nurtured the sport in the early days of the twentieth century. Their rivalries were a regional phenomenon at first. But in trying to outdo each other, the four neighboring schools drove each other to greater and greater heights and turned the term "Tobacco Road" into a shorthand for the nation's college basketball heartland.

It didn't start out that way. Originally, *Tobacco Road* was the title of an Erskine Caldwell novel about poor, rural degenerates in Georgia. But North

Carolina, not Georgia, is the center of the tobacco industry—and over the years, Caldwell's pejorative term came to be accepted as a description of the four basketball programs that blossomed like the bright leaf in the Carolina soil. It's not clear who first used the term, but by the 1950s it was a standard description in North Carolina newspapers for the schools that also styled themselves as "The Big Four."

Tobacco was very much at the heart of the modern Tobacco Road.

Durham, the home of Duke University, was founded on the tobacco industry. Washington Duke, who built his empire on Bull Durham chewing tobacco, lured tiny Normal College from Randolph County to his new factory town in the late nineteenth century. His son and heir, James Buchanan Duke, endowed what had become Trinity College with a huge gift in 1924—and the school changed its name to Duke University to honor the tobacco magnate.

The new West Campus built with Duke's money was barely eight miles as the crow flies northeast of Chapel Hill, where the University of North Carolina had been educating planters' sons since the eighteenth century. When UNC welcomed its first student in 1796, it became the nation's first state-supported institution of higher learning. It was the largest university in the South before the Civil War—and even though the school suffered a brief decline in the reconstruction era, North Carolina bounced back before the end of the nineteenth century to reclaim its place as one of the nation's premier public institutions.

One of its rivals grew barely twenty miles to the east, where in 1887 North Carolina A&M was founded in the state capital of Raleigh. A land-grant institution, the school quickly became a recognized leader in agricultural science and engineering. Even though the school's student population soon topped its rival in Chapel Hill, N.C. State College only became a university during a bitter reorganization of the state's university system in the mid-1960s. Even then it was a close call: State College almost became the University of North Carolina at Raleigh, but emerged instead as N.C. State University.

Wake Forest, a small private school established by the Baptist State Convention in 1834, was also designated a "college" for most of its history. The smallest of the four schools on Tobacco Road, Wake Forest grew up in the sleepy farming hamlet of the same name, located just north of Raleigh's city limits and equally close to the eastern edge of Durham. The small school remained in the shadow of its neighbors until 1956, when another tobacco giant intervened. The

Smith Reynolds Foundation, based on another tobacco fortune, made a large endowment to the school with the stipulation that Wake Forest move seventy-five miles west to Winston-Salem, a blue-collar Tobacco city very much like Durham. An entire new campus was built, and Wake Forest College in Wake Forest was reborn as Wake Forest University in Winston-Salem.

Coincidentally, the move occurred just as basketball was overtaking football as the most important sport on Tobacco Road.

THE FIRST NATIONAL TITLE

It all started innocently enough. In 1905—fourteen years after Dr. James Naismith came up with his original thirteen rules for the sport in Springfield, Massachusetts—Wake Forest's Richard "Red" Crozier, a student in charge of the school's gymnasium, formed a team to play "basket ball" (as it was usually referred to in those days) against various YMCA and club teams.

His team attracted the interest of a young instructor at Trinity College. Wilber Wade Card—known as Cap after captaining the Trinity baseball team as an undergraduate—had done graduate work at Harvard, where he met Naismith and saw the new game played. Card brought basketball back to Durham, planting the seed that would blossom under Cameron, Bubas, and Krzyzewski.

Card and Crozier arranged for Trinity to play Wake Forest in what was long believed to be the first intercollegiate basketball game played south of the Mason-Dixon line. Some historians believe that Wake Forest may actually have faced a team from Guilford College about a month before the first Trinity–Wake Forest meeting on March 2, 1905, but the evidence is contradictory.

The Wake-Trinity game—played almost exactly a hundred years before the dramatic conclusion of the 2005 regular season—was clearly the first clash of the future Tobacco Road juggernauts. It was played on the undersized court in the Angier Duke Gym on the Trinity Campus, built in 1898 and still standing today on Duke's East Campus. Crozier's more experienced Battling Baptists won that first matchup 24–10 as forward Vanderbilt Couch scored fourteen points to single-handedly outscore the entire Trinity team. Wake Forest would win their first six games in the series before Card's Methodists finally beat their first rivals in 1909.

The other two future Tobacco Road powers were slow to pick up the sport. Neither North Carolina nor N.C. A&M (the future N.C. State) fielded a team until 1911. Basketball had been a part of physical education classes in Chapel

Hill for several years before a student named Marvin Ritch convinced track and field coach Nat Cartmell to put together a team to represent the university. That same year, a faculty committee in Raleigh suggested that the agricultural school form a team in the new sport and The Farmers took the court.

The Tobacco Road rivalries that would become so prominent in the second half of the twentieth century were remarkably slow to form. Wake Forest appeared to be a catalyst: the other three schools may not have played each other, but they all played the Baptists from the beginning. The A&M Farmers played Trinity for the first time in 1912 and a year later took on North Carolina for the first time. But that future rivalry was allowed to lapse and the two state schools wouldn't meet again until after World War I.

North Carolina and Trinity were even slower to ignite what would become the greatest rivalry in college sports. It's not quite clear why the two neighboring schools refused to meet in basketball until 1920—fifteen years after the game sprouted in the state. It's possible that the university in Chapel Hill was upset by Trinity's refusal to field a football team. The Methodist school, alarmed by what it saw as growing professionalism at UNC, had dropped the popular sport in 1895.

Duke and North Carolina finally began to play each other in basketball in the early 1920s, just as North Carolina was beginning to emerge as one of the South's first basketball powers. It really began late in the 1922 season, when the team from Chapel Hill traveled to Atlanta for the inaugural Southern Conference Tournament. The new league, formed earlier that year, included twenty-two teams (many of which would later break off to form the Southeastern and the Atlantic Coast conferences). The league's new tournament—the inspiration for the ACC's famous postseason event—was originally a matter of necessity. There were just too many teams in the league to play a round-robin schedule. UNC—led by the Carmichael brothers, Billy and Cartwright—had to win five tournament games to claim the title, beating such diverse schools as Samford, Newberry, Georgia, Alabama, and Mercer on successive days.

That 1922 triumph would be just the forerunner for UNC's first era of basketball glory. The 1923 team finished 15–1, losing only to Ole Miss in the Southern Conference championship game. And in 1924, as senior Cartwright Carmichael was joined by the talented Jack Cobb and Carolina moved into its new home—an all-metal structure dubbed the Tin Can—the White Phantoms didn't lose at all, winning twenty-six straight games and a second Southern Conference championship.

That 26–0 season also set the stage for the first great Tobacco Road controversy. It stems from a 1942 decision by a committee of basketball historians appointed by the Helms Foundation to retroactively award North Carolina the 1924 national championship. That's an award that the UNC faithful cherish and their Tobacco Road rivals reject out of hand.

Is North Carolina's 1924 championship a valid national title? In the absence of an NCAA playoff, which didn't begin until 1939, it's impossible to tell. UNC was the nation's only major undefeated team that season, but in an era when the best basketball was being played in the East and Midwest, North Carolina played nothing but Southern teams. The Southern Conference champs did not participate in the only national tournament played that season—the AAU championships in Kansas City, won by Butler University. The Indiana school beat a field that included teams from as far away as New York and California and was acclaimed at the time as the nation's best team.

While the exact merits of UNC's 1924 "national championship" are open to debate, there's no doubt that basketball remained a secondary sport on Tobacco Road. Football was still king on Tobacco Road, especially at Duke, which resumed the sport with a vengeance in 1920, building a massive stadium on the new West Campus and hiring celebrated coach Wallace Wade away from Alabama.

Basketball remained on the fringes of the action. All four Tobacco Road programs enjoyed moments of regional success in the late 1920s and through the Depression years—but nothing that attracted the attention of the North Carolina sporting public, much less the national press. It wasn't until the dying days of the 1930s that a very special character would propel the winter sport into the limelight.

BONES

Horace Albert "Bones" McKinney was larger than life, a curious amalgam of basketball ability and comic presence. Take future Tobacco Road products Meadowlark Lemon and Andy Griffith and put them together and you'd have someone like McKinney.

Bones was a 6-foot, 6-inch forward whose weight varied between 174 and 210 pounds, "depending on how much I was a'sweatin'," he said. His slender frame had nothing to do with his nickname, which was derived from a character he played in a school play.

"I don't remember exactly when people started calling me Bones," he recalled. "But with a name like Horace Albert, the sooner the better, right?"

The gangly big man was the centerpiece of the revolutionary style of basketball that Durham High coach Paul Sykes unleashed upon the unsuspecting fans on Tobacco Road. Taking advantage of a 1937 rule change that eliminated the center jump after every made basket, Sykes installed a running game that showcased the talents of his young stars. McKinney was the key to the new strategy, starting fast breaks with his outlet passes after rebounds or even after made baskets—when he would rip the ball out of the net and push it up the court. In an era when winning scores were usually in the thirty- and forty-point range, Durham High routinely topped fifty, sixty, and even seventy points a game.

Sykes's Durham High greyhounds soon became a sensation. After losing the opening game of the 1938–39 season to the Wake Forest freshman team, McKinney and company would win seventy-two straight games over the next three seasons, beating all manner of competition from across the Eastern Seaboard.

"They are a team of basketball professionals masquerading under the name of Durham High," a sportswriter from Daytona, Florida, wrote after Durham routed the Florida state championship team 54–14. Later that season, Sykes's team traveled to Glen Falls, New York (just outside Buffalo), where Durham defeated three of the top teams in the East and was proclaimed the nation's best high school team.

Naturally, the four Tobacco Road coaches cast covetous eyes at the Durham High stars. Duke's Eddie Cameron had the advantage of a new arena and a family connection through burly 6-foot-2 forward Bob Gantt, the son of former Duke baseball star Bob "No-Hit" Gantt. The Blue Devils figured to get the bulk of Sykes's players.

But an incident one night at Duke Indoor Stadium cost Cameron a chance to land Durham High's biggest star.

As Bones used to tell it, his rejection of hometown Duke was due to a campus policeman. You see, when he was young and unknown, he used to sneak into Duke's games. When the Durham High team became famous, Cameron used to leave tickets for all of the team's players to get in for free.

"But I was a stubborn cuss and I didn't like taking the easy way out," Bones explained. "So I kept sneaking into Duke games."

At least he did until one night when a Duke campus cop caught him trying to squeeze his lanky frame through a narrow window into the men's restroom on the first floor of the Indoor Stadium (the one just beside the door where the students now enter). Instead of merely ejecting or perhaps arresting the young trespasser, the policeman sat down, pulled the teenager onto his lap, and delivered a spanking in front of a crowd of jeering college students.

"I was so embarrassed. That's when I decided I'd never play at Duke," he said.

Instead, Bones traveled twenty miles southeast to Raleigh and helped turn a Pack team that had been 8–11 and 6–9 in the two previous seasons into a 15–7 contender that earned a spot in the Southern Conference championship game. Unfortunately for McKinney, that game was against Duke, which featured his former teammates Gantt and two of the three Loftis brothers. The Blue Devils won their second straight Southern Conference title that night, wrapping up a brilliant 22–2 season with a 45–34 victory.

Bones would have to wait four years for his revenge. He left N.C. State after the 1942 season and entered the service. After World War II, he returned—not to Raleigh, but to join Ben Carnevale's burgeoning program at North Carolina. There he teamed with John "Hook" Dillon and Jim Jordan on a team that swept thirteen of fourteen Southern Conference games. Although the White Phantoms (the nickname still being used at that time) were upset by Wake Forest in the Southern Conference Tournament, UNC was selected to represent the league in the eight-year-old NCAA Tournament. McKinney helped Carolina beat New York University and Ohio State to reach the NCAA championship game in New York's Madison Square Garden.

The championship contest turned into a showcase for Oklahoma A&M's Bob Kurland, college basketball's first dominant seven-footer. Kurland started slowly against McKinney's aggressive defense. The White Phantoms were within three points when Ol' Bones fouled out and Kurland was able to take over. The Oklahoma giant scored seven straight points and the Aggies held on for a 43–40 victory over the first Tobacco Road team to reach what would become known as the Final Four.

After the season, Carnevale left UNC to take a better job offer from the Naval Academy—a pretty good indication of the low status that basketball still had on Tobacco Road.

The UNC coach was not the only one to go. McKinney would pass up his final year of collegiate eligibility to join Red Auerbach's Washington Capitals in the fledgling NBA. He would later return to Tobacco Road for a second career as a coach and later still for a third career as a TV commentator. But when McKinney left Chapel Hill in the spring of 1946, it seemed as if a little of the spark had gone out of the game.

Who could have imagined that Bones was only laying the groundwork for the messiah of Tobacco Road basketball?

2

THE GRAY FOX

N.C. STATE TURNED TO EVERETT CASE OUT OF NECESSITY.

The Raleigh school, saddled with a small and inadequate football stadium, was tired of being overshadowed by the football juggernauts at Duke and North Carolina. But when the school's athletic officials explored the possibility of upgrading their program to challenge those of their rivals, they were appalled at the projected cost. Instead, they made a conscious decision to go in a different direction.

If they couldn't beat UNC and Duke at football, why not focus on a cheaper sport—like basketball?

The decision to emphasize the winter sport was made in the days just before World War II. The first step in the plan was the construction of a new basketball arena to replace the aging and inadequate Walter Thompson Gym. The steel frame for the new arena, modeled closely after Duke's Indoor Stadium, began to rise on N.C. State's campus in the fall of 1941. However, construction was halted by the sudden onset of World War II; for the next four years, the bare skeleton of the new arena stood as a reminder of the school's unfulfilled ambition to become a basketball power. H.A. Fisher, the chairman of the school's athletic council, was anxious to restart the school's scheme as soon as the war ended and normalcy returned. He knew N.C. State not only needed to resume construction of its new arena: it also needed to find a new coach capable of guiding the Raleigh school to national prominence. But where would N.C. State find such a coach?

Dick Herbert, the editor of Raleigh's morning newspaper (and, ironically, a Duke graduate) suggested that Fisher ask Chuck Taylor, a former semi-pro basketball star who had made a career of traveling the country and selling Converse products directly to coaches and their teams. In turn, Taylor told Fisher (as related in a 1951 story in the *Saturday Evening Post*), "The best basketball coach in the country is a lieutenant commander in the U.S. Navy. His name is Everett Case."

Case was already famous in Indiana, where he had been one of the most successful and controversial high school coaches in the history of that hoop-crazy state. Hired at age twenty-two to coach hapless Frankfort High School, he led the Frankfort Hot Dogs to state titles in 1925, 1929, 1936, and 1939. However, his success was marred by a series of battles with "King" Arthur Trestler, the head of the Indiana High School Athletic Association, who accused Case of recruiting players and of arranging jobs in Frankfort for their parents. He was twice suspended for recruiting violations—a problem that would crop up again during Case's reign at N.C. State.

The man who would soon be known as the Gray Fox was forty-six years old when he arrived on Tobacco Road at almost the same moment as Bones McKinney was leading North Carolina to the NCAA championship game.

The first thing Case did in Raleigh was to demand the redesign of the arena that existed only as a rusting steel frame just below the railroad tracks that cut through the campus. He didn't want a carbon copy of Duke's now-six-year-old arena. He wanted something bigger . . . much bigger. His experience in Indiana had taught him that the school with the biggest gym hosts the postseason games—and he wanted N.C. State to have the biggest gym. The problem was that the new design had to encompass the already existing steel frame. The only way to increase capacity without prohibitive cost was to extend the two end zone areas. As a result, William Neal Reynolds Coliseum would end up looking like an elongated shoebox with a handful of excellent seats on the sidelines and thousands of bad seats in the end zone.

Still, those seats were there: 12,400 of them in all. The arena had more seats than any arena in the South at that time. When it was finished in 1949, it would remain the largest on-campus arena on Tobacco Road for thirty-seven years. Case would use his huge new arena to showcase basketball to a growing audience in North Carolina.

However, he didn't wait until Reynolds was finished to begin his education of Tobacco Road fans. His first lesson was delivered in his first season, in 1946–47, when he imported six Indiana high school products and instantaneously turned a team that had been 6–12 the year before into a 26–5 juggernaut.

Several of Case's Hoosier Hotshots were service veterans who had refined their games during the war. The best of these was 6-foot-1 Dick Dickey, a Navy veteran from Alexandria, Indiana, who perfected the one-handed jump shot that had only recently been introduced into the college game by Stanford's Hank Luisetti. He was the key to the pressing, fast-break style of ball that Case installed in Raleigh. If Sykes's Durham High teams had run before the war, Case's "Red Terrors," as they were known that first season, sprinted after it. N.C. State scored a school record 83 points in a victory over Duke in 1947 and the next year topped 100 points twice, including an unbelievable 110 points in a 60-point victory over High Point.

That first class also included guard Norm Sloan from Indianapolis, who was disgusted to lose his starting job a year later to another Hoosier import. His replacement, Vic Bubas of Gary, Indiana, was part of a 1948 class that also included another Gary product, Sammy Ranzino. The 6-foot-2 forward would become the first three-time All-American at N.C. State as the Wolfpack (the new nickname officially adopted the year Bubas and Ranzino were freshmen) launched a decade of domination.

Yet, for all Case's success on the court, he was even more successful as a salesman. His product was basketball; his market, the fans on Tobacco Road who had grown up worshipping football and baseball as their primary love. He showed them just how thrilling basketball could be. Much of it was his fast-breaking style of play—a far more entertaining version of the sport than the sedate tempo in vogue before the war. Like the fans who had thrilled to Sykes's running teams at Durham High, thousands more discovered that Case's Hurryin' Hoosiers brought a new dynamic to the game.

"When he brought basketball to North Carolina, he packaged it as a way to make it more attractive to the fans," Bubas said. "Basketball was kind of a second-class citizen at the time. He changed that and everybody else had to keep up."

Case wasn't content to let basketball sell itself. He was a promoter who introduced dozens of frills that we now take for granted. He started the first pep band in the South. When N.C. State won the 1947 Southern Conference Tournament, he introduced Tobacco Road to a tradition that he had invented at Frankfort: cutting down the nets to celebrate a championship. Case introduced the now-familiar pregame introductions. He hung a noise meter from the Reynolds rafters: a long pole with a line of lightbulbs that would light up as the noise reached a crescendo. (Only later would it be revealed that the noise meter was phony; the lights were controlled by a dial that a State official twisted at whim.)

Case also turned himself into an ambassador of the game. He traveled the back roads of North Carolina, speaking to civic groups and occasionally stopping to give away a basketball or one of the hoops that he kept in his trunk. He told his listeners that he dreamed of the day when every young boy in the state would have a basket in the driveway and he could replace his Hoosier mercenaries with homegrown talent.

That day must have seemed very far off when Case started his crusade. Football was never bigger on Tobacco Road than in the years immediately after World War II. Wade was back at Duke after a stint in the service, and the Blue Devils were aiming to recapture their prewar gridiron glory. D.C. "Peahead" Walker had Wake Forest in bowl games in 1946 and 1949. In Chapel Hill, the arrival of swivel-hipped halfback Charlie "Choo Choo" Justice ignited football's Golden Age at the state's flagship university. Justice led UNC to three major bowl games and kicked off a football hysteria that has never been matched on Tobacco Road.

The crowning moment came on November 19, 1949, when more than 57,500 fans packed Duke Stadium to watch Choo Choo and the Tar Heels edge the Blue Devils 21–20. The crowd was the largest ever to see a football game in North Carolina, a record that would stand for more than a quarter century. On that thrilling afternoon in Durham, it seemed as if football would reign as King of Tobacco Road forever.

THE DIXIE CLASSIC

Case, however, had a secret weapon—one that he would unleash exactly five weeks after UNC's dramatic gridiron victory over Duke.

It was a three-day, eight-team basketball tournament that was scheduled for the week after Christmas in his newly opened Reynolds Coliseum. Butter Anderson, Case's lone assistant coach at the time, suggested the name: the Dixie Classic.

But while the name belonged to Anderson, the idea was all Case's. He schemed to appeal to the regional pride of North Carolinians, who often felt left out or ignored when it came to national coverage of sports. The tournament was designed to test the four Tobacco Road teams against four national powers each year.

N.C. State rolled through the University of Rhode Island, Georgia Tech, and Penn State University to win the inaugural Dixie Classic in 1949. Case's Wolfpack also won in 1950, 1951, and 1952. When N.C. State was upset by Navy in the 1953 Dixie Classic semifinals, Duke was there to prevent an outsider from winning, knocking off Ben Carnevale's Midshipmen in the title game. The partisan N.C. State crowd cheered as lustily for Duke's Bernie Janicki and Joe Belmont as they did for State's Bobby Speight and Mel Thompson. The Wake Forest and UNC fans joined the chorus as all so-called "Big Four" fans set aside their bitter rivalries to adopt an us-against-the-world mentality for the holiday tournament.

"What really solidified the Big Four was the Dixie Classic," Bucky Waters, a reserve at N.C. State, said. "I remember we all pulled for each other; we'd even pull for Carolina and Duke and Wake Forest. There was a real synergy to Tobacco Road."

That was what Case wanted. He watched the Tobacco Road fans bond in his big new stadium, growing a passion they didn't know existed. It became a point of pride that no outside school ever won the Dixie Classic: not Iowa, Oregon State, Minnesota, Seton Hall, or Princeton. In 1958, Case brought in No. 2 Cincinnati with Oscar Robertson and No. 7 Michigan State with "Jumpin' Johnny" Green and beat them both. To add to the triumph, North Carolina handed Robertson and the Bearcats a second defeat in the consolation game.

The Dixie Classic rapidly became one bookend to the basketball season. The other was the postseason conference tournament—which was played to decide the Southern Conference title until 1953, and after 1954 used to crown the champion of the new Atlantic Coast Conference.

Case used the Dixie Classic to provide a national stage for all four programs on Tobacco Road. He used the postseason conference tournaments to establish his dominance over his four local rivals. No coach has ever had a run of postseason tournament success quite like the one Case had between his first season in 1947 and his tenth in 1956. In that span, he won six Southern Conference championships and the first three ACC titles—winning twenty-nine of a possible thirty tournament games.

THE NEW CONFERENCE

When seven members of the Southern Conference broke off to form the new Atlantic Coast Conference in the spring of 1953, they were looking for football glory. None could foresee that Case and his rivals were on the verge of making basketball the new league's money sport.

The first ACC Tournament—held March 4–6, 1954 at Reynolds Coliseum—might have provided a clue for the astute observer. Tobacco Road newspapers unanimously predicted that the first day in tournament history would produce four blowouts. Maybe that's why just 6,800 fans showed up for the initial afternoon session. Those lucky spectators got to see an overtime thriller as unheralded South Carolina led favored Wake Forest almost all the way—before sub John Devos hit a shot to force overtime and star Dickie Hemric finally asserted himself as the Deacons advanced with a 57–56 victory.

The 8,500 fans who arrived for the night session saw an even more intense game, matching Case's heavily favored Wolfpack against Frank McGuire's second, and worst, North Carolina team. The outmanned Tar Heels, playing without leading scorer Al Lifson, relied on a packed-in zone in an attempt to neutralize N.C. State's trio of stars: guards Vic Molodet and Mel Thompson and sophomore center Ronnie Shavlik.

Case, disgusted by McGuire's tactics, ordered his guards to hold the ball outside for long stretches at a time, leading the writers at courtside to describe the game as a "walkathon." Case, for once more intent on winning than pleasing the fans, ignored the boos from the crowd as N.C. State nursed a 47–42 lead into the game's final minutes. But the Tar Heels rallied, closing to within one point when Gerry McCabe scored with eleven seconds left. UNC's Tony Radovich then tackled N.C. State's Davy Gotkin, who jumped to his feet and smashed the ball into Radovich's head.

The two benches emptied and pandemonium reigned before the coaches and officials could sort things out. Radovich was ejected for a flagrant foul, and Gotkin was called for a technical. N.C. State managed to hang on for a 52–51 victory that set the tone for a half century of tournament hysteria.

Case's Wolfpack eventually won that first ACC Tournament, edging Wake Forest in overtime in the title game in front of 12,400 screaming fans. The string of thrilling games was a sign of things to come in the ACC Tournament, and the sellout crowds for the final two sessions insured a profit of $72,000—

a sum lucrative enough to assure that the tournament would continue, despite the opposition of seven of the league's eight coaches.

As exciting and as profitable as it proved to be, the three-day tournament wasn't the best sendoff for ACC teams into postseason play—especially in an era when the ACC champion had to play an early-round game, usually in Philadelphia or New York, on Monday night, just forty-eight hours after cutting down the nets in Raleigh.

Case's teams, for all their regular season success, rarely did well in the NCAA Tournament. The Wolfpack coach ignited the passion of North Carolina fans for the winter sport, but it would take another coach at another program to make Tobacco Road a national phenomenon.

3

THE FIRST RIVAL

N.C. STATE'S DOMINATION WAS BECOMING INCREASINGLY FRUS-trating to its rivals on Tobacco Road.

Duke actually beat Everett Case when he first visited Durham, but the Gray Fox would win twelve of the next thirteen games from the Blue Devils. Wake Forest lost thirteen of fifteen to N.C. State; then after three wins in four games in 1953 and 1954, the team went on another ten-game losing streak to the Wolfpack between 1954 and 1957.

It's not as if the two programs were struggling during that period. Duke had a national player of the year in guard Dick Groat. The future Major League shortstop twice led the nation in scoring and once (unofficially) in assists. The Deacons fielded powerful teams built around powerful big man Dickie Hemric, who would end his four-year career as the top scorer in ACC history.

The only team that didn't put up much of a fight in Case's early days was North Carolina. The once-proud Tar Heels saw their program gradually decline after its 1946 success, collapsing with back-to-back losing seasons under Tom Scott in 1951 and 1952. UNC, which had won eight straight from N.C. State before Case's arrival, lost the first fifteen games it played against the Gray Fox. That dramatic reversal didn't make Scott, who was to become one of college basketball's most influential administrators, a popular man in Chapel Hill. North Carolina officials began looking for a replacement who could stand up to their rival.

Ironically, they found him in Reynolds Coliseum.

UNC Athletic Director Chuck Erickson was in the stands on the night of March 21, 1952 when St. John's University of New York manhandled N.C. State's newly crowned Southern Conference champions in the East Regional semifinals. One night later, Erickson was back in his seat in Reynolds, and he watched as the Redmen (as they were known in that politically incorrect age) upset Adolph Rupp's defending national champions, the Kentucky Wildcats, to earn a trip to the Final Four.

Erickson was taken with St. John's slick but fiery young coach, Frank McGuire. He had just proven he could beat Case head-to-head, even on his own turf. And even if his Redmen did fall just short of Kansas in the national title game, McGuire had proven he could win on a national stage.

When McGuire first arrived in Chapel Hill, the Tar Heel faithful didn't quite know what to make of him. The son of an Irish cop, he had grown up in Queens; if his neighborhood was not quite on the mean streets of New York, his bedroom window overlooked them. McGuire used basketball to claw his way up the social ladder, first at Xavier High School then at St. John's. He affected the veneer of a successful businessman. His hand-tailored suits and his flashy cufflinks were his trademark. But the tough, combative New York street kid was never far from the surface.

McGuire ended UNC's fifteen-game losing streak in his very first game against Case and the Wolfpack. By almost sheer force of will, he guided the Tar Heels to a 70–69 victory in Reynolds Coliseum on January 24, 1953. Freshman Jerry Vayda hit an off-balance, left-handed, over-the-head shot with twenty-six seconds left to give UNC the win. The cocky Irish coach celebrated by throwing Case's favorite tradition back in his face—by cutting down the nets in Reynolds, just as Roy Williams would do in the Smith Center fifty-two years later after an equally significant win over Duke.

Case would bounce back to beat McGuire six times in a row (including two lopsided wins later in the 1953 season), but that first encounter gave promise of what was to come. The real rivalry would have to wait until the new UNC coach upgraded his talent.

McGuire, like Case, was a charismatic salesman. And just as Case mined his homeland of Indiana for talent, McGuire stocked his first Tar Heel teams with the best players his home city of New York had to offer. McGuire's Underground Railroad (as it was later labeled by *Sports Illustrated*) first delivered Lennie Rosenbluth, a slender 6-foot-5 Jewish forward from the Bronx, in the fall of 1953. Four Catholic stars would arrive from the city a year later: Pete Brennan, Tommy Kearns, Joe Cunningham, and Joe Quigg.

"The reason I went to North Carolina was Frank McGuire," Kearns said. "In those days, the priests at the Catholic schools up North were reluctant to send transcripts to schools in the South. My parents were worried about it too. Coach McGuire convinced them that we'd be missionaries, going South to convert the Baptists."

Later runs of McGuire's Railroad would bring South such New York stars as Larry Brown, Doug Moe, York Larese, and finally Billy Cunningham. But those first two classes, those four Catholic players and their Jewish teammate, became the heart of McGuire's first great team—and the only perfect team in Tobacco Road history.

"FOUR CATHOLICS AND A JEW"

It would be an exaggeration to suggest that greatness was expected from the 1957 North Carolina Tar Heels: high hopes, yes, but greatness, no.

UNC entered the 1956–57 season with all five starters returning from an 18–5 team. The Tar Heels thought in terms of finally surpassing N.C. State as the ACC's best team. The Pack, dealing with the graduation loss of four senior starters, had star guard John Maglio back as a senior and a strong crop of sophomores, including dazzling guard Lou Pucillo and powerful big man John Ritcher; but the team didn't appear to have the experience to contend with McGuire's patiently constructed squad.

Rosenbluth, the slender Jewish forward from the Bronx, was a star from the moment he stepped on the campus in Chapel Hill. He averaged 25.5 points as a sophomore for a 10–11 team in 1955 and remained the team's top-scoring option a year later, when sophomores Joe Quigg, Pete Brennan, Tommy Kearns, and Joe Cunningham graduated from the freshman team and immediately turned UNC into the second-best team on Tobacco Road.

UNC began the 1956–57 season ranked No. 6 in the first AP poll, just ahead of No. 8 N.C. State. The Tar Heels—getting twenty-eight points a game from Rosenbluth, almost fifteen from Brennan, and double-figure averages from Kearns and Quigg—climbed to No. 2 in the rankings after a northern swing that saw McGuire's team, labeled by the press as "Four Catholics and a Jew," beat NYU in Madison Square Garden and then sweep Dartmouth and Holy Cross at the Boston Garden on the next two nights.

The Tar Heels improved to 11–0 after beating Utah, Duke, and Wake Forest to win the Dixie Classic. UNC was 16–0 and ranked No. 1 for the first time in school history when the streak appeared to be coming to an end on a cold February night at Maryland. Down four points with two minutes left, McGuire called time-out and told his players to take their first loss like men. Only UNC didn't lose: they rallied to win in double overtime.

"That game was the turning point of the season for us," Kearns told sportswriter Ron Morris. "It gave us the lift we needed in the close ones that followed. When things got bad after that, we just reminded ourselves that we did it at Maryland and we could do it again."

The fans on Tobacco Road, long mesmerized by Case's magic act in Raleigh, were starting to get excited about the unbeaten Tar Heels. How long could the streak last? N.C. State, playing without the injured Ritcher, couldn't come close in Raleigh; but four nights after the close call at Maryland, Duke almost spoiled UNC's perfect season in Woollen Gym. The Tar Heels led most of the way, but with McGuire's five overworked starters wearing down, the Blue Devils mounted a furious comeback and erased a 73–65 lead in the final two minutes. After two quick Duke baskets, guard Bobby Joe Harris stole a pass and fed teammate Bob Vernon for a layup to cut the lead to two points . . . then moments later, Harris came up with another steal and again fed Vernon for another easy basket to tie the game with twenty-four seconds left.

But the frantic action had confused the Duke guard, who didn't realize the Blue Devils had just tied the score. He looked over at the hand-operated scoreboard—but the scoreboard operator was so caught up in the game, he forgot to flip the cards. Harris, thinking Duke was still down two, committed a quick foul in desperation. Kearns hit the two free throws with sixteen seconds left, and UNC escaped defeat at home.

"I lost the game and on purpose, but I didn't know it at the time," Duke guard Harris complained. "I wouldn't have fouled him, if I had known it was tied. They didn't beat us. That scorekeeper did. They were no better than we are."

That sentiment was repeated by UNC's rivals on Tobacco Road.

"They had nice players, but they weren't imposing defensively," Bucky Waters, a junior that season at N.C. State, said. "They did nothing flashy. It just seemed like Rosenbluth was always getting a basket when they needed it. There was nothing commanding about them. We always felt we could beat them. We just never did."

The pressure on the Tar Heels—and the excitement on Tobacco Road—continued to build as UNC completed the regular season at 24–0. But that would mean nothing if McGuire's team didn't win the ACC Tournament. As it turned out, the great season came terrifyingly close to disaster in the Friday night semifinals against the same Wake Forest team that had bounced the Tar Heels out of the 1956 tournament.

Technically, the Deacons were coached that night by Murray Gleason, who was completing the final year of a distinguished twenty-three-year career. But it was an open secret that the team was actually being run by Gleason's assistant and designated successor, our old friend Horace "Bones" McKinney.

Wake Forest had moved to Winston-Salem the previous summer, but McKinney brought his team back to familiar Gore Gym in Wake Forest to prepare them for their tournament matchup with McGuire's unbeaten Tar Heels. He devised a unique defensive scheme—a variation of the 1-3-1 zone he called the Fruit Salad defense—to stop Rosenbluth and stifle the UNC offense.

McGuire's confident team still forged an early lead with a 10–0 first-half run and clung to their advantage until Deacon center Jim Gilley sank two free throws with fifty-five seconds left, to put Wake on top 59–58. Suddenly, UNC's dream season was in jeopardy: a second straight ACC Tournament loss to Wake Forest would have ended UNC's great season and prevented the Tar Heels from playing in a postseason tournament.

Years later, Bucky Waters would attend a coaching clinic when another young coach asked McGuire what tactics he used in late-game situations with his team behind.

"He said, 'Very simple, get the ball to Lennie,'" Waters recalled.

That's what the Tar Heels did in their crisis against Wake Forest. Cunningham got the ball to Rosenbluth, who turned and dribbled into the lane. Deacon sub Wendell Carr tried to defend the play and collided with the UNC star just as the shot went up.

"I knew it was in the moment it left my hand," Rosenbluth said. "I could just feel it go in the basket—like it had eyes."

Referee Jim Mills blew his whistle as the ball swished through the net. The 12,000-plus fans in Reynolds held their breath, waiting for Mills to make the call. Although McKinney would contend to his dying day that Rosenbluth should have been called for charging on the play, Mills called Carr for blocking and Rosenbluth added a free throw to give UNC the 61–59 win.

The ACC title game, played twenty-four hours later, was anticlimactic. UNC routed South Carolina to give McGuire his first ACC championship and the school its first official league title since 1940.

There was little time for celebration. Three nights later, North Carolina had to beat Yale in Madison Square Garden to earn a trip to Philadelphia for the East Regional semifinals. It wasn't as easy as the final score of 90–74 would suggest, for the uptight Tar Heels were tied with the Ivy League champs at the half. But the second-half explosion not only impressed the skeptical New York media, a jaded group used to seeing heralded ACC teams wilt in New York; it also seemed to release the pressure that had been building during the streak. UNC took the train to Philadelphia, where the team dubbed the "Yankee Tar Heels" rolled past Canisius—much the same team that had upset Case's greatest team the year before—on Friday night in the Palestra, then defeated Syracuse on Saturday night.

Hysteria seemed to grip the state as UNC prepared for the trip to Kansas City and the Final Four. Even McGuire was taken aback when he showed up for practice one day only to find his office buried in mail from adoring grade-school students.

"This is something," McGuire told reporters. "It's one thing when we get the adults excited. But when second-graders take it this seriously, I'm wondering if it's good to keep winning?"

Saturday night was to be the big showdown: No. 1 North Carolina against No. 2 Kansas. Just as national writers had speculated about a potential matchup between N.C. State and San Francisco in 1956, all the talk before the '57 Final Four was about the possibility of the unbeaten Tar Heels facing the hometown favorite Jayhawks, with Wilt Chamberlain, in the title game. But Michigan State, which had upset No. 3 Kentucky in the regional finals, almost got in the way of that dream matchup.

Foddy Anderson's Spartans, with young star "Jumpin' Johnny" Green in the middle, turned out to be a surprisingly difficult hurdle for the Heels in the semifinals. The Spartans almost won in regulation, but Jack Quiggle's miraculous shot from midcourt was launched just after the buzzer. Green had a chance to clinch the win in the first overtime, but with the Spartans up two points and eleven seconds left, the sophomore star missed two free throws. Brennan rebounded the second miss, drove the length of the court, and sank a fifteen-footer from the foul line to tie it up again with four seconds left.

Rosenbluth missed the final shot in the second overtime, but in the third extra period he scored four straight points to give UNC a 72–68 lead. Then he came up with a steal that reserve Bob Young converted into a basket, and the Heels were able to hang on for a heart-stopping 74–70 victory.

Although UNC was unbeaten at 31–0 and ranked higher than its opponent in the title game, the No. 2 Jayhawks were ten-point favorites in the betting line. Not only did Kansas have a distinct homecourt advantage, but Chamberlain was perceived as an unstoppable force in the middle.

"I told them, 'We're not playing Kansas, we're playing Chamberlain,'" McGuire said. "I told them, 'Kansas can't beat you . . . Chamberlain can beat you.' We had the whole team playing Chamberlain."

The wily Irish coach tried to neutralize the intimidating Kansas big man with a stunning psychological ploy—one suggested by assistant coach Buck Freeman. When the two teams lined up for the center jump, the Kansas giant found himself facing not the 6-foot-9 Quigg, but 5-foot-11 Tommy Kearns.

"Wilt looked ten feet tall towering over Tommy," McGuire said. "They made such a ridiculous figure that Chamberlain must have felt no bigger than his thumb. That's the state of mind we wanted to get him into. We wanted him thinking, 'Is this coach crazy? What other tricks does he have up his sleeve?'"

The bizarre start did seem to unnerve Chamberlain—who was not much of a factor early on, as UNC jumped to a 9–2 lead. The Tar Heels shot almost 65% to maintain that advantage through the half, but foul trouble sent first Quigg, then Rosenbluth to the bench, allowing the Jayhawks to fight back and take a 40–37 lead. At that point, Kansas coach Dick Harp made a tactical blunder of epic proportions, pulling the ball out to give McGuire some of his own slowdown medicine. But McGuire, with two key players on the bench beside him in foul trouble, was delighted to shorten the game. He let Kansas hold the ball for five minutes before extending his zone.

The Tar Heels fought back to tie the game at 46, even as Rosenbluth fouled out. For the second straight night, UNC went into overtime, then into a second overtime, then into an incredible third overtime.

Most of the state of North Carolina was watching the black-and-white television broadcast of the game as Gene Elston hit two free throws to put Kansas up 53–52 with twenty-five seconds remaining in the third extra period. In Durham's Washington-Duke Hotel, the Sertoma Club suspended its annual ball to gather around four portable television sets and watch the finish. Chapel

Hill was described as a ghost town as students and townsfolk followed the telecast or listened on their radios. Much the same happened in Greensboro, Charlotte, and in all the little towns on Tobacco Road. The state of North Carolina was united—wondering if McGuire's miracle workers had one last miracle in them. But with Rosenbluth on the bench with five fouls, who would McGuire turn to?

It turned out to be Joe Quigg, who took the ball on the right side and drove the baseline. Before he could challenge Chamberlain at the basket, Kansas defender Maurice King was whistled for a foul. There were six seconds left when McGuire stunned onlookers by calling time-out to ice his own free-throw shooter. But the Irish magician had one more psychological ploy up his sleeve. McGuire confidently told his team, "*After* Joe makes the shots, we'll go to a zone."

That's exactly what happened. Quigg made both free throws to give UNC a 54–53 lead. Then he dropped back in the zone and deflected a pass meant for Chamberlain toward Kearns, who grabbed it with two seconds left.

The final image, seen by the hundreds of thousands of fans watching the regional telecast, was Kearns, who had started the game by jumping center against Chamberlain, throwing the ball toward the rafters to run out the final two seconds. The pandemonium that followed on the court in Kansas City was nothing compared to the hysteria that rocked Tobacco Road.

North Carolina's 1957 national title was a landmark for the region. Neither Wade's great prewar Duke football teams nor Choo Choo's postwar heroics had ever brought a national championship to the state. Even Case's great Wolfpack basketball teams always seemed to stumble on the national stage.

But McGuire's "Four Catholics and a Jew" had not only earned the ultimate title: they had done it in the most dramatic fashion, in front of a statewide television audience. Just eight years after North Carolina and Duke had carried football to the pinnacle of the North Carolina sports scene, McGuire and his Tar Heels had completed the work of Bones McKinney and Everett Case: basketball was King of Tobacco Road.

THE RIVALRY HEATS UP

North Carolina's success in 1957 changed the face of Tobacco Road. The basketball revolution ignited by Everett Case in 1947 had come to fruition under Frank McGuire. North Carolina owned (and still owns) the largest fan base in the state—maybe as large as the other three schools put together. When the Tar Heels returned triumphant from Kansas City, fans from every school in the state celebrated and thousands of new fans were created. But in the coming months, the prospect of a Tar Heel dynasty began to terrify its neighbors.

To those fans on Tobacco Road who wore colors other than the baby blue and white, the euphoria of UNC's triumph faded quickly, replaced by an intense desire to see the Tar Heels humbled. It was the birth of the ABC (Anybody But Carolina) brigade. And just as North Carolina had reacted to Case's success by hiring McGuire from St. John's, UNC's rivals on Tobacco Road took steps to challenge the new power in Chapel Hill.

Wake Forest acted first, finally giving Bones McKinney the title to go along with the job that he had been doing for several years. The Baptist school had to act to keep from losing the charismatic coach. Throughout the 1957 season, there had been rumors that Bones would be leaving Wake after the season. Several NBA teams were reported to be pursuing him. Chuck Taylor of Converse wanted to hire him to coach clinics and sell shoes. Murray Olderman, the chief basketball writer for the Associated Press in New York, even reported that Bones would be hired to replace Case at N.C. State!

That rumor was fueled by speculation that Case would step down in the wake of his second recruiting scandal in less than five years. The first was a fairly minor affair. Charges that N.C. State had used illegal inducements to lure Ronnie Shavlik from Denver to Raleigh proved unfounded, but in the course of investigating that charge, the NCAA had discovered that Case was holding illegal tryouts for prospects.

That violation cost N.C. State a one-year probation that prevented the Pack from competing in the 1955 NCAA Tournament. But the Jackie Moreland case—and the revelations that emerged from it—proved far more serious.

Moreland was a 6-foot-7 post player from Minden, Louisana, who had previously signed letters of intent with Kentucky and Texas A&M before landing in Raleigh in the fall of 1956. In his first game in a Pack uniform, Moreland scored thirty points in a scrimmage with the Wolfpack varsity, despite sitting out the last eight minutes.

That would be his last appearance in the red-and-white. N.C. State spent most of the 1956–57 season trying to refute the charges of recruiting improprieties brought by the NCAA and the ACC. Moreland blamed his troubles on an ex-girlfriend, who turned out to be the chief witness in the investigation.

"We sorta broke up," Moreland said. "I should have broke her."

N.C. State wound up with a four-year postseason ban from the NCAA. The penalty not only blocked the Wolfpack from the NCAA Tournament for four years, it covered all sports, preventing the 1957 football team from playing in the Orange Bowl. The ACC followed by ruling Moreland ineligible to play at N.C. State.

The penalties in the Moreland case incensed Case, who argued that he wasn't doing anything that his rivals weren't doing.

"If you're going to convict schools on charges like these, I can tell you there wouldn't be very many left to play basketball," he said.

His point was illustrated by a 1957 story in *Sports Illustrated*, celebrating McGuire's Underground Railroad. The story reported that UNC paid scouts in the New York area. It quoted UNC alumnus Mike Tynberg as saying, "I'm on the North Carolina payroll. So is Uncle Harry [Gotkin]. We're listed as assistant coaches."

McGuire rapidly denied that Tynberg, Gotkin, or anyone else was paid to scout talent for him. No investigation followed, which merely fed the growing paranoia in Raleigh. The situation spotlights another of those Tobacco Road controversies: just how bitter was the rivalry between Case and McGuire?

At the time, the two rivals were portrayed as very real enemies who wouldn't even shake hands with each other. McGuire made headlines in 1954 when he ripped Case for using a full-court press to run up the score against one of his teams, telling reporters, "I am declaring war against Everett Case." Case fired back, "When did he get to the place where he could coach my ball club?"

Long after the fact, both coaches claimed that their early battles were nothing more than a publicity ploy and that the Case-McGuire feud was a fraud.

"Case told him, we can turn this into something," Bucky Waters said. "If we don't shake hands, that will be the lead in the papers for three days."

Dean Smith, an assistant under McGuire for three seasons, said his former boss was reluctant at first to go along.

"That was kind of a funny deal," Smith said. "Everett said, 'Don't shake my hand; that will be good for the fans.' Frank said that shaking hands was just good sportsmanship. He used to chase Everett downstairs [where the locker rooms were in Reynolds] to shake his hand."

Smith insisted that he never saw the two coaches act like enemies off the court.

"I know when I was there, Frank and I went over to Everett Case's house for dinner on several occasions and we'd laugh and tell stories," he said.

However, there is some evidence that the phony feud wasn't a total fabrication, especially after McGuire finally pushed his program past N.C. State in 1957. The apparent (to Case anyway) inequities of the NCAA in regards to recruiting didn't soothe the Old Gray Fox. And McGuire's criticism of N.C. State's response to the probation only made things worse.

The North Carolina coach thought it outrageous that N.C. State would continue to participate in the ACC Tournament, where the Pack could perhaps knock an eligible team out of NCAA consideration. That belief was behind McGuire's inflammatory action in the 1959 ACC championship game. The contest should have been a classic. UNC and N.C. State had tied for the ACC regular season title and both were ranked in the top 10 nationally: 21–4 N.C. State, led by the senior Philadelphia duo of big man John Ritcher and flamboyant point guard Lou Pucillo, was ranked No. 6 going into the tournament; 20–3 UNC—powered by the balanced trio of center Lee Shaffer, forward Doug Moe, and sharp-shooting guard York Larese—was ranked No. 9.

But because of N.C. State's probation, the Tar Heels clinched an NCAA bid by beating surprisingly tough Duke in the semifinals. McGuire's thoughts leapt past the matchup with State and turned to the upcoming NCAA playoffs and a Tuesday night matchup with Navy in Madison Square Garden.

"What would happen if I didn't start my first five," he asked reporters after the Duke game. "It would give us some badly needed rest."

Apparently thinking out loud, he decided, "No, I don't think I can do it. We'll have to play them, but if [my players] begin to look bad or tired, I won't hesitate to pull them."

That's exactly what happened the next night. N.C. State, with the 5-foot-9 Pucillo dominating play, jumped to an early eight-point lead. McGuire, who usually rode his starters until they dropped, subbed frequently during the first half and early in the second half. UNC rallied to within four points with ten minutes to play. But when the Wolfpack spurted to a thirteen-point lead in the next two minutes, the UNC coach pulled all of his starters and let his scrubs finish out the 80–56 rout.

McGuire's tactics infuriated the ABC crowd. One irate Wolfpack fan snuck into the basement of Reynolds and turned off the lights, forcing an eight-minute delay in the game. And with four seconds left to play, a State reserve called a very unnecessary time-out. That was a deliberate slap at McGuire, who used to do the same thing quite often, huddling with his team and telling them to enjoy the victory.

Afterwards, Case halfway apologized for the time-out, but he took some thinly veiled shots at his rival.

"We just wanted it," he said when asked the difference in the game.

And UNC didn't?

"I don't know if Carolina wanted it or not," Case answered.

McGuire, who joked that his team should have slipped out of Reynolds during the blackout, got quite irate when a reporter asked about his unusual substitution pattern.

"That's my business," he snapped. "You don't mind if I coach my own ball club do you? I don't want to lose my temper. I think you're trying to intimate that we were not trying."

If McGuire thought resting his regulars in the ACC Tournament title game would pay off in the NCAA Tournament, he was wrong. The well-rested, and heavily favored, Tar Heels trailed all the way and were thrashed 76–63 by unranked Navy in the first round of the playoffs. In a small touch of irony, Navy was coached by the same Ben Carnevale who had guided UNC to the 1946 NCAA championship game, then left for a better job in Annapolis. But by 1959, there weren't any better basketball jobs than those on Tobacco Road.

4

NEW BLOOD

Bones McKinney was, of course, already a star on Tobacco Road long before he became head coach at Wake Forest. The tall, fast-talking showboat first burst on the region's consciousness as the star of Durham High's fabulous prewar teams. As a freshman at N.C. State, he led the Southern Conference in scoring and almost single-handedly transformed a losing Wolfpack team into a winner that came within a single game of the Southern Conference title. And after a stint in the military during World War II, Bones returned to lead North Carolina all the way to the national championship game.

McKinney left the Tar Heels with a year of eligibility remaining to play for Red Auerbach in the NBA. He was a first-team All-NBA pick as a twenty-eight-year-old rookie in 1947. But because of his late start, his career was short—just three years with the Washington Capitals and two years with the Boston Celtics.

Bones returned to Tobacco Road in 1952, enrolling at the Baptist Theological Seminary, which was at the time a part of Wake Forest College. Murray Gleason, who had coached the Deacons since 1934, asked McKinney to join his staff as an unpaid assistant. Over the next five years, Bones took a larger and larger role in coaching the team, eventually becoming the head coach in reality, if not in name. He finally got the official title on March 26, 1957—just two weeks after the Deacons were eliminated from the ACC Tournament by unbeaten UNC.

McKinney, always clad in his trademark red socks, proved to be as colorful a coach as he had been as a player.

"The trouble with officials," he once pronounced solemnly, "is that they don't care who wins."

Behind the humor was a sharp basketball mind and a coach with a burning desire to succeed. McKinney built a championship team out of an unusual variety of pieces. There was Len Chappell, a burly 6-foot-8 forward from Pennsylvania, who picked Wake Forest because he liked Bones and because he wasn't sure he was good enough to play at Duke.

"When I finished high school, I didn't have any confidence in myself," Chappell said. "I went to Wake Forest where I felt I'd get to play."

Dave Weideman, a talented guard from New Jersey, was a big-time recruit. But Bones also lured burly Bill Hull from the football team and helped walk-on Alley Hart develop into one of the best guards in the ACC.

Then there was Billy Packer, the son of Lehigh basketball coach Tony Packer. The two-sport star grew up idolizing hometown hero Dick Groat, who went to Duke and became an All-American in basketball and baseball before moving on to the Pittsburgh Pirates. Packer dreamed of following the same path and tried his best to commit to Duke. But when he told assistant coach Fred Shabel that he was ready to sign, Shabel told him that Duke wasn't ready to offer him. Head coach Hal Bradley was trying to decide whether to offer his final scholarship to Packer or to another guard. The news infuriated Packer—who decided on the spot to attend Wake Forest, because he knew the Deacons played in the same league as Duke and he'd get repeated chances to prove the Duke coaches wrong.

Bradley wouldn't be there to suffer for his recruiting mistake. Before Packer's sophomore season, the Duke coach left Durham to take a lucrative offer from Texas. He left behind a program that had been good, but not great, during the 1950s. Bradley's Blue Devil teams won a Dixie Classic title and twice finished first in the ACC regular season standings. But Duke never won an ACC championship under Bradley, lost its one and only NCAA game, and hadn't produced an All-American quality player since the departure of Groat in 1953.

Still, a lot of basketball insiders saw potential in the program. Blue Devil Athletic Director Eddie Cameron reviewed applications from 135 candidates for the job. Many were from established head coaches. However, the former Duke coach kept returning to the young assistant coach who was Case's right-hand man.

When Vic Bubas finished his playing career at N.C. State in 1951, Case hired him as his third assistant. It wasn't long before Bubas was running practice, making tactical decisions during games, and—most importantly—heading N.C. State's recruiting efforts.

Bubas extended the school's reach far beyond Case's old stomping grounds in Indiana. It was Bubas who found Ron Shavlik in Denver. It was Bubas who found Lou Pucillo in Philadelphia. And it was Bubas who pursued Jackie Moreland in Louisiana.

The latter concerned Cameron, who knew the administration at the small, academically exclusive private school would insist on a coach with a squeaky clean image. It was only after he received assurances from friends at N.C. State that Bubas had nothing to do with the illegal inducements allegedly offered to the Louisiana schoolboy that Cameron decided to gamble on the thirty-one-year-old assistant coach.

Cameron introduced Bubas to the media on May 5, 1959 with the words, "Gentlemen, this is our new basketball coach. We hope he is our coach forever."

Privately, he had another message for his new coach: "Don't you think it's time you go recruiting?"

Indeed, Bubas wasted little time before pulling off one of the great recruiting coups in Tobacco Road history. He knew that Long Island prep star Art Heyman, the latest passenger on McGuire's Underground Railroad, just might not be as locked in at Chapel Hill as McGuire thought.

Heyman, a powerful 6-foot-5 forward, had visited Duke early in the spring, when Cameron was still looking for a replacement for Bradley. It was a perfunctory tour of the campus. Heyman—and everybody else—knew he was going to play at Carolina, where he was slated to room with his longtime Long Island playground rival, Larry Brown.

But Bubas had heard that Heyman's stepfather harbored a deep dislike for McGuire. The new Duke coach continued to woo Heyman, even after he signed with the Tar Heels. His tactics paid off when Bill Heyman and McGuire got into a shouting match one night at the Carolina Inn—an argument that nearly came to fisticuffs.

"I had to step in between them," Art Heyman said. "My stepfather called Carolina a basketball factory and McGuire didn't like that. They were about to start swinging at each other."

According to the rules at the time, Heyman's letter of intent did not become binding until July 1, and as that date approached, Bubas continued to recruit the Long Island star. Or more precisely, he recruited his parents.

"He charmed my mother and stepfather," Heyman said. "They made me go to Duke. All my friends from New York were at Carolina. If Duke hadn't picked me up at the airport, I would have gone down the road and started school there."

Bubas' "theft" of Heyman energized the Duke program. It also propelled the rivalry with UNC to unprecedented heights. Duke's new freshman star became the focus of abuse from the Tar Heel faithful. Much of that abuse was anti-Semitic in nature, ironically coming from a fan base that had idolized Jewish star Lennie Rosenbluth and adopted Jewish guard Larry Brown at the same time as it abused Heyman.

Bubas had to bide his time while waiting for Heyman to join the varsity. He had to make do with the junior-dominated team that he inherited from Bradley. He guided Carroll Youngkin, Howard Hurt, Doug Kistler, and company to surprising victories over Alabama and Navy in a tournament in Birmingham, Alabama, then directed an upset of No. 6 Utah State in the first round of the Dixie Classic. But Bubas' first team just wasn't strong enough to compete with its Tobacco Road rivals, and Duke finished the regular season at a modest 12–10 and a fourth-place ACC finish.

N.C. State, feeling the effects of that massive four-year probation, was down, finishing in the second division for the first time ever under Case. But in Winston-Salem, Bones McKinney's recruiting efforts were finally starting to pay off. Chappell was a star from the moment he stepped on the court, averaging 17.4 points and 12.5 rebounds as a sophomore. Packer averaged exactly 13 points a game and helped the Deacons to two lopsided regular season victories over the Blue Devils, the team that had rejected him.

Wake Forest tied North Carolina for the regular season title. Early in the week before the ACC Tournament opened in Raleigh, a snowstorm dumped sixteen inches on Tobacco Road. On Wednesday night, another storm dropped twelve more inches, forever branding the 1960 tournament as "The Year of the Big Snow." But the tournament would become memorable for another reason.

It started placidly enough with all four North Carolina teams winning in the first round. The only surprise was not really a surprise: sixth-seeded N.C. State "upset" third-seeded Maryland to reach the semifinals of the conference tournament for the fourteenth straight year under Case.

But Friday night's double-header was a bit more unpredictable. It started when fourth-seeded Duke jumped to a big early lead on North Carolina. The

Tar Heels had dominated the season series with the Blue Devils, winning by twenty-two points in the Dixie Classic, by twenty-six points in Chapel Hill, and by twenty-five points in Durham. McGuire's cocky team couldn't believe it when they trailed by twelve at the half in the tournament semifinals.

"There was no way they could beat us," Lee Shaffer later said. "We knew it and they knew it."

But early foul trouble bothered UNC's big man and Duke's Carroll Youngkin took advantage of it, scoring a career-high thirty points as the ABC crowd at Reynolds began to roar for the Blue Devils. The Tar Heels, getting twenty-five points from York Larese, staged a furious rally. But Hurt and tiny guard Johnny Frye each hit two clutch free throws down the stretch to help Duke hold on for the mind-boggling 71–69 victory.

"I'll bet you they'd trade all three [regular season wins] for this one," Duke's Youngkin told reporters.

Bubas, who appeared to be stunned by the unexpected victory (and maybe thinking about the piles of snow on the ground), said, "It's like Christmas in March."

Duke's upset of UNC was just the first act in a memorable semifinals. With eighteen seconds left in Wake Forest's 71–66 victory over N.C. State, Deacon senior Dave Budd and Wolfpack guard Anton Muehlbauer traded punches, touching off a controversy that still rankles Wake Forest fans.

Budd, a pugnacious 6-foot-6 forward from New Jersey, had been involved in a multitude of fights and brawls in his career, including a confrontation with Oscar Robertson in the 1958 Dixie Classic. Early in the 1959–60 season, Maryland coach Bud Milliken had written ACC commissioner Bob Weaver a letter complaining about Budd's conduct and asking that an earlier probation be extended through the 1959–60 season.

After the fight with Muehlbauer, Weaver decided to suspend Budd for the title game against Duke. However, Wake Forest requested that the league's executive committee review the decision. Three hours before the tipoff of Saturday night's game, the league's faculty chairmen overruled Weaver and reinstated Budd.

McKinney later claimed that the controversy was a major factor in the championship game, which was the first ACC/Southern conference title game to be played without N.C. State or North Carolina since 1946.

"We would have beaten the hell out of Duke without Budd," the Wake Forest coach said. "When they called his name and they threw that spotlight on him, the fans started to boo. Then they started to applaud. Then they gave him a standing ovation."

The Wake team, expecting Budd to face brutal treatment from the fans, was surprised by the generous reaction of the Reynolds crowd.

"That made pussycats out of us . . . pussycats," Bones said.

Budd played thirty-nine minutes against Duke and turned in his typical game: ten points and fifteen rebounds. But Kistler outscored Chappell twenty-two to nineteen. Packer—perhaps trying too hard to stick it to the team that rejected him—was a miserable two of eleven from the floor, and the Deacons fell 63–59 to Duke and the Devils' first-year coach.

After cutting down the nets, Bubas dedicated the win to his old mentor.

"I'm deeply grateful to Coach Case," Bubas said. "No words can explain what he's done to make this moment possible. He's put so many pages in my book that I can never call it my own."

Yet, even as Case was being honored by his star pupil, his N.C. State program was in decline. The harsh NCAA penalty after the 1956 season had taken its toll, making it harder to lure top talent to Raleigh. And just as that penalty ended and Case could think about restoring N.C. State's status as the premier team on Tobacco Road, the Pack basketball program suffered another crushing blow. In the spring of 1961, four Wolfpack players were indicted for point-shaving.

The scandal stretched twenty-five miles down Highway 54 to Chapel Hill, where reserve guard Lou Brown (no relation to Larry) was alleged to be the go-between between the gamblers and the players. He testified that he helped arrange fixes for seven games and had put teammates Doug Moe and Ray Stanley in contact with his gambling friends. Although no evidence was ever offered that Moe or Stanley had ever participated in a fix, both were suspended from school after the 1961 season for not reporting the approaches from the gamblers.

Far more serious for McGuire's program was the response of UNC system president William Friday, who reacted to the point-shaving scandal by ordering a de-emphasis of basketball at the two major state universities. He severely limited out-of-state recruiting, temporarily cut back schedules, and—worst of all from the fans' point of view—he killed the Dixie Classic.

The immediate result of Friday's action was to set back Tobacco Road's two most successful programs for half a decade. His action opened the door for the state's two small private universities to dominate the early 1960s. Bones McKinney and Vic Bubas would reap the passion that Case and McGuire had sewn.

THE BIG BRAWL

Frank McGuire, true to his nature, was not about to go quietly into that good night, not even after the NCAA placed his 1961 team on probation for "excessive recruiting entertainment." The root of UNC's problem turned out to be McGuire's habit of spending money lavishly, usually without bothering to get receipts.

"That's the way Frank operated—freewheeling and first class," Dean Smith said. "It just wasn't in Frank's nature to worry about details."

The 1960–61 Tar Heels, with talented point guard Larry Brown joining seniors Moe and Larese in the starting lineup, showed their strength after a slow start, climbing into the top 10. Bubas' Blue Devils, with Heyman joining four starters from the 1960 ACC title team, had opened with nine straight wins before running into the Tar Heels in the Dixie Classic title game in Raleigh. Duke's sophomore star had averaged twenty-six points in his first nine games, but Moe—one of the best defenders in the league—stifled Heyman and the Tar Heels handed Duke its first defeat.

Heyman reacted by ripping a picture of Moe out of the Durham newspaper and pasting it on his dorm wall. He was primed for the next rematch, when UNC visited Duke Indoor Stadium on Saturday night, February 4, 1961.

An ice storm swept the state on the night before the game, which may have contributed to the huge TV audience that tuned in to see No. 4 Duke (15–1) take on No. 5 North Carolina (14–2). It was the first (but far from the last) time the two rivals would both be ranked in the top five when they met.

The night would start ugly and end ugly. In the freshman game, which preceded the varsity contest, future star Jeff Mullins helped Duke's Blue Imps (as the Blue Devil freshmen were known) rout the Tar Babies (the politically incorrect term then used for the UNC freshman teams) 79–52. But the score didn't tell the story of a violent game marked by a number of fights. UNC actually ended the contest with just three players on the floor, after five players fouled out and three were ejected for fighting.

The varsity contest almost turned into a brawl in the first half as Heyman and Moe squared off. It was reported that Heyman was upset at a Moe elbow that nearly hit his nose, but Heyman said there was another reason for his anger.

"He spit on me," the former Duke star said. "Every time I took a shot, he spit on me. I told him I was not going to take that."

Officials Jim Mills and Charlie Eckman finally got the situation under control and the game continued with the two teams trading the lead throughout the first half. Heyman was on fire, hitting nine of his first eleven shots and getting Moe in foul trouble. But the Tar Heels nursed a narrow lead throughout the second half—until there were three minutes to play and UNC was up 73–70. Frye hit a free throw and Heyman scored five straight points to give Duke a 76–73 lead. Two free throws by Heyman with fifteen seconds left stretched that advantage to 80–75. That's when the tension that had been building ever since Heyman had reneged on his commitment to UNC exploded into the ugliest scene in ACC history.

The trouble began when Brown took the inbounds pass after Heyman's free throws and raced toward the basket. The Duke star grabbed Brown by the shoulders as he went up for the shot—a hard, and unnecessary, foul. Brown reacted by throwing the ball at Heyman, then threw a punch at his former friend from Long Island. Heyman responded with a flailing blow of his own. At that point, UNC reserve Donnie Walsh—the future NBA executive—raced off the bench and slugged Heyman from behind, knocking him down. Walsh raced away after his cheap shot and Heyman got up and tried to follow, but Brown and several other UNC players piled on the Duke star and began pummeling him. Fans began to pour out of the stands, throwing punches at everyone in sight.

Heyman later claimed that he was kicked by a pair of alligator shoes—supposedly those worn by McGuire, but films of the fight show McGuire briefly trying to restrain his players, then walking away from the fight. Oddly, not a single Duke player rallied to Heyman's defense.

The melee continued for more than ten minutes as ten Durham policemen struggled to stop the violence. When order was finally restored, Heyman was ejected for fighting, although his foul of Brown was already his fifth foul. Amazingly, Brown was not ejected and was allowed to stay in the game to shoot his two free throws. Duke added a free throw in the final seconds to finish with an 81–77 victory.

"Duke won the game, but lost the fight," Durham sports editor Jack Horner wrote.

Horner was just about the only writer at the game who did not write that Heyman threw the first punch. Even referee Charlie Eckman, who claimed that he gallantly tried to break up the fight, reported that Heyman had punched first. Bubas, incensed by the accusations, took the unusual step of scheduling a press conference for the next Wednesday. At the conference he reran the film footage of the fight for more than forty reporters, proving that Brown had thrown the first punch and the heroic Eckman had spent the entire fight hiding behind a basket support.

Weaver, the ACC commissioner, saw the same film. In his report, he acknowledged that Brown was guilty of starting the fight and Walsh's "hit-and-run tactics" (as Weaver termed it) turned the brief scuffle into a major brawl. The commissioner handed down the most severe punishment ever delivered for on-the-court misbehavior, suspending Heyman, Brown, and Walsh for the remainder of the ACC regular season.

For Carolina, that meant that Brown and Walsh would not play again that season. McGuire had convinced the school to withdraw from the ACC Tournament after learning that the Heels would be on probation for one year. It proved to be his parting shot at his old rival Case, who had refused to take similar action during N.C. State's four-year probation.

While Dean Smith insisted that the action had nothing to do with N.C. State, he admitted that it was perceived that way at the time.

"Frank and I went over for the first [ACC Tournament] game in 1961 and sat on the front row," he said. "We had detectives around us, like they were afraid somebody would shoot us."

The loss of Heyman proved devastating to Duke's title chances. The Blue Devils lost four of its final six conference games without him and finished third in the ACC regular season standings. UNC claimed the regular season title with an overtime victory over Duke in the rematch in Chapel Hill. Despite some hysterical talk from McGuire, who predicted the game would be a "bloodbath" and suggested the governor call out the National Guard, the tight contest, played under intense security, was without incident.

Duke got Heyman back for the ACC Tournament and he played well, scoring eighty points in the three games. He led the Blue Devils into the finals against Wake Forest, a replay of the 1960 title game. But this one would have a different outcome as Chappell scored thirty-three points and completely dominated a foul-played Kistler. Packer scored sixteen points and played a superb floor game—and he finally got his revenge against the school that didn't want him.

Representing the ACC in the NCAA Tournament, Wake Forest moved on to New York City and knocked off St. John's in Madison Square Garden, then

returned to North Carolina to beat St. Bonaventure in the Charlotte Coliseum—a large new stadium with a bright, shiny dome and 11,666 seats. Wake
Forest came up one game short of the Final Four in a 96–86 loss to St. Joseph's.

The deep tournament run in 1961 only whetted the team's appetite for
more success in 1962. And with the gifted trio of Len Chappell, Billy Packer,
and Dave Wiedeman returning, that success seemed guaranteed. Only
Duke—where heralded sharpshooter Jeff Mullins and giant center Jay Buckley were slated to join Heyman in the lineup—appeared to stand in Wake
Forest's path.

North Carolina's program was in turmoil. Frank McGuire, disappointed in
his lack of support from the school's administration and frustrated by the
penalties heaped on his program, decided to leave UNC. On August 3, 1961,
without any hint or warning, the news broke that McGuire was indeed leaving
to take over the Philadelphia Warriors, where he would coach the same Wilt
Chamberlain he had outfoxed in the 1957 Final Four.

McGuire was replaced by his self-effacing assistant coach, Dean Smith. At
the time, little was known about or expected from the thirty-year-old Kansas
graduate. When Chancellor William Aycock introduced Smith as the new Tar
Heel coach, he had to go out of his way to assure the media that the quiet, unknown assistant coach was actually replacing the flamboyant McGuire and not
just stepping in as an interim coach.

"In a few years, he's going to be viewed as one of the best coaches in the
country," McGuire said of his former assistant.

It would be years before McGuire's prediction would be validated. But
with UNC and N.C. State hobbled by Friday's sanctions, Wake Forest and
Duke would dominate the ACC in the near future, starting in 1962.

The Deacons, shaken by an early season loss to Ohio State, rallied to edge
the Blue Devils by a game in the ACC regular season race. Chappell proved to
be the catalyst for Wake Forest's title run. The powerful senior—an immensely
strong 6-foot-8, 255-pound forward—was in the midst of one of the great offensive seasons in ACC history. He averaged 30.1 points and 15.1 rebounds,
while shooting 54.8% from the floor.

"If you let him get his hands on the ball, he'll put it in the basket—and
you along with it," an admiring Case said. Maryland's Bud Milliken was
equally in awe of the Deacon big man.

"Chop him off at the knees," he said. "That's the only way you'll stop him."

Chappell proved to be unstoppable in the ACC Tournament that March. After coasting through the opener against hapless Virginia with a mere eighteen points and sixteen rebounds, the Deacon star poured in thirty-eight points in the semifinals against South Carolina, then pounded surprising Clemson with thirty-one more in the finals.

The easy tournament title launched Wake back into the NCAAs with a lot of confidence and momentum. The Deacons needed all of it to survive overtime games with Yale and St. Joseph's. A more comfortable victory over Villanova in the East Regional finals set up a rematch with No. 1 Ohio State in the national semifinals in Louisville. McKinney had insisted after the early season loss to the Buckeyes that he still thought he had the better team. Now, riding a twelve-game winning streak, his Deacons had a chance to prove it.

"We've come a long way since the last time we played Ohio State," the Wake Forest coach told reporters. "I just hope we can keep it going."

It didn't happen. Ohio State jumped to the early lead and was never threatened en route to an 84–68 victory. The only difference between the early season loss and the Final Four defeat was that on the second occasion, Chappell outplayed national player of the year Jerry Lucas with twenty-five points and eighteen rebounds (to Lucas's nineteen and sixteen). However, Ohio State forward John Havlicek more than made up for Lucas's troubles with twenty-five points and sixteen rebounds.

"I thought Ohio State played as great a game as any college team I ever saw," a disappointed McKinney said. "Any doubt in my mind that they were not great was certainly dispelled by their magnificent performance."

One night later, Ohio State was upset in the championship game for the second straight year by Cincinnati. Very few people outside Tobacco Road paid attention to the consolation game, played two hours earlier. Yet, Wake Forest's narrow 82–80 victory over UCLA in the third-place game would have significant long-term consequences. Historically, it would turn out to be the last NCAA loss for John Wooden's Bruins before their run of thirty-eight straight NCAA wins (including nine national titles)—a streak that would finally be halted by another team from Tobacco Road.

Far more important was the benefit Wake Forest's win was to provide for future ACC champions. It had to do with the NCAA rules at the time, which awarded first-round byes in the tournament based on a league's historical strength. As it turned out, Wake Forest's consolation game victory over UCLA raised the ACC's tournament record to 24–16 (60.0), just ahead of the Mid-Atlantic Conference at 17–12 (58.6), which had owned the bye.

"It's the first time a consolation game has ever given me consolation," Bones said, adding with a smile, "Tell Vic Bubas we did it for him."

Indeed, Bubas' Blue Devils were to reap the benefits of Wake Forest's success. Duke, which would win three of the next four ACC titles, would no longer have to play in that dangerous Monday/Tuesday game that had derailed so many promising ACC teams. Now, the ACC champion would have six days to recover from its ACC Tournament ordeal before starting NCAA play the next Friday night in the East Regional semifinals.

That was a gift that was to prove of incalculable advantage in the coming years—not just to Duke, but also to UNC when it began its run later in the decade. Wake Forest in 1962 was just the second ACC team in nine years to reach the Final Four. In the next seven years, six ACC champions would reach the Final Four—all from Tobacco Road.

Unfortunately, the Deacons would not be one of them.

THE RECRUITING MACHINE

Bones McKinney had put together one of the best teams in ACC history. But his rival in Durham was building a mini-dynasty, based on far more than a single great class.

It was just what Eddie Cameron expected when he lured Bubas away from Case. The energetic redhead from Gary, Indiana, had already revolutionized the recruiting business by pursuing top prospects wherever they might be—instead of concentrating on a single talent base, as Case first did in Indiana and McGuire would do in New York. He personalized the process, sending a stream of letters and cards to his recruiting targets and their parents.

"Vic taught us all to recruit," Dean Smith said.

Bubas obviously started quickly at Duke, stealing Heyman from UNC within weeks of taking the job in May of 1959. However, that was actually his second great recruiting coup that spring. Before being hired at Duke, Bubas offered Case and N.C. State one last recruiting gift, when he snuck into Lexington, Kentucky, and stole promising guard Jon Speaks from under Adolph Rupp's nose.

Speaks would become a fine player at N.C. State, a first-team All-ACC performer before his tragic death in a traffic accident just weeks before his graduation. But it turned out that Bubas' successful pursuit of Speaks for State paid dividends for Duke. Speaks's high school team in Lexington included a junior who was even more highly thought of: forward Jeff Mullins.

"Mullins, he was the golden boy," Waters recalled. "The thing that made it possible for us to get him is he didn't grow up in Kentucky, listening to Cawood Ledford. His dad was with IBM and he only moved to Lexington when Jeff was a sophomore. His roots weren't there."

Mullins watched Rupp and Bubas fight for his teammate and came away impressed by the young Wolfpack assistant. And when Bubas returned to Lexington a year later as head coach at Duke, the prep star was receptive to his overtures.

Getting Mullins out of Lexington was a great coup, but it was just a piece of a strong all-around recruiting class. Mullins joined Jay Buckley, a slender 6-foot-10 center from Maryland with an IQ of 160, and Buzzy Harrison, a strong, steady guard from Charleston, West Virginia, as sophomore starters in 1961–62. The talent kept coming. Bubas added 6-foot-11 Hack Tison from Geneva, Illinois, in 1961; forward Jack Marin and guard Steve Vacendak, both from Pennsylvania, in 1962; sweet-shooting guard Bob Verga from Sea Girt, New Jersey, in 1963; and powerful big man Mike Lewis, all the way from Missoula, Montana, in 1964.

The haul might have been greater. Bubas almost lured prep star Rod Thorn out of West Virginia in 1959, but the youngster changed his mind and stayed home after being declared a West Virginia natural resource in a vote by the state legislature. Two years later, Bubas turned down big man Fred Hetzel from Washington, D.C.—a future All-American at Davidson who would be the first player taken in the 1965 NBA draft—to take Buckley instead. The next year, Bubas received a signed letter of intent from 6-foot-5 Missouri sensation Bill Bradley. The future U.S. senator (not to mention All-American, national player of the year, and all-pro) changed his mind at the last minute—just as future congressman Tom McMillen was to do to North Carolina a decade later.

The defections hardly slowed the momentum of Bubas' program, which won thirty-three of thirty-four ACC games in 1963 and 1964 and became the first team on Tobacco Road to play in back-to-back Final Fours.

Heyman—who became the ACC's first consensus national player of the year—had a spectacular senior season in 1963, averaging twenty-five points and eleven rebounds while dominating games with his passing, his defense, and his sheer force of will. He went out on a high note, scoring forty points and pulling down twenty-four rebounds in his final home game against North Carolina—an echo of the forty-eight points that Groat scored in his home finale, also against Carolina.

"Everybody talks about how great Dick Groat was," Bubas said after the game. "Groat was a great player. I guarded him. But Heyman is bigger and stronger. He's got to be the best player ever to put on a Duke uniform."

Mullins, after two years of playing in Heyman's shadow, stepped up and became a superstar in 1964, averaging twenty-four points a game and taking the big shots that Heyman used to demand. He was at his best in the 1964 NCAA East Regionals, when the soft-spoken Kentucky product hit nineteen of twenty-eight shots and scored forty-three points in an 87–73 victory over Villanova. Mullins and the ultra-intelligent Buckley, who took his game to another level midway through his senior season, carried Duke to the 1964 title game in Kansas City, where the Blue Devils became the first victim of UCLA's soon-to-be-famous zone press.

"We just lost our poise against their pressure defense and went to pieces," Bubas said.

While the loss in the title game was a huge disappointment for Bubas and the Blue Devils, the future appeared bright. More than five thousand fans turned out at the Raleigh-Durham Airport to welcome the team home. It demonstrated the optimism Duke fans felt about the program. The talent was still flowing and Duke's Tobacco Road's rivals were still struggling to catch up.

Who would have guessed that Bubas' dynasty would be interrupted by a blast from the past?

CASE'S FAREWELL

As always happens on Tobacco Road, the success of one program spurs changes in its rivals. That was happening at N.C. State, where Everett Case imported former Clemson head coach Press Maravich to help him rebuild his stagnant program.

It was widely assumed that Maravich would soon succeed Case. The Gray Fox was known to be in poor health. He was hospitalized for surgery before the 1963–64 season and took a ten-day leave of absence midway though the year. However, it was not reported at the time that the aging Wolfpack coach was beginning to suffer from the cancer that would soon kill him. Case complained of headaches and fatigue, but he was determined to coach the 1965 Wolfpack.

He believed that after five years of mediocrity, his new team—with talented sophomore guard Eddie Biedenbach joining all-star forward Larry Lakins—would be strong enough to challenge Duke for supremacy on Tobacco Road.

As it turned out, Case's estimation of his team proved accurate—but the ailing coach couldn't make it on the bench. Two games into the season, after a tough loss at Wake Forest, N.C. State announced that after more that eighteen years at the helm, Case was stepping down. He watched from his sickbed as Maravich, whose son Pete was turning heads with his play at Raleigh's Broughton High School, brought the Wolfpack home a game behind Duke in the ACC standings.

The Blue Devils won seventeen of eighteen games during one stretch as juniors Marin and Vacendak rose into starring roles, along with sophomore Bob Verga, who dazzled opponents with a unique jump shot that seemed to be slingshotted from behind his head. Duke, employing a relentless full-court press and a frantic fast break, led the nation in scoring and appeared headed for a third straight trip to the Final Four.

But Bubas' team had to get through the ACC Tournament first—and that meant beating N.C. State in Reynolds in the championship game. The Blue Devils had won easily in Raleigh in early February, but the March rematch included two new elements. The first was the ghostly presence of Case, now widely known to be dying. He was too ill to attend the first two rounds of the tournament, but on the night when N.C. State faced Duke for the title, he was at courtside, providing an emotional spark for his underdog team.

"We would all like to win it for him," Lakins told reporters before the title game.

The victory was made possible by N.C. State's second unexpected weapon—an unheralded sub named Larry Worsley, who grew up in Oak City, North Carolina, and was an early product of Case's "basket in every driveway" campaign. The 6-foot-5 junior had averaged just seven points a game that season. But when starter Billy Moffitt got in foul trouble in the ACC title game, Worsley proved unstoppable: he hit fourteen of nineteen shots from the floor for a career-high thirty points to propel N.C. State to a 91–85 victory over the heavily favored Blue Devils.

"Worsley was no surprise to me," Bubas said. "The first thing I said to my team before the ballgame tonight was that Larry Worsley would bear watching. And I still say, it was too much Worsley for us tonight."

The Wolfpack celebration was marked by one of the most emotional moments ever seen on Tobacco Road, when the N.C. State players raced en masse to courtside and hoisted the ailing Case on their shoulders, so that he could take the final cut in the net-cutting ceremony he'd brought to Tobacco Road.

"I've never been happier," Case said. "The last taste is always the best."

Barely one year later, Case passed away at his Raleigh home. His will left almost $200,000 to his sister, but also divided $69,525 among his former players. Case's will contained one further request—that he be buried in a Raleigh cemetery overlooking Highway 70, so, as he wrote, "I can wave to the team when it goes to Durham to face Duke."

THE LANDMARK GAME

Despite State's dramatic victory, Duke was still the class of Tobacco Road and the Blue Devils proved it in 1966, bouncing back from their 1965 ACC Tournament disappointment to win a fourth ACC title in seven years and make their third Final Four trip in four years. Both Jack Marin and Bob Verga had achieved All-America status, while burly Montana big man Mike Lewis proved more than an adequate replacement for Tison in the middle.

Duke's season got off to a fast start when the Blue Devils routed No. 1 UCLA in back-to-back games, playing on a Friday night in Durham and a Saturday night in Charlotte. Bubas prepared his team for Wooden's now-feared zone press by stealing an old trick from Everett Case: he worked his starters in practice against six defenders.

The twin triumphs vaulted Duke to No. 1 in the national polls, a position the Blue Devils would hold for the next eight weeks. But it also brought a bit of unfavorable national attention, a story that would foreshadow some significant changes in college basketball and on Tobacco Road. *Sports Illustrated*'s account of the two games focused on an ugly racial incident in the stands at Duke Indoor Stadium. Author Frank Deford suggested, "There was blood on the Carolina Moon," and his story detailed racial slurs directed at the family of UCLA senior Kenny Washington—the Beaufort, South Carolina, native who had played a large role in the Bruins' victory over Duke in the 1964 NCAA title game.

The story was a reminder that Tobacco Road remained all-white.

The situation was about to change. UNC's Dean Smith had already tried to change it, pursuing Greensboro's Lou Hudson in the early 1960s and arranging for William Cooper, a black prospect from Elm City, to join the Tar Heel freshman team in 1964. But Hudson didn't have the SAT score required to play in the ACC, so the future NBA all-star opted to sign with Minnesota. And Cooper, after actually playing a season of freshman ball without incident, declined a chance to play for the varsity and break the ACC's color line, choosing instead to concentrate on his studies.

As a result, sophomore Bill Jones of Maryland was the only black player in the ACC during the 1965–66 season. Bubas was one year behind—guard C.B. Claiborne from Danville, Virginia, was playing for the Duke freshman team that season. The other three Tobacco Road schools would desegregate over the next two seasons, but only one of the first wave of black players on Tobacco Road would turn out to be a significant player.

That was in the future as an all-white Duke team marched toward its third ACC title in four years, surviving ACC Tournament tests from North Carolina—which unveiled Dean Smith's soon-to-be-infamous Four Corners offense in a 21–20 Blue Devil win—and from N.C. State, which led Bubas' team late in the title game before senior guard Steve Vacendak rescued the Devils. The senior guard was so impressive that he not only won the Case Award as the tournament MVP, he also won the next week's vote for ACC Player of the Year, despite being named in a vote the week before as a second-team All-ACC performer.

Duke, still enjoying the first-round bye first earned by Wake Forest four years earlier, won two games in Raleigh to earn another trip to the Final Four. Duke arrived in College Park, Maryland, tabbed as the co-favorite of the bettors and the national press. The one thing everybody agreed on was the semifinal matchup of No. 1 Kentucky and No. 2 Duke was the "real" national title game.

"Duke is the best team I've seen all year," UCLA's John Wooden said. "But I haven't seen Kentucky. Let's just say [the champion will be] the winner of Duke-Kentucky."

Bubas went into the game under a considerable handicap. All-American guard Bob Verga was hospitalized all week with a throat infection. When Kentucky's Rupp heard the news, he sent Larry Conley to the infirmary, telling reporters that his senior guard had the flu. Several years later, when Duke participated in the Kentucky Invitational Tournament, a member of Rupp's staff bragged that Conley's illness was phony and that it was actually all a clever ploy by the Baron of Bluegrass to prevent Duke from earning a physiological advance from Verga's illness.

Whatever the truth, Conley played a normal game and scored ten points (his average for the season), while Verga missed five of seven shots and finished with a mere seven points (eleven under his average). Bubas got twenty-nine points from Marin, twenty-one from Lewis, and seventeen from Vacendak. But with Verga below par, Duke fell just short in an 83–79 loss to the Wildcats.

"I don't want a man to go out of this room and write that I said we could have beaten Kentucky with a well Bobby Verga," Bubas told reporters afterward. Naturally, Duke fans thought that—and so did Bubas.

"I know Bobby is a better player than he showed and we are a stronger club when he is well," Bubas said. "We are better, a whole lot better, when he is healthy."

In hindsight, Rupp may have wished that his Wildcats had lost to the Blue Devils in the semifinals. In the title game, Kentucky was not only upset by Texas Western but was beaten in a game that would come to symbolize the racial revolution in college basketball. Don Haskins started five blacks against Rupp's all-white team—and won. Somehow, over the years, Rupp and the 1966 Kentucky team, which was just one of many all-white teams in the South, have come to symbolize the racism that kept blacks off the court for so many years.

Would the same thing have happened if Verga had been healthy and Duke would have beaten Kentucky in the semifinals?

The Blue Devils, like Kentucky, were an all-white team in 1966. However, the young, articulate Bubas would have been harder to demonize than the long-established Rupp. He didn't have a history of resistance to racial change and he could have pointed to Claiborne, who was about to move up to the varsity, as evidence that Duke was integrating with all due speed.

It's also possible that Duke would not have lost to Texas Western.

The Blue Devils, a superb ball-handling team that had handled UCLA's pressure with ease, might not have wilted as Kentucky did under the pressure of Willie Worsley, Orsten Aris, and Bobby Joe Hill. And Bubas had something that Rupp's Runts didn't: a genuine big man to match up with David Lattin in the post.

"If we could have been at full strength, I'd have welcomed a shot at Texas Western," Bubas said, when asked about such speculation. "I don't say we would have beaten them, but we could have given them a whirl."

Who knows how the history of college basketball might have changed had Bob Verga not gotten sick before the 1966 Final Four? But two facts are fairly certain: The racial walls in college basketball were going to tumble with or without the example of Texas Western; and Bubas' run at the top of Tobacco Road was going to end—no matter what happened that spring weekend in College Park.

5

THE RISE OF DEAN SMITH

Dean SMITH ALWAYS SEEMED TO BE IN FRANK MCGUIRE'S SHADOW during his three seasons as an assistant coach at North Carolina. Even when he was introduced as UNC's new head coach at a hastily called press conference at a Chapel Hill restaurant, almost all the stories written at the time focused on McGuire and his reasons for leaving. Reporters weren't even sure of Smith's age, which was variously reported at twenty-nine and thirty, or his hometown, which was reported to be either Emporia or Topeka, Kansas.

Unlike McKinney and Bubas, who were collegiate stars on Tobacco Road, Smith had been a marginal player at Kansas, halfway across the country. He was so obscure that his brief appearance in the 1951 NCAA title game—when the Jayhawks knocked off McGuire's St. John's Redmen—was originally not recorded. Smith later had to provide photographic evidence that he got in the game with twenty-nine seconds left to secure a place in the NCAA record-book.

Smith, born in Emporia and raised in Topeka, was an assistant coach at the Air Force Academy when he first met McGuire during the 1957 Final Four. The Tar Heel coach shared a hotel suite in crowded Kansas City with Navy coach Ben Carnevale and Smith's boss at Air Force, Bob Spear. The young Air Force assistant slept on a couch and got to know McGuire, who told him that he was going to need a replacement soon for aging assistant coach Buck Freeman.

When Freeman retired after the 1958 season, McGuire's first offer went to Smith. He hired the young coach for $7,500 a year, then allowed the new-comer to handle much of the detail work involved in the coaching business that he found distasteful. That included preparing UNC's appeal of the NCAA charges of "excessive recruiting expenditures." When McGuire shrugged off the accusation and refused to get involved in the case, Smith was forced to track down and document several years of expenditures, often obtaining affidavits to explain the missing receipts. While the appeal failed, Smith's hard work and his integrity impressed UNC Chancellor William Aycock.

So when McGuire left UNC late in the summer of 1961, Aycock picked the thirty-year-old Smith to run a program that was just about to be wrecked by UNC President William Friday's draconian response to the point-shaving scandal that had unfolded the previous spring.

"Don't worry about winning and losing," Smith recalls Aycock telling him. "Give me a team that won't embarrass the university. Do that and I'll support you."

Smith needed Aycock's support in his first few years. While his Tobacco Road contemporaries, McKinney and Bubas, were winning ACC titles and going to Final Fours, his Tar Heels were struggling to overcome the handicaps of recruiting and scheduling. In retrospect, Smith's record for those dry years looks surprisingly good—although it didn't seem that way to UNC fans who were used to McGuire's contending teams.

Their frustration reached a peak in the early morning hours of January 7, 1965 when UNC returned to Chapel Hill after suffering a dispiriting 107–85 loss at Wake Forest. The defeat was Carolina's fourth loss in a row and dropped the team to 6–6 on the season with a trip to No. 8 Duke coming up in three days.

As the team bus pulled up in front of Woollen Gym, about a hundred students gathered across the street, surrounding a dummy of Smith that was hanging from a tree.

"I could tell it was me because of the long nose," Smith said.

Smith ignored the scene, but senior Billy Cunningham raced off the bus, grabbed the dummy, and ripped it down. The Tar Heel players walked past in silence, several pausing to kick the effigy of their coach in disgust.

"You never forget a thing like that, ever," Smith wrote in his autobiography. "But it wasn't as traumatic for me as it has been made out to be over the years. My standard response was that I was glad there was an interest in basketball here and I'm just happy they used a dummy and not the real thing."

Smith's critics got a taste of his mettle just days after the ugly scene outside Woollen Gym. He took his staggering Tar Heels to Duke and staggered the heavily favored Blue Devils with a perfectly executed gameplan. He spread the floor and worked to get shots for his two stars, Cunningham and sophomore Bob Lewis. Defensively, UNC focused on stopping Marin and Verga, holding the two Duke stars to twenty-one points between them. The impatient Blue Devils took seventeen more shots than the visiting Tar Heels, but UNC made one more field goal and silenced the Duke fans—and Smith's critics—with a 65–62 victory.

"I would prefer not to be hung in effigy to motivate a team," Smith said, "but the incident helped. We were a fired-up bunch."

When UNC returned to Chapel Hill after the game, there was another large crowd waiting—this time to cheer the embattled coach. The fans yelled for Smith to speak.

"I can't," he told them. "There's something around my neck that keeps me from speaking."

That was a glorious moment for the young Tar Heel coach, but it would be a mistake to see that as a turning point in his program. In fact, four days after the win at Duke, UNC lost at home to N.C. State and, afterward, Smith was again hung in effigy.

The truth was that Smith, in his fourth year, was still a long way from the top of the ACC. He was able to cover up many of his team's deficiencies by using his tactical acumen and exploiting the talent of Cunningham—an amazing leaper nicknamed The Kangeroo Kid, who led the ACC in scoring and rebounding in 1965.

"I don't know whether it will be John Glenn or Cunningham who will make the first trip to the moon," Wake Forest's McKinney said. "Cunningham is already in striking distance."

But Cunningham could not carry North Carolina past Duke to the top of Tobacco Road. That would have to wait for a new generation of Tar Heel players.

DEAN FINALLY STEPS UP

When Duke returned to Durham in 1966 with another NCAA third-place trophy, it would have been easy to think that the Blue Devils would continue to rule Tobacco Road.

True, Jack Marin and Steve Vacendak were graduating; but Vic Bubas had replaced Art Heyman and Jeff Mullins without faltering. Who would argue that he couldn't build a new champion around Bob Verga and Mike Lewis?

And his recruiting touch seemed as good as ever. As the new season opened, the Duke coach was lining up what would become his most celebrated recruiting class—headed by diminutive point guard Dick DeVenzio from Pennsylvania, giant center Randy Denton from Raleigh, and two-sport superstar Brad Evans from Durham.

It would have taken a perceptive observer to predict that after five seasons of relative mediocrity, North Carolina's Dean Smith was about to assert himself and his carefully constructed program. But Smith, who had watched his freshman team rout his varsity in a preseason scrimmage before the 1965–66 season, suspected that his time had finally come.

The key to UNC's revival was the construction of Carmichael Auditorium. The new facility was an odd compromise with legislators who couldn't see the value in spending money to build a new basketball facility, especially in the wake of the point-shaving scandals. Technically, Carmichael wasn't a new facility. It was an "extension" of Woollen Gym, a three-sided structure that shared one wall with the old building. It was designed to seat 8,600 fans, but jamming a few extra seats in boosted capacity to exactly the same 8,800 that could pack Duke Indoor Stadium.

Smith didn't wait until Carmichael Auditorium was completed in 1965 to put it to use. He brought recruits to view the hole in the ground and told them that's where they would play. It helped him lure a five-man class that moved up to the varsity in the fall of 1966. Three of the newcomers—6-foot-11 center Rusty Clark of Fayetteville, North Carolina, slender 6-foot-8 forward Bill Bunting of New Bern, North Carolina, and 6-foot-3 point guard Dick Grubar from Schenectady, New York—moved right into the starting lineup. They joined senior Bob Lewis, who had led the ACC in scoring the year before, and 6-foot-4 junior forward Larry Miller, who was perhaps the most significant player Smith ever recruited.

"Miller was the first guy we got that Duke wanted," Smith said.

Miller was a powerful wing player from Catasauqua, Pennsylvania. For months, everybody thought Duke was the favorite to land him. But UNC assistant Kenny Rosemond practically lived in Catasauqua, getting to know the Miller family and finally convincing the star prospect to visit Chapel Hill with the line, "You know, Larry, the saddest thing is, if you went from here to Duke, you'd be going all that way and you'd still be five minutes from heaven."

Miller enjoyed his visit and hit it off with Smith. And just as Heyman's reversal changed the balance of power in the rivalry five years earlier, Miller's decision to cast his lot with the young Tar Heel coach would turn the rivalry back in Carolina's favor.

That point was driven home in Durham on January 7, 1967, in the final seconds of North Carolina's first matchup with Duke. The Tar Heels led most of the way, but with the Duke crowd egging them on, the Blue Devils fought back to tie the game with less than a minute to play. On the UNC bench, Smith stood up and tried to call time-out to set up a winning play. Miller ignored his coach. He took a pass from Clark and slashed through the Duke defense to score the go-ahead basket. "I can't tell you how much I was hoping no one had seen my time-out signal," Smith told reporters. "Fortunately, they hadn't."

North Carolina had entered the game 10–1 and ranked No. 3 in the nation, but getting past Duke that Saturday afternoon in Durham proved to be an important psychological hurdle as UNC climbed to the top of the ACC standings.

It was a very different ACC than the one that Duke had dominated in the previous years. Bones McKinney was no longer at Wake Forest and there was a new but familiar face in Raleigh. And there was trouble brewing south of the North Carolina border, where another familiar character was sparking controversy once again.

McKinney's departure had actually come a year earlier, after the 1965 season. He joked that he was fired: "I had a lifetime contract, then [Wake Forest President] Dr. [Harold] Tribble called me one day and pronounced me dead." The truth was more prosaic. McKinney had tried to cope with the pressures of the job by using (and then abusing) alcohol and amphetamines. His immediate replacements, Jackie Murdock and Jack McClosky, would have little success.

N.C. State had better luck replacing Press Maravich. Case's successor was disappointed that N.C. State wouldn't match the huge salary offer he had received from LSU. He was also frustrated by his son's inability to meet the ACC's notorious qualifying standard: a minimum score of 800 on the SATs. Pete Maravich, who had completed his career at Raleigh's Broughton High as the top scorer in North Carolina prep history, attended prep school in 1966 in an effort to boost his academic credentials. When he still failed to meet the

ACC standards, Maravich and son took their act to Baton Rouge, where the money was better and the admissions standards were a bit more lenient.

N.C. State responded by luring former Wolfpack guard Norm Sloan back to Raleigh from Florida, where he had recorded a good, but not great, record as head coach of the Gators. Sloan, already known as "Stormin' Norman" for his volatile temper, would take a while to get going in Raleigh.

For the time being, the greatest threat to Smith's new powerhouse in Chapel Hill would come from his old boss. Frank McGuire had returned from a brief stint in the NBA to rebuild the South Carolina program. His Underground Railroad was quickly delivering the same kind of New York talent that he had used to make UNC a power a decade earlier.

The young Gamecocks upset UNC in Columbia and were thought to pose a major threat to the league's regular season champs in the ACC Tournament. After years of complaints by rival coaches that playing the tournament in Raleigh was an unfair advantage for N.C. State, the ACC had finally moved its showcase event to a neutral site: the Greensboro War Memorial Coliseum. But if the site was new, the finalists were quite familiar as UNC and Duke advanced to the title game. The Blue Devils knocked off South Carolina in the semifinals—an impressive win that convinced quite a few ACC veterans that Duke would continue its dominance of the ACC Tournament.

"Duke to Win Tournament," screamed a headline in the Greensboro newspaper, topping a column written by respected writer Smith Barrier. Larry Miller cut the headline out and pasted it inside his locker. Then he went out and almost single-handedly proved Barrier and all the other skeptics wrong. Miller hit thirteen of fourteen field goal attempts and finished with thirty-two points and eleven rebounds, and the Tar Heels were in control almost all the way in their 82–73 victory. Lewis added twenty-six points as UNC won its second conference championship since 1940.

It was finally clear that Smith had constructed a powerful, balanced team. One of the keys was Lewis, who sacrificed much of his offense to produce that balance. One year after leading the ACC at 27.4 points a game, he was content to average just 18.4 points and to surrender team scoring honors to Miller, who earned ACC Player of the Year honors.

It was still a very young team, with the three sophomore starters. And while the Tar Heels were disappointed by their loss to Dayton in the Final Four, one game short of a championship matchup with UCLA, it was still a great season for Tobacco Road's most popular program. Now that Smith had finally guided his program to the top of Tobacco Road, he wasn't about to go away again.

BREAKING THE BARRIER

Late in the 1966 season, North Carolina was returning to Chapel Hill after a heartbreaking loss at Virginia when UNC radio man Bill Currie—promoted as "The Mouth of the South"—happened to mention to Dean Smith that Davidson's Lefty Driesell was about to sign his first black player.

"I had never heard of Charles Scott," Smith said. But when he learned that the former New York playground legend was, in fact, an excellent student on an academic scholarship at North Carolina's Laurinburg Institute, he sent assistant coach Danny Lotz to check him out. At the same time, assistant Larry Brown traveled to Lebanon (Ind.) to scout Indiana prep legend Rick Mount. When the two assistants returned to Chapel Hill, they got into an argument as to which one was the better prospect: it was a debate that was not settled until Brown watched Scott and agreed that Lotz was right.

Smith learned that while Scott had originally committed to Davidson, he had since backed off and was looking at Duke, West Virginia, and several Ivy League schools.

The reason for Scott's change of mind is the stuff of legend—and like most legends, the facts are often confused. It was not, as is so often repeated, that Scott was refused service in a Davidson restaurant. Actually, when Scott visited the establishment in question with Driesell, he was treated well. However, when Laurinburg headmaster Frank McDuffie and his wife visited the same restaurant in company with Davidson assistant coach Terry Holland, the black couple was refused service.

In contrast, Scott had a spectacular visit to Chapel Hill. Freshman guard Dick Grubar took him to a concert on campus, but Scott slipped away from his hosts for a few hours and wandered the town on his own.

"He wanted to see how he would be treated," Smith said. "He reasoned that if he were with a coach, he might be treated differently."

Scott was also impressed that Smith asked him what he preferred to be called. To everybody else in the basketball universe, he was Charlie Scott. "That was never my name," said Scott, who asked to be called Charles.

It's hard to believe now, but over the next four years, Smith's insistence on referring to his black star as Charles Scott infuriated the ABC crowd. It was a flashpoint for those who had trouble accepting not just a black player, but the ACC's first great black player. For Scott was clearly a great player, almost from the moment he stepped on UNC's campus. A slender 6-foot-5 guard, he played with intelligence and grace—plus an athleticism that few players, of any color, could match.

His freshman year, when Smith's varsity was driving toward its first ACC title, Carmichael was packed for freshman games. And as the 1967–68 season opened, Scott slid comfortably into the starting lineup, replacing high-scoring senior Bob Lewis. Opponents soon learned that the transition did little to make their job easier.

"We're doing a pretty good job of containing Larry Miller and Scott is tearing us apart," Bubas said after losing to UNC in Chapel Hill. "I'm thinking, we're covering Superman and Zorro is killing us."

The combination of Miller and Scott anchored a North Carolina team that bounced back from an early loss at Vanderbilt to win twenty straight games—the most for the Tar Heels since the 1957 team's thirty-two straight wins. The streak finally ended in Carmichael when Frank McGuire's Gamecocks pulled off a stunning 87–86 upset as a skinny sophomore guard named Bobby Cremins converted sixteen of seventeen free throws down the stretch. Just three days later, the No. 2-ranked Tar Heels were again upset in the regular season finale at Duke (amazingly by the same 87–86 score). Forever known as the "Freddie Lind" game, it took three overtimes and one of the most unlikely performances in the history of Tobacco Road to win for the Blue Devils.

Lind was a little-used junior big man from Highland Park, Illinois. Unlike Larry Worsley, who was a top sub before his surprising showing against Duke in the 1965 ACC Tournament, Lind hardly ever got off the bench. He had played in just thirteen of Duke's previous twenty-four games, scoring a grand total of twelve points on the season. But with backup center Warren Chapman hurt and starter Mike Lewis in foul trouble, Bubas had to turn to Lind in desperation.

Surprisingly, Lind responded—playing, as one writer put it, "with fire in his eyes and ice-water in his veins." He made play after play as the Blue Devils pulled out the unexpected victory. Long after the game, hundreds of Duke students gathered in the walkway between Duke Indoor Stadium and Card Gymnasium and waited for Lind to finish in the locker room. When he finally emerged, the unlikely hero was hoisted on the shoulders of admiring students and carried toward the Duke Chapel.

But the loss at Duke proved to be just a bump on UNC's return path to the Final Four. The Tar Heels stormed through the ACC Tournament, routing N.C. State by thirty-seven points in the title game.

"I believe this is a better Carolina team than the one last year," Smith said. "And as you know, that was one of the greatest in Carolina history."

Unfortunately, the 1968 Tar Heels had the misfortune to be great in the same year that John Wooden's UCLA program hit its peak with All-American center Lew Alcindor and a brilliant supporting cast. The mighty Bruins, playing in front of a home crowd in Los Angeles, rolled to a 78–55 victory in the national title game—which was at that time (and was to remain for twenty-two more years) the most one-sided game in championship history. Alcindor finished with thirty-four points on seventeen of twenty-four shooting and single-handedly destroyed UNC's delay game with his defense around the basket.

"UCLA has to be the best basketball team ever assembled," Smith told reporters.

GREAT SCOTT!

Scott was the No. 3 vote-getter on the All-ACC first-team as a sophomore, trailing only teammate Larry Miller and Duke's Mike Lewis in the voting.

His strong play was in sharp contrast to the black players who had preceded him in the ACC. Bill Jones at Maryland averaged 2.1 points a game when he broke the ACC's color barrier in 1965–66. C.B. Claiborne, bothered all year by an injury, played little as a sophomore at Duke in 1966–67 and was still a marginal player a year later when Scott arrived in Chapel Hill. Norwood Todmann—a guard from New York City who debuted at Wake Forest in the same season that Scott first played at UNC—was better, but he was still far from an elite player. Al Heartley, a walk-on guard from Clayton (N.C.), joined N.C. State a year after Scott's debut but played little in his first two years.

Scott became the focal point of a Carolina team trying to win its third straight ACC title. While Rusty Clark, Bill Bunting, and Dick Grubar returned to start for the third straight season, Miller was gone and he was replaced in the lineup by junior guard Eddie Fogler—a solid player but no superstar. Scott had to take over the leadership role for a team that spent most of the season ranked No. 2 to unbeaten UCLA.

The Tar Heels took an 18–1 record and a No. 2 national ranking to Charlotte on February 14 to meet South Carolina in the annual North-South

Doubleheader. Former UNC coach Frank McGuire had his new team ready for his old, unleashing sophomore guard John Roche—a tough New York kid who scored thirty points in a 68–66 upset of the Tar Heels. Two weeks later, North Carolina traveled to Columbia (S.C.); despite thirty-seven points by Roche and what Smith called a barrage of "the worst possible racial taunts," Scott led UNC to a 68–62 victory.

The two UNC–South Carolina matchups would assume major importance after the ACC Tournament, becoming the focal point in another great controversy on Tobacco Road. But before that story erupted, the league was consumed by the unexpected decision of Duke's Vic Bubas to step down at the end of his tenth season.

Bubas—the coach Cameron hoped, "would coach forever"—was just forty-one years old. But just after Christmas, he told his two assistants (future NBA coaches Chuck Daly and Hubie Brown) that he would be quitting at the end of the season. Although Duke made no official announcement, the news leaked out. Just before UNC traveled to Durham for the 1969 regular season finale, Bubas acknowledged that he was quitting at the end of the season to take an administrative job in Duke's Development Office.

His last team gave him a spectacular sendoff, upsetting No. 2 North Carolina for the second straight year in Duke Indoor Stadium. Although senior Steve Vandenberg led Duke with thirty-three points and Lind had another big day, Smith credited the victory to sophomore point guard Dick DeVenzio.

"Now all of you saw why I recruited Dick DeVenzio so heavily," Smith said. "I think we lost this game when he decided to go to Duke."

DeVenzio, a celebrated prospect out of Ambridge, Pennsylvania, had also been heavily recruited by John Wooden at UCLA and by Lefty Driesell at Davidson. He ended up having a disappointing career after Bubas' departure and became very bitter about his collegiate experience. He would become a leading advocate of athletes' rights before his death in 2002 from cancer.

But in March of 1969, DeVenzio appeared to be living up to the hype. After sparking Duke's upset of UNC in Durham, he scored twenty-four points in a first-round ACC Tournament victory over Virginia, then fourteen more as Duke upset second-seeded South Carolina in the semifinals. DeVenzio was once again on fire in the title game as the Blue Devils took a 43–34 halftime lead over heavily favored UNC. Everything seemed to be going Duke's way:

Gubar was carried off the court after suffering a knee injury that would end his career; both Clark and Bunting were in serious foul trouble.

When Duke scored the first basket of the second half to go up eleven, Bubas said that for a moment, he thought victory was in his grasp.

Then he saw Charles Scott.

"I looked down at the Carolina bench and I felt like everybody except Charlie Scott looked like the thing was over," Bubas said. "He was yelling, 'Give the ball to me . . . I'll win the game.' I'm afraid that's what happened. But when a guy hits thirty-foot jump shots, going to his left, falling in the crowd, all you can say is 'nice going.'"

One writer described UNC's slim junior as "a leaping, whirling, twisting ball of fire."

Scott, who had scored twelve first-half points, hit thirteen of fourteen shots in the second half, many from long range. His twenty-eight second-half points (forty for the game) propelled the Tar Heels into the lead with five minutes left. Then he triggered the Four Corners down the stretch as UNC pulled away for an 85–76 victory.

"It was one of the great individual displays you've ever seen," UNC's Smith said. It was one of the great individual displays anybody on Tobacco Road had seen—or ever would see. Scott's heroics not only earned the Tar Heels a third straight ACC championship, they also demonstrated in the clearest way possible that the black athlete had arrived and would forever change the way basketball was played on Tobacco Road.

Some of the league's old-timers had been resisting that revelation. That became obvious on the Monday after the ACC championship game, when the league announced the voting for ACC player of the year. South Carolina's John Roche won the award with fifty-six votes compared to thirty-nine for Scott. Worse, Roche was a unanimous choice for first-team All-ACC, while Scott was left off five ballots. It was a slight that Scott refused to swallow without gagging.

"They put a guy ahead of me because he's white," Scott told the *Washington Post*. "It's a frustrating thing when you go to the Olympics and you represent your state, your country and your conference. It really makes you think. It makes you wonder."

When reporters ran to Smith with Scott's comments, he backed his star up—although at the time, he denied that the voting slight was racist in nature.

"It just shows the lack of basketball knowledge of those writers," he said. Many years later, in his autobiography, Smith was more open about the vote.

"It was transparently racist," he wrote. "The real telltale sign of what happened was that five voters did not even put Charles on their all-conference team—despite the fact that he was an Olympian and a first-team All-American. It was a clear insult."

Scott responded to the insult by leading UNC to its third straight Final Four. He capped the run by almost single-handedly shooting down Driesell's Davidson Wildcats in the regional finals. The player Smith had stolen from Driesell poured in thirty-two points, including the game-winner from the top of the key at the buzzer.

"If you can't do it under pressure, what good is it to be out there?" Scott said.

Unfortunately, Scott's storybook season didn't have a storybook finish. Matched against Purdue in the national semifinals in Louisville, Scott was clearly outplayed by Rick Mount—the gunner than both Brown and Lotz had scouted four years earlier. Another thorn in UNC's side that afternoon was Winston-Salem guard Herm Gilliam, who had tried to enroll at Wake Forest and only went to Purdue when he came up a few points short of 800 on his SAT score.

Scott finished the season with a thirty-five-point outburst against Drake in the consolation game. His season ended without a national title or without ACC player of the year honors. But, later that summer, the same ACC writers and broadcasters who had snubbed Scott as the ACC basketball Player of the Year, voted him the ACC's Athlete of the Year.

It was a small, but significant, admission that "Great Scott" was changing the atmosphere on Tobacco Road.

6

STORMIN' NORMAN

THE DEPARTURE OF BUBAS AFTER THE 1969 SEASON MARKED THE beginning of nearly a decade-long decline for Duke basketball and created a void on Tobacco Road.

The league was undergoing major changes. At Duke, Bubas was replaced by his young protégé, Bucky Waters, who had established himself with a strong four-year run as head coach at West Virginia. Duke alum Lefty Driesell wanted the job badly; he even drove to Durham before the Southern Conference Tournament to meet with Duke officials. He learned that the powers at Duke still remembered his intemperate remarks after a 1965 loss to Duke, when he called Bubas "yellow" for not playing him in Charlotte; and he didn't feel he'd fit the image that the elite private school wanted to project.

Duke would get a good chance to see what they missed. One day after Driesell's Davidson Wildcats were knocked out of the 1969 NCAA Tournament by Charlie Scott at Cole Field House in College Park (Md.), Driesell toured the Maryland campus and was soon introduced as Maryland's new coach. He boldly proclaimed that his goal was to make Maryland, "the UCLA of the East."

But the real challenger—and eventual conquerer—of the mighty Bruins would be constructed on Tobacco Road, by the heir to Everett Case.

Norman Sloan, a member of Case's first recruiting class, had slowly climbed the coaching ladder. He started at tiny Presbyterian College in Clinton, South Carolina, where he also worked as an assistant football coach with young Midwesterner Bo Schembechler. After a year as an assistant at Memphis, Sloan took the head job at The Citadel and then moved on to Florida, where he made himself unpopular by constantly arguing that the football-crazy Gators treat basketball with respect. During one debate with football coach/athletic director Ray Graves, Sloan made his boss so mad that Graves slammed his fist on his desk, shattering the glass desktop. Sloan admitted that he earned his nickname "Stormin' Norman" in those days.

"I had trouble arguing," he admitted. "I could fight, but not argue."

The opportunity at N.C. State offered Sloan more than the chance to return to his alma mater: it offered him a chance to coach at a school that put basketball first. He took special delight one weekend a few years later when Florida visited Raleigh to play N.C. State in football, just as preseason basketball practice was beginning. He hosted a pig-picking for his old friends from Gainesville.

"All they could talk about was how the front pages of all the Carolina papers that morning were covered with basketball practice stories," Sloan recalled.

The colorful coach didn't find immediate success in Raleigh—although it didn't take him long to get the program moving in the right direction. The Pack slowly climbed from last in the ACC in his first season (1967) to second in his fourth (1970). That year, he engineered a stunning 42–39 double-overtime victory over South Carolina in the 1970 ACC Tournament title game.

That early triumph merely laid the groundwork for what Sloan would achieve in the coming years. While his rival Dean Smith was locked in a long, bitter recruiting battle (and ultimately an unsuccessful one) for celebrated Pennsylvania big man Tom McMillen, Sloan was mining the talent on Tobacco Road, reaping the bountiful harvest of Case's campaign to put "a basket in every driveway."

In back-to-back years, the Wolfpack coach beat Smith head-to-head for two gifted players from the western part of the state—starting with 7-foot-4 stringbean Tommy Burleson. Sloan knew he had the edge in the battle for the farm boy who had dreamed of studying agriculture at N.C. State ever since visiting the Raleigh campus on a 4-H tour as a fourteen-year-old. During the trip, Burleson visited the N.C. State basketball office and asked to meet Coach Sloan. The Wolfpack coach, in a meeting with his staff, graciously agreed to meet the curious eighth grader.

"Then Burleson walked in and he had to bend over to keep from hitting his head on the door," Wolfpack assistant coach Sam Esposito told writer Tim Peeler. "We almost had a heart attack."

Burleson actually committed to N.C. State very early in the process, but he asked Sloan to keep his decision secret. He was working that summer at Grandfather Mountain, a resort owned by Hugh Morton, a fanatic UNC basketball supporter. Burleson was afraid that if Morton learned he was going to State, he'd be fired. UNC's Smith was furious when he learned what had happened and blamed Sloan.

"Maybe Norm wanted me to spend my time recruiting Tommy instead of anybody else," he said. "I spent a lot of time going to the mountains to show interest."

Smith would have been even more angry if he'd known the impact Burleson's choice would have on another prospect from western North Carolina. David Thompson was a 6-foot-4 wing player from just outside Shelby, where he grew up in a small house at the end of a long dirt road. He was the youngest of eleven children.

Playing in the same western North Carolina prep conference, Thompson and Burleson met and became admirers first, then friends. They talked about going to school together; since Burleson, who was one year ahead of Thompson, was determined to go to N.C. State, they talked about winning a national championship in Raleigh. Sloan's new assistant coach, Eddie Biedenbach, played much the same role that Ken Rosemond had in UNC's successful pursuit of Larry Miller: he practically lived in Shelby and convinced Thompson that State wanted him more.

N.C. State ended up paying a price for its successful recruiting effort. The NCAA levied a one-year postseason ban on the school for a number of minor infractions, including providing free rooming for Thompson at the school's basketball camp (he slept on the floor of a dorm room with two friends from Shelby) and an illegal tryout (assistant coach Eddie Biedenbach joined a pickup game in which Thompson was playing). Duke drew a similar penalty for a couple of minor violations committed by a Shelby businessman who was trying to help the Blue Devils land Thompson.

Sloan's twin recruiting victories in western North Carolina in 1970 and 1971 were to change the balance of power on Tobacco Road once again.

THE GREATEST

David Thompson was not that well known when he first took the floor as a member of N.C. State's 1971–72 freshman team. Many fans knew he was the target of an intense recruiting battle among N.C. State, Duke, and UNC; but in an era when there was no summer camp circuit, just one national prep all-star game, and just one recognized prep All-American team, even the most celebrated recruits were unknown quantities.

Thompson, for all the hoopla over his recruiting, wasn't nationally celebrated. And even when he played in the North Carolina East-West High School All-Star Game, Greensboro guard Ray Harrison, who had signed at UNC, was voted the MVP after outscoring Thompson 26–24. The Greensboro paper wondered in print: "Harrison or Thompson, which is No. 1?"

But it didn't take long for word to filter out of Raleigh that the 6-foot-4 freshman from Shelby was in a class by himself. In his third freshman game, Thompson set a Reynolds Coliseum record by scoring fifty-four points against Isothermal Community College. When a strong North Carolina freshman team visited Raleigh, Thompson scored forty-nine points and abused Harrison as State won by twenty-six points.

Fred Schaus—who had coached Jerry West, both at West Virginia and with the Lakers—watched the precocious freshman play and announced, "Thompson is better right now than Jerry West was as a college senior. Thompson is one of the ten best basketball players in the nation, pros included." Other observers started to compare the Wolfpack's young prospect to Oscar Robertson or Elgin Baylor.

"No matter what you say about David, you can't exaggerate," Norm Sloan answered when asked about his freshman prodigy. However, he did squelch one rumor: "He cannot jump up, take a quarter off the top of the backboard and leave change in nickels and dimes."

Maybe not, but Thompson's leaping ability was no myth. A representative from Guinness World Records arrived in Raleigh with masking tape and a tape measure and after extensive tests, announced that Thompson's measured vertical leap from a standing start was a world record 42 inches. That otherworldly leaping ability was combined with outstanding quickness, better-than-average strength, and superb agility. Although standing just 6-foot-3½ inches, Thompson had a 7-foot wingspan. He also owned a deadly long-range jump shot out to modern three-point range, excellent defensive and ballhandling skills, and an innate understanding of the game.

Fans began arriving early on game nights in the winter of 1971–72—packing Reynolds Coliseum to see the freshman team perform its magic, and often leaving at the half of the less magical varsity games. Thompson, who averaged 35.6 points and eight rebounds, wasn't the whole show. The freshman team also featured Tim Stoddard, a powerful 6-foot-7 forward from East Chicago (Ind.), and Monte Towe, a 5-foot-7, 145-pound point guard from Converse (Ind.).

Midway through the freshman season for Thompson, Towe, and Stoddard, the NCAA voted to change its bylaws, allowing freshmen to compete at the varsity level. While it was primarily a cost-cutting measure (with freshmen on the varsity, schools could give less scholarships overall), the excitement generated by Thompson was used as evidence that freshmen would be able to contribute on the varsity level.

It would not be the last time that Thompson had a hand in changing the face of college basketball.

He changed the face of basketball on Tobacco Road in his sophomore season, when he and Towe joined Burleson in a lineup that would win fifty-seven of fifty-eight games over the next two years. Burleson had enjoyed a productive sophomore season in 1972 as the Pack finished 16–10. Known as the Newland Needle, he averaged 21.3 points and led the ACC with 14.0 rebounds a game while earning first-team All-ACC honors as a sophomore. Blocked shots weren't counted in that era, but Burleson was as much a force at the defensive end as he was on offense.

Great things were expected from the Pack in 1973, but the reality turned out to be far better than the expectations.

Thompson's varsity debut came against Appalachian State, coached by former Wolfpack coach Press Maravich. The father (and college coach) of the celebrated Pete Maravich had to watch as Thompson, playing with strained knee ligaments, scored thirty-three points and pulled down thirteen rebounds in a 130–53 N.C. State win.

"He's a damn good ballplayer," Maravich said of the young State star. "He can shoot. He jumps well and he's smart. He has all the tools and all the moves to be an All-American."

The Pack's opening win was followed up by lopsided victories by the equally ridiculous scores of 110–40, 144–100, and 125–88. Thompson continued to dazzle all observers, averaging 35.8 points in the Pack's first four victories.

"He's too much for one man and sometimes too much for three," South Florida coach Don Williams said.

Even Thompson called the early season slate "a bunch of creampuffs," but after the Big Four Tournament in early December it became obvious that State's early success was more than an illusion created by a weak schedule. The Big Four Tournament was an attempt to fill the void created by the cancellation of the Dixie Classic. No outsiders were involved this time: just the four Tobacco Road powers and as many fans as could jam their fannies into the expanded Greensboro Coliseum. The fans loved it. The coaches, faced with two extra games against their most bitter rivals, hated it.

In the 1972 Big Four opener, Thompson scored twenty-nine points to carry the Pack into the title game. Expectations had already grown to the point that his twenty-nine-point, twelve-rebound performance against Wake Forest was labeled "disappointing" in several newspaper accounts of the game. Still hampered by a sore knee, Thompson scored a mere nineteen points the next night against No. 11 North Carolina, although that was enough to lead all scorers in a 68–61 Wolfpack win.

That weekend in Greensboro established Thompson as the biggest superstar on Tobacco Road. It would be another month before he exploded onto the national scene.

The stage was a Super Bowl Sunday matchup between No. 3 N.C. State (11–0) and No. 2 Maryland (10–0) in College Park. The Terps had added spectacular freshman guard John Lucas out of Durham's Hillside High School to a powerful lineup that had won the 1972 National Invitational Tournament with Tom McMillen and Len Elmore starting up front.

But it wasn't the magnitude of the matchup that made that State-Maryland game so important. The real significance was the brainchild of N.C. State Athletic Director Willis Casey.

"Willis was sick and tired of sitting through two weeks of hype before the Super Bowl," Frank Weedon, the former N.C. State sports information director, said. "He brought up the ideal for a Sunday game at the ACC's spring meetings." Both Sloan and Driesell liked the idea. "I never particularly liked playing on Sunday," Driesell said. "But it was the same day as the Super Bowl and everybody in the nation would be watching."

Philadelphia-based TV producer C.D. Chesley, who managed the ACC's regional game of the week, was able to sell the noon game to most of the CBS stations that would be televising Super Bowl VII later in the afternoon.

The contrast between the college basketball game at noon and the pro football championship game later in the afternoon couldn't have been more striking. Miami's 14–7 victory over Washington in the latter was an incredibly dull affair, enlivened only by Gary Yepremian's feeble attempt at a forward pass on a botched field goal attempt. State-Maryland was a classic in every way. McMillen was spectacular with twenty-nine points and fourteen rebounds, and freshman John Lucas introduced himself to the nation with eighteen points and eight assists. Burleson had twenty points and fifteen rebounds to outplay Elmore in the middle.

Still, there was no question that the star of the show was the high flying Thompson. He already had thirty-five points when N.C. State called time-out to set up a play with sixteen seconds left and the score tied at 85. Sloan recalls designing a play for Burleson to feed Thompson for the game-winning shot.

"But Maryland was determined to keep the ball from David," he said. "They had all their players, their ushers and everybody else between Tommy and David."

Burleson, standing just beyond the foul line, couldn't see a way to get the ball to Thompson, so he launched a jump shot that clanked high off the front of the rim.

On TV screens across the nation, an estimated audience of 25 million viewers saw Thompson soaring into the picture as if he had dropped from the rafters to grab the rebound and gently lay it in the basket as the buzzer sounded.

"I knew this was the biggest game of my life and I really wanted to do well," Thompson said. "I felt I had to prove myself in this one."

He did just that. There was no going back. From that moment on, Thompson was a national figure and college basketball had found a national audience. Within a year, both CBS and NBC began scheduling regular Saturday afternoon telecasts. The NCAA changed its Final Four format—moving the championship game to Monday night and playing the semifinals on Saturday afternoon so, for the first time, both games could be televised nationally.

It was the second—but not the last—time Thompson would help change the face of college basketball.

Unfortunately, N.C. State's one-year probation prevented Thompson and the 1973 Wolfpack from challenging UCLA's dominance of the college game.

"If we can go unbeaten, that will be as good as getting a crack at UCLA," Thompson said after his seven straight second-half field goals beat Maryland 89–78 in the rematch in Raleigh.

N.C. State, which settled into the No. 2 spot in the national polls after its first victory over Maryland, ran through the ACC season without a loss. The Wolfpack was naturally favored in the ACC Tournament in Greensboro—but the Pack's probation created the same situation as in 1959, when Case's probation-plagued team was ineligible to claim the ACC's automatic bid. Maryland clinched the ACC's bid to the NCAA Tournament with a victory over Wake Forest in the semifinals. And echoing McGuire's lackadaisical approach to the meaningless 1959 title game, Driesell elected to rest hobbled center Len Elmore in the 1973 finals. His presence might have made a difference as the short-handed Terps still hung with the Pack until David Thompson's two free throws with ten seconds left clinched the 76–74 title.

"It's a happy feeling, but an empty one," Tournament MVP Tommy Burleson said.

The 27–0 Wolfpack, just the second (and last) unbeaten team in ACC history, had to watch as Bill Walton led UCLA to its seventh straight NCAA title by beating Memphis State in St. Louis. Thompson, Burleson, and company could only wonder how they'd have fared against the Bruins.

They'd get a chance to find out in the coming season.

THE GREATEST GAME
Sloan knew he had a powerhouse team coming back in 1973–74—once Thompson rejected a $2 million under-the-table offer from the Kentucky Colonels of the fledgling ABA, and he returned to the team with Burleson and Towe. N.C. State was the preseason favorite in a league that was very much divided into the haves and the have-nots. Former Tobacco Road heavyweights Duke and Wake Forest were in the latter group.

Wake Forest coach "Gentleman Carl" Tacy, a West Virginia native who replaced Jack McClosky a year earlier, was just beginning to rebuild his program. Duke was in even worse shape after a bizarre off-season coaching transition.

Bucky Waters, the early promise of his program wrecked by a parade of player transfers, suspected that he was going to be fired after his contract ran out in the spring of 1974. He asked for a vote of confidence from the administration, and when it was not forthcoming, he resigned on September 14—a month before the start of preseason practice. The timing was awkward for Duke Athletic Director Carl James, who responded with a scheme that was either brilliant or insane. He called retired Kentucky coach Adolph Rupp and offered the seventy-one-year-old known as the "Baron of the Bluegrass" a one-year contract to coach Duke.

Amazingly, Rupp accepted and was getting ready to travel to Durham for the introductory press conference when his farm manager died and he decided he couldn't leave his Lexington home. James, with no other option, gave thirty-one-year-old Neill McGeachy, Waters's top assistant, the job. Although he wasn't officially labeled an interim coach, James didn't hesitate to tell reporters that he was conducting a nationwide search to find Duke "a super coach."

North Carolina already had a super coach. And with freshman Walter Davis—a lithe swingman from the Charlotte suburb of Pineville—joining senior forward Bobby Jones and sophomore center Mitch Kupchak in the lineup, the Tar Heels had a powerful team, one that would spend almost the entire season ranked between No. 4 and No. 6 in the nation.

But as good as the Tar Heels were, both State and Maryland were better. The matchups between the Terps and Wolfpack remained the focus of the ACC, even when the two teams weren't playing each other.

Maryland, with sophomore guard Mo Howard joining Lucas to form the ACC's best backcourt, opened the season at UCLA and had the Bruins on the ropes in Pauley Pavilion—before Dave Meyers stole the ball from Lucas in the final seconds to preserve a 65–64 UCLA victory. The win protected the Bruins' seventy-seven-game winning streak. The thriller was in sharp contrast to N.C. State's December bid to knock off the seven-time defending NCAA champs.

That made-for-TV matchup netted both teams an astronomical (for the time) sum of $125,000. The game was played in St. Louis, where that hypothetical 1973 championship game would have been played between the No. 1 Bruins and the No. 2 Wolfpack.

The real thing proved a horrifying experience for Sloan's cocky warriors. State led by 1 at the half, and the game was tied at 54 with 9:30 left. Forward Keith Wilkes sparked a Bruin blitz that blew the Pack into the Mississippi River. The UCLA All-American scored twenty-seven points and limited Thompson to seventeen points, and the Bruins outscored N.C. State 30–12 down the stretch for a lopsided 84–66 victory.

"I hope we're better than this," Sloan told reporters. "We'll just have to wait and see."

Maryland might have been able to take consolation in its far more impressive performance against mighty UCLA if the Terps could have just handled N.C. State—just once. But in a second Super Bowl Sunday matchup, this time in Raleigh, Thompson scored forty-one points in an 80–74 Wolfpack victory. Three weeks later, Thompson scored thirty-nine in Cole Field House as the Pack pulled out yet another close victory over the Terps.

"There was nothing you could do to stop him," Maryland defensive ace Tom Roy complained. Driesell agreed.

"I've guarded him with 6-10 people and 6-4 people and 6-6 people," the Maryland coach said. "You just couldn't stop him. He was unstoppable."

North Carolina came close on a couple of occasions, including the Big Four Tournament, when big man Ed Stahl missed a potential game-winning shot with three seconds left in a 78–77 Pack win. The Tar Heels also came close in Chapel Hill, but twenty-six points by Thompson and twenty-one by the tiny Towe were just too much for UNC to overcome.

"He will just not let them lose," UNC's Bobby Jones, who was later named to the NBA all-defensive team in eight straight seasons, said of Thompson. "If State needs something, Thompson will get it for them. He's just the best I've ever been around."

N.C. State closed out the regular season with twenty-two straight wins following the UCLA loss, becoming the first (and still only) team to record back-to-back unbeaten seasons in ACC play.

But like UNC's 1957 Team of Destiny and South Carolina's 1970 Team of Disappointment, the Wolfpack would have to repeat its success in the ACC Tournament to earn a chance at the national title.

And Sloan's Wolfpack found Maryland—a team N.C. State had beaten in five straight close games over the two previous seasons—once again standing in its path. There were a couple of interesting angles leading up to the championship game.

One was Driesell's approach to Maryland's semifinal victory over North Carolina. The Terps simply destroyed Lefty's old nemesis, jumping to a sixteen-point halftime lead and coasting to a 105–85 victory. It was an impressive rout of the nation's No. 6 ranked team; but curiously, Driesell elected to go almost all the way with his starters. Elmore, Howard, and forward Owen Brown played forty minutes each, while Lucas and McMillen each played thirty-eight minutes—even though the outcome was never in doubt.

"That was a hate game," Maryland assistant coach Dave Pritchett told writer Ron Morris. "We were going to beat their butts as bad as we could beat them."

N.C. State, which enjoyed a first-round bye, was much more rested. Sloan's five starters averaged just twenty-nine minutes in an easy semifinal victory over Virginia.

The fatigue factor may have played a huge role in a title game that would stretch into overtime. The game was played at a terrific pace with superstars on each side making spectacular play after spectacular play. Several players on both sides would battle leg cramps in the hot, humid atmosphere.

"You got the feeling that you had to play better than you'd ever played before or the season would be over," Towe said. "Maryland was playing that well."

As the game progressed, it became obvious that another pregame story line was bearing fruit. At the heart of the controversy was another All-ACC voting snub. Starting that season, the league's media decided to select its all-conference team by position, rather than merely pick the league's five best players. That forced voters to choose between State's Burleson and Maryland's Elmore at center. Statistically, it was a tough choice: Burleson averaged 18.1 points, 12.2 rebounds, and shot 51.6% from the floor; Elmore averaged 14.6 points, 14.7 rebounds, and shot 52.5% from the floor. Both were exceptional defenders.

Burleson, the first-team All-ACC center in each of the two previous years, believed he should get the edge because he anchored the league's championship team, sacrificing statistically to make N.C. State a winner.

"When I was first with David at the beginning of my junior year, the first game we played, I had twenty-six shots and David had twenty-five," Burleson said. "Coach Sloan called me in and said, 'Tom, David needs to be taking the most shots on this team. He needs to be our premier player.' I said, 'You're correct,' so I became more of a defender and playmaker. I averaged over twenty-one points a game as a sophomore. I could have scored a lot more, but I did what was best for the team."

The N.C. State senior was infuriated when the voters gave Elmore the edge in their all-star vote.

"I was quite upset," he said many years later. "I felt like I'd dominated play in the ACC for three years. I would have been the first player at State to be

All-ACC first team three years in a row. I was pretty perturbed that the media didn't think I was a great player."

He transferred some of that anger to his rival when Elmore told reporters to send Burleson the message, "that I am *the* center in the ACC." Sloan clipped the note when it appeared and had assistant coach Eddie Biedenbach paste it in Burleson's locker on the day of the title game.

The 7-foot-4 senior answered his rival on the court. David Thompson, who usually bedeviled the Terps, scored "only" twenty-nine points and shot poorly (10 of 24). Towe was his usual dynamic self, contributing eighteen points, eight assists, and just one turnover in forty-one minutes. But it was Burleson, enjoying the greatest night of his great career, who seized the spotlight in what would be recognized on Tobacco Road as the greatest game ever played.

The center in the ACC scored thirty-eight points on eighteen of twenty-five shooting and added thirteen rebounds against one of the best big men in college basketball.

"He's a great ballplayer, but thirty-eight points against me is unbelievable," Elmore said. "Nobody has ever done that to me and I just can't believe it."

Neither could Driesell.

"We did everything we could to stop the guy," the Maryland coach said. "He just had a fabulous, fabulous night. He was super fired-up."

N.C. State needed every bit of Burleson's brilliance to overcome the equally inspired Terps. Maryland shot almost 65% from the floor and got stellar performances from McMillen, Howard, and Lucas.

"They can't keep shooting like that," Sloan told his players during a second-half time-out, imploring them to turn up the defensive pressure.

But Maryland could—and did. When Elmore banked in a short jumper with just over a minute left, the two teams were tied at 97. N.C. State tried to hold for a final shot, but with Towe (the team's primary ballhandler) out of the game with leg cramps, McMillen stole a pass and gave Driesell a chance to set up a potential game-winner with twelve seconds left.

He designed a play for Lucas, a charismatic native of Durham (N.C.), whose brilliance had come as a shock to those Tobacco Road coaches who half-heartedly recruited him out of Hillside High School.

Sloan asked Moe Rivers, his backcourt stopper, to check Lucas coming out of that final time-out. But Towe, who was supposed to be guarding Mo Howard, slid over to keep the Maryland star out of the lane. Lucas quickly found his backcourt mate—wide open, twelve feet or so to the left of the basket.

For an instant, all of N.C. State's hopes and dreams nestled in Howard's hands. Maryland was just a short jump shot from victory and he was a deadly jump shooter.

But Howard hesitated, perhaps remembering that Driesell wanted Lucas to take the final shot. Instead of launching the short jumper that was there, he kicked the ball out to Lucas, who had to heave an off-balance twenty-five-footer to beat the buzzer.

"We wanted [Lucas] to go one-on-one at the end, but he was physically exhausted and gave the ball up," Driesell complained, ignoring the fact that Lucas had in fact set up a teammate for a relatively easy shot. "If Lucas hadn't been so tired, I think we'd have won."

The overtime went back and forth. Elmore hit a free throw to put Maryland up one, but Burleson countered with a sweeping sky hook to put the Pack up one. Howard hit two free throws to give the Terps a 100–99 edge. Once again, victory seemed to be within Maryland's grasp when Thompson uncharacteristically missed a short jumper, McMillen rebounded, and Lucas was fouled. He had a chance to stretch the lead to three points, but his free throw missed.

"He was just exhausted," Driesell repeated, defending his young star. He didn't mention the extra minutes he'd asked Lucas to play the night before and how that may have impacted his stamina in the title game.

State converted Lucas's miss into a fast break as Towe fed reserve forward Phil Spence for the layup that put the Pack back on top—this time for good. Maryland had two chances to regain the lead—but Burleson blocked a shot by Howard, and the fatigued Lucas overthrew a pass to Elmore that sailed out of bounds. Towe, the fastest free throw shooter in ACC history, sank two free throws with six seconds left to clinch the 103–100 victory.

"That was one of the greatest college games that has ever been played," Sloan said moments after it was over, voicing the sentiment that would be echoed by historians for the next thirty years. (Frank Dascenzo, who covered ACC basketball for more than thirty years—and was at the famous 1992 Duke-Kentucky game—later wrote: "The greatest game ever played? That's easy. It was March 9, 1974. The stakes were terribly high, as were the emotions. It was such a storied night that time seemed to stop. People couldn't sit—not anymore. They stood, and they weren't quite sure whether to applaud . . . or cry. Instead, they gawked at one another—like children watching their siblings open Christmas gifts—to see what in the whole wide world could be so fulfilling.") Sloan then said something else that had a more immediate impact on history: "I think we beat the second-best team in the nation tonight," he told reporters.

But the second-best team in the nation wouldn't be going to the NCAA Tournament. That organization had long invited just one team per conference, a practice that helped independents and top-heavy leagues but hurt deep, balanced conferences such as the ACC.

"It makes me sick," Driesell said. "I see who is getting bids in this NCAA Tournament and I know that [our team] and Carolina and State are better than most of them. But only one team is going. It's not fair."

An increasing number of fans and coaches were beginning to agree. The national attention that the N.C. State–Maryland game attracted added momentum to the debate. Starting in 1975, the NCAA changed its rules to invite as many as two teams per conference. Five years later, the NCAA Tournament took on its present form and invited the best at-large teams, regardless of conference affiliation.

Of course, none of that did Driesell or his Terps any good. They voted not to return to the NIT and sat on the sidelines and watched as N.C. State began its march to the NCAA title. The Wolfpack, playing the East Regionals on its own home court in Raleigh, looked unstoppable in the regional semifinals against Providence as Thompson poured in forty points against All-American Marvin Barnes.

"Now you know why we call him Superman," Barnes said. "I was just trying not to let him get fifty."

But ten minutes into the Sunday afternoon East title game against Pittsburgh, disaster struck State's Superman.

Thompson, upset at what he perceived as a rough treatment by the Panthers, lost his temper for an instant. He raced downcourt, determined to block Pitt's next shot, a jumper by Keith Starr. As the Wolfpack star soared unimaginably high, his foot caught the shoulder of the 6-foot-8 Spence. Thompson flipped and landed head-first on the hardwood court, making a sickening sound that echoed through Case's basketball palace.

"It was unbelievably frightening for me," Burleson said. "I was looking right at him when he fell. I've never seen a person take a fall like that in my life. It was the worst accident I've ever seen."

For four interminable minutes, Thompson laid motionless where he had fallen. Many spectators feared that he was seriously injured—even dead. The crowd of 12,400 had gone deathly silent when Thompson fell and it stayed that way until Thompson finally showed signs of life. The fans nervously applauded as he was strapped into a stretcher and carried off the floor to a waiting ambulance. The game seemed secondary at that moment, although Sloan tried to fire up his shaken team by telling them to win it for Thompson.

CBS news anchor Walter Cronkite, watching the game in New York, phoned Raleigh's Rex Hospital to get a report on Thompson's condition. He was told the same thing the Wolfpack players and the spectators at Reynolds were told at halftime: X-rays showed no broken bones and Thompson was not in any danger.

Towe found that he could breathe again. "I thought David had broken his neck," he said.

Buoyed by the good news—along with twenty-six points from Burleson and strong play by Towe and Rivers—State broke the game open early in the second half. The Pack was leading 79–59 with just under seven minutes left when Thompson made his reappearance, walking slowly on his own and wearing a white bandage around his head to protect the fifteen stitches used to close his bleeding head wound.

Reynolds went crazy.

"The response was overwhelming," Thompson said. "Just the show of affection from my teammates and fans—it was probably the greatest feeling I've ever had in my life."

As it turned out, Thompson, his modest afro shaved to a short buzz cut, was able to play against UCLA six days later. In fact, he played far better than he did in the first meeting with the Bruins three months earlier.

The N.C. State faithful made up the vast majority of the 15,000-plus fans who packed the Greensboro Coliseum for the Final Four. The Pack would need their help to overcome not only UCLA's talent, but also the mystique of a program that had won seven straight NCAA championships and nine of the last ten titles. The Bruins had not lost a tournament game since falling to Wake

Forest in the 1962 Final Four consolation game. In two championship game matchups against Tobacco Road's best, John Wooden's warriors had routed Vic Bubas' best Duke team and Dean Smith's best Carolina team.

Of course, Wooden's greatest weapon was his talent: Center Bill Walton had been the Final Four MVP only a year earlier; forwards Keith Wilkes and Dave Meyers were both future all-pro players; guard Greg Lee had started on two national championship teams and had set a championship game assist record the year before. But State had Burleson to offset Walton, Towe to break down the Bruins' pressure, and Thompson to do everything else.

"David was like the queen on the chessboard," Maryland's Elmore said. "He could go everywhere—inside, outside, rebounding. His impact was felt all over the floor."

This game, like the December matchup in St. Louis, was close at the half. And just as in St. Louis, UCLA threw a second-half run at the Pack—racing to an eleven-point lead. This time, Burleson scored six straight points to start the Pack's long comeback. Thompson hit a pair of jumpers and converted a lob from Stoddard into a three-point play to finally give the Pack a 62–60 lead as the noise in the Greensboro Coliseum reached a crescendo.

When UCLA regained the lead on a bank shot by Walton, Thompson tied it—soaring so high over Walton and Meyers on a lob that his elbows were over the rim.

Burleson blocked a shot by Walton in the final minute to give N.C. State the last shot in regulation, but Stoddard's wide open twenty-three-footer rimmed out and the Pack went into overtime for the second time in two weeks on the Greensboro court.

"I thought we had the game in hand," Wooden would tell reporters later. "We took some bad shots when we had the eleven-point lead and State had the poise and ability to take advantage or our mistakes."

The first extra period was a tactical duel with each team slowing it down and scoring a single field goal. Burleson had a chance to win for the Pack, but his hook shot over Walton clanked off.

"I couldn't believe it," Thompson would late write. "Two chances to win at the end and both missed. Monte came over to me and said, 'David, if it comes down to that situation again, either you or I are going to take that shot.'"

But it didn't look like State would get that chance. UCLA seemed to catch the Pack off-balance by turning up the tempo in the second overtime. The

Bruins took a 74–67 lead with just over three minutes left. This time it was Towe who brought the Wolfpack back—Towe and the thousands of hysterical Tobacco Road fans screaming for an upset.

"It always helps to have the crowd on your side, especially when you're making a run like State was," Wooden said, then quickly added: "There's nothing wrong with this place. We've already had the national finals in Los Angeles, so I'm not complaining."

Burleson missed a chance to tie when he hit just one of his two free throws with 1:38 left, but after UCLA's Meyers missed the first of a one-and-one, Thompson decided to take the game in his own hands. He rebounded the missed free throw and pushed the ball up the left side of the court, with Wilkes in his face all the way.

A week earlier, Marvin Barnes's had scoffed at the notion that Wilkes had shut down Thompson in St. Louis.

"I watched the game," Barnes said. "Thompson was getting his shot off over Wilkes whenever he wanted to. He was just missing."

Thompson was to justify Barnes's scouting report in that frenzied moment at the end of the second overtime in Greensboro. He pushed the ball to within twelve feet of the basket, then soared over Wilkes to launch a jump shot that dropped in, giving the Pack a 76–75 lead.

When Lee missed a long jumper at the other end, Thompson again leaped over Wilkes for the rebound. The UCLA All-American fouled out trying to block the State superstar. Thompson's two free throws (his 27th and 28th points) gave State a three-point lead with thirty seconds to play.

When Burleson knocked a long pass from Lee to Walton away, the game was essentially over, especially after the unflappable Towe added two free throws to negate Walton's meaningless basket at the buzzer.

The 80–77 victory ended the most dominant run in NCAA history.

"Before the season began, I told our team that we had a chance to be one of the greatest teams of all time," Sloan said. "I'm not making that claim now, but we beat one of the greatest of all time."

Of course, beating UCLA didn't give N.C. State the national championship. The Wolfpack still needed to beat Al McGuire's Marquette Warriors in Monday night's title game. The big man combo of Maurice Lucas and Bo Ellis proved to be a problem, combining for thirty-two points and twenty-four rebounds, but star guard Earl Tatum was shut down by Rivers, scoring just four points on 2-of-7 shooting. The game was close until McGuire's intemperate tirade late in the first half earned him a pair of technical fouls and sparked N.C. State to a 10–0 run in a fifty-three-second span. That spurt gave N.C. State a working margin that it protected the rest of the way for a 76–64 victory and the championship.

"We wanted it so badly," Sloan said. "The players deserved to be national champions. I would have been heartbroken if they hadn't won it."

Thompson, who followed his 28-point performance against UCLA with 21 points in the victory over Marquette, earned the Final Four MVP trophy. But the title wouldn't have been possible without Burleson's postseason run; starting with the ACC title game against Maryland, he averaged 22.8 points and 14.8 rebounds against such future pro big men as Len Elmore, Marvin Barnes, Bill Walton, and Maurice Lucas.

A new bypass connecting Raleigh with Greensboro and the western part of the state had recently opened. But on the seventy-five-minute drive back to campus, Sloan made the bus driver turn off the new superhighway and follow the old Highway 70 route into town, past the graveyard were his mentor Everett Case was buried.

Sloan stopped the bus and had his players step out to pay homage to the man who had laid the groundwork for the title they had just achieved.

THE GREATEST PLAYER

Burleson takes a kind of perverse satisfaction at what happened to N.C. State in the year after its national championship.

"The year after I graduated, Coach Sloan said they'd be a better team without me," Burleson said a quarter-century later. "I was the only starting senior [in 1974]. David, Monte, Stoddard, and Rivers all came back. They had Phil Spence back and they added another All-American-to-be in freshman Kenny Carr."

But just as UNC couldn't recapture the magic of 1957 in 1958, the veteran Pack couldn't quite duplicate its 1974 success in 1975. Although N.C. State started the season ranked No. 1 in the nation, the Pack's two-year domination of its Tobacco Road rivals ended in the Big Four Tournament, which had moved to the first week of January. Resurgent Wake Forest, using a 2-3 zone that limited N.C. State to 34.9% shooting, got twenty-five points from sophomore guard Skip Brown and defeated the defending national champs

83–79. The upset snapped State's thirty-six-game overall winning streak and a thirty-two-game streak against ACC opponents.

Thompson still enjoyed a memorable senior season, despite his team's occasional stumble. He put his personal stamp on the team in State's second game, when he scored an ACC-record fifty-seven points in a victory over Buffalo. He kept scoring at an incredible pace as the Pack won twenty-two of twenty-eight games, including eight of twelve in the ACC. He topped forty three times and scored thirty-six in his home finale against UNC Charlotte. He would have had thirty-eight that night, but he ended the game with a political statement, taking the ball on a breakaway and slamming it home—an intentional violation of the rules at the time.

"I got a technical foul and a standing ovation at the same time," Thompson said.

That was his only dunk in three seasons of college basketball. Because of the no-dunk rule (put in place after the 1967 season to limit Lew Alcindor's dominance), Thompson had to find another way to finish around the basket. What he came up with was a dazzling play called the "alley oop." Towe or often Stoddard would lob the ball toward the rim. Thompson would catch it somewhere in the stratosphere and gently lay the ball in the basket.

Thompson's statement dunk in his home finale got national attention. Is it just coincidence that the NCAA rules committee reinstated the dunk before the next season? Or did Thompson once again change the face of college basketball?

Freshman eligibility, nationwide TV broadcasts of college basketball, the expansion of the NCAA Tournament, the return of the dunk: Thompson didn't single-handedly bring any of those changes about, but he played a significant role in all of them. It's one of the reasons that many who saw him play believe that the N.C. State superstar was the best ever to play in the ACC—and maybe in the college game itself.

"I still think David Thompson is the greatest player in college basketball," said Maryland's Elmore, who followed his pro career by becoming a college broadcaster.

Sports Illustrated recently conducted a poll of experts to pick the top 20 players in college history. Thompson finished third, behind Lew Alcindor and Oscar Robertson.

Thompson averaged 29.9 points as a senior, shooting just under 55% from the floor. After beating out Walton for the AP's national Player of the Year award in 1974, he swept every major national player of the year as a senior. He's the only player in the history of Tobacco Road to be a three-time consensus All-American or to win three ACC Player of the Year awards. But his college career didn't end in storybook fashion.

Thompson was spectacular as his final ACC Tournament opened in Greensboro. The Wolfpack team, ranked No. 8 in the nation, was determined to grab one of the two available NCAA bids, so they could try to defend their NCAA championship. It certainly looked possible as Thompson scored thirty-eight points in the opener against Virginia and thirty in the first thirty minutes in the semifinals against Maryland. At that point, the Wolfpack star left the game with what seemed to be a simple case of leg cramps. But there was nothing simple about what Thompson was going through.

"Those were the most severe leg cramps I ever experienced," Thompson said. "My legs totally locked up on me. The trainer and doctor said they had never seen cramps like that. They had to carry me off the court and into the dressing room."

Without their superstar, the Pack lost a fifteen-point lead but pulled out the victory on a dramatic three-point play by freshman Kenny Carr. That pushed State into the ACC title game for the third straight year. But with Maryland, the ACC's regular season champions, certain to claim one of the ACC's two NCAA bids, all N.C. State's upset did was make it imperative that the Pack win the title game to get the other bid.

And with the greatest player in ACC history still hobbled the next night by those mysterious leg cramps, the 1975 title game was to provide the coming out party for another Tobacco Road superstar.

7

FORD CORNERS

ROCKY MOUNT IS A SMALL MILL TOWN ABOUT AN HOUR'S DRIVE east of Raleigh, in a part of the state where N.C. State's lure was very strong.

But Wolfpack coach Norm Sloan was just one of many coaches who flocked to Rocky Mount in the spring of 1974 and tried to lure a talented young point guard named Phil Ford. Maryland's Lefty Driesell spent most of the spring of 1974 burning up I-95 between Petersburg (Va.), where he was courting big man Moses Malone, and Rocky Mount, where Ford was holding court. Driesell had an ace in the hole: John Lucas had actually grown up in Rocky Mount before moving to Durham, and the two young guards remembered each other from the town's playgrounds, where the younger Ford used his mother's cookies to bribe the older boys into letting him play with them. The Maryland coach reminded Ford that he had taken Lucas, a prospect the To-bacco Road coaches were lukewarm about, and helped him become a star. He painted beautiful pictures about the two of them playing in the same backcourt with Malone dominating down low.

Ford liked Driesell and he was intrigued by the idea of replacing David Thompson as the star at State, but he was more impressed by the quiet, scholarly coach from North Carolina. Dean Smith immediately won over Ford's mother, who joked to her son how nice it was that UNC would send a "Dean" down to recruit him. Unlike so many other coaches, Smith never promised Ford playing time. But he sold him on the prospect of joining the Tar Heel program. Just a few days after N.C. State cut down the nets in Greensboro, Ford signed with North Carolina.

In later years, Smith would grow disgusted at all the attention given recruiting. He would shrug off his rare recruiting losses with the line, "You can't lose a prospect because you never had him in the first place." He would take rejection calmly, knowing there was an equally promising young player out there somewhere.

But Ford was different. He was Smith's most important recruit since Miller—and there probably hasn't been one as important since. Ford picked UNC at a time when it appeared that the Tar Heel program was slipping behind Sloan's national champs at N.C. State and Driesell's recruiting machine at Maryland. Anybody who watched the Terps run UNC into the ground in the 1974 ACC Tournament semifinals had to come away thinking not about the promise of Mitch Kupchak and Walter Davis, but about how badly UNC's guards were outplayed by John Lucas and Mo Howard.

Ford would remedy that weakness, but not right away.

His freshman season would be a series of ups and downs. He was outstanding as UNC lost the Big Four consolation game to N.C. State, but awful as the Heels lost to the Pack in Raleigh (the team's ninth straight loss to its rival). He was outstanding again a month later as UNC finally snapped that streak with a two-point victory over State in Chapel Hill. Ford was outplayed twice by Wake Forest's Skip Brown, even though the Tar Heels narrowly won both games.

As the regular season ended, Ford was recognized as a very good young player, but he wasn't regarded as the best freshman in the ACC. That honor went to Clemson's Skip Wise, who became the first freshman voted first-team All-ACC. Maryland freshman Brad Davis, who played in a three-guard alignment with Lucas and Howard (you wonder where Driesell would have fit Ford in?), was a second-team All-ACC pick.

But during the 1975 ACC Tournament, Ford finally fulfilled the promise that so many had seen in him. It started in the opener against Wake Forest, when for the first time, Ford held his own against the Deacons' talented Brown. However, Ford's twenty-four points didn't appear to be enough as Wake took an eight-point lead with fifty-six seconds left. At that point, Ford hit a long jumper to trim the margin to six, and after a turnover, Kupchak scored inside. It was 90–86 with thirty-four seconds left.

What followed was perhaps the single most controversial play in Tobacco Road history. Jerry Schellenberg took the ball out under the UNC basket and looked for Brown, breaking long against the UNC press. He hit his teammate with a perfect high arching pass. Brown caught the ball without breaking stride and without needing to dribble, laid the ball in for what appeared to be the game-clinching field goal.

Only it wasn't: referee Fred Hikel blew his whistle and ruled that Schellenberg's pass had grazed the overhanging scoreboard at the Greensboro Coliseum. That negated the Wake basket and gave UNC the ball under its own goal.

"I did not see it hit the scoreboard," Smith admitted to reporters. "I thought he'd thrown a curveball."

UNC used the reprieve, plus two missed one-and-one opportunities by the Deacons, to tie the game and force overtime. In the extra period, UNC went to its Four Corners offense and pulled out a 101–100 victory. North Carolina's second-round game was no easier. Ford was again magnificent, pouring in twenty-nine points as UNC ran the Four Corners, with the freshman point guard in the middle, for the final 11:30 of the second half. With the score tied at 64, Clemson got the final shot in regulation and Tree Rollins's short hook shot seemed to go halfway down the basket before it spun out. UNC, again reverting to the Four Corners in overtime, scored ten of its twelve points from the foul line in the extra period to secure a 76–71 victory.

That set up a title game matchup with David Thompson and N.C. State. Only Thompson, hurting from the cramps that had sidelined him the night before, wasn't David Thompson on this occasion. The N.C. State superstar, playing what turned out to be his last collegiate game, limped through thirty-nine painful minutes and finished with just sixteen points on 7-of-21 shooting.

Thompson's struggles left Ford the dominant player on the floor. The UNC freshman, again operating out of the middle of the Four Corners for much of the second half, scored twenty-four points and passed out five assists.

"The Four Corners was unfair with Ford," Smith said several years later. "He could drive, take it in, bring it out and pass it off. He was unstoppable."

The tactic infuriated the ABC crowd and helped provoke sentiment for an NBA-style shot clock. Smith, who believed a shot clock would actually help the more talented teams, threw his support behind the proposal. But as long as the Four Corners was legal, he planned to use it—fair or unfair.

And the Four Corners would help make Phil Ford the heir to Thompson's mantle as the ACC's most important player.

THE PERFECT POINT

"I think he might have been the greatest competitor ever to play in the ACC," Maryland's Driesell said of Ford. "He just hated to lose."

The Tar Heels didn't lose very often with Ford at the point. He quarterbacked teams that won three straight ACC regular season titles and two ACC Tournament titles. In between his sophomore and junior seasons, he quarterbacked a U.S. Olympic team with six players from Tobacco Road to the gold medal in Montreal. He was a three-time first-team All-American and the national Player of the Year as a senior.

"You can't measure his heart," Dean Smith said. "He said I gave him confidence—he gave me confidence."

Unfortunately, an incredible series of physical problems—both to Ford and his teammates—curtailed his postseason success after 1975. Ford, taking advantage of a few days off after the 1976 ACC Tournament, suffered a knee injury in a pickup game that crippled him in an NCAA loss to Alabama. A year later, he suffered a bruised elbow in a regional victory over Notre Dame, joining an injury list that also included center Tom LaGarde (out with a knee injury) and wing player Walter Davis (playing with a broken finger). Ford was still able to lead the crippled Tar Heels to the national title game. His senior year was spoiled by an ankle injury that hobbled star forward Mike O'Koren in an NCAA loss to San Francisco.

Ford finished his career with the most points (2,290) and most assists (753) in school history. His assist total was the best ever recorded in the ACC to that time.

In the light of the astronomical assist totals piled up by guards who came after Ford, it's worth noting his numbers in the historical context of the game. Awarding of assists became much more liberal in the 1980s, which is one reason that Ford's career total of 753 assists is so impressive. He still ranks tenth in ACC history. He is the only player from the 1970s on the ACC's career list. Ford also ranks ninth on the ACC career scoring list. Throw in the facts that he also ranks fourteenth in ACC history in steals and his career shooting percentage of 52.7% is miles ahead of any other point guard rival, and it's easy to see why Ford is generally considered the greatest point guard to ever play on Tobacco Road.

8

DUKE RINGS THE TINKERBELL

O<small>N THE FRIDAY NIGHT BETWEEN</small> UNC'<small>S</small> E<small>AST</small> R<small>EGIONAL</small> V<small>ICTORY</small> over Notre Dame and the Tar Heels' Saturday night victory over Kentucky in College Park, a very odd scene played out in the Washington, D.C. Armory, located just beside Robert F. Kennedy Stadium.

West Philadelphia High School had just defeated Georgetown Prep. Outside the visiting team's locker room, a handful of North Carolina reporters—in the area to cover UNC in the NCAA Tournament—waited to talk to Duke's newest basketball recruit. But before they could speak to Philadelphia's Gene "Tinkerbell" Banks, they had to wait and watch as Notre Dame's Digger Phelps engaged in a long and apparently passionate conversation with the celebrated schoolboy star.

Phelps's determined pursuit of Banks, after the Philadelphia star's well-publicized announcement that he would sign with Duke, evoked memories of Vic Bubas' theft of Art Heyman, Bill Bradley's defection to Princeton, and Tom McMillen's last-second decision to renege on his commitment to UNC.

Banks later told reporter John Feinstein, "The last thing [Phelps] said to me was, 'Sure Duke is a good school, Gene, but so are we. Choosing their basketball program over ours is like choosing a Volkswagon over a Cadillac.'"

Would Banks surrender to Phelps's blandishments and deal Bill Foster's rebuilding efforts a mortal blow?

Duke's Carl James had lured Foster from Utah to Duke after the 1974 season. The veteran coach had vowed to play an uptempo game in Durham, and indeed his early Blue Devil teams did score a lot of points. Unfortunately, they surrendered a lot too—and his first three teams finished last or tied for last in the ACC standings.

But Duke had begun to show signs of life as Foster used his connections in prep circles to uncover some hidden recruiting gems. The high-strung coach had long run a popular prep summer camp in Pennsylvania's Pocono Mountains, along with former Temple coach Harry Litwack. That experience gave the Duke coach an insight into prospective players that some of his contemporaries lacked. Foster's edge first paid off for Duke when he lured Jim Spanarkel, a relative unknown playing in the shadow of the more famous Mike O'Koren, from Jersey City to Durham. He was rewarded when the slow, pigeon-toed wing man won the ACC's first Rookie of the Year award in 1976 and developed into an All-American.

Before the 1976–77 season, Foster pulled a giant recruiting rabbit out of his hat, landing 6-foot-11, 250-pound Mike Gminski out of Monroe, Connecticut. It was not that Gminski was an unknown. Coaches all over the country had seen and appreciated Gminski's strength, his good hands, and his sweet jump shot. But what Foster knew that many of his rivals didn't was that Gminski was in position to graduate from high school a year early.

"We still had him listed on our records as a junior," Maryland's Lefty Driesell said when he learned that Gminski had signed with Duke.

The player called "The G-Man" would average 15.3 points and 10.7 rebounds as a seventeen-year-old freshman. He combined with Spanarkel and sweet-shooting senior Tate Armstrong to give Duke the firepower to compete with its powerful Tobacco Road rivals. And when the Devils opened 10–1 in 1977, it looked like a new dawn had arrived for the program in Durham.

Alas, it proved to be a false dawn for the Blue Devils. Early in an overtime victory at Virginia, Armstrong fell and suffered a broken wrist. He finished the game—scoring thirty-five points to help Duke snap a twenty-seven-game ACC road losing streak—but his college career was over. The loss of the talented guard would ruin Duke's season. The team was 11–3 before Armstrong's injury, and just 3 and 10 afterward.

A number of those ten losses were excruciating defeats. Steve Gray, a guard from California who possessed wonderful athleticism (he had been a top football prospect on the West Coast), tried to take over for Armstrong, but he seemed to possess an uncanny ability to screw up at the wrong moment.

He dribbled the ball off his foot to cost the Devils a certain victory against N.C. State in Durham. And three weeks later, Duke had Maryland beat—up three with just seconds remaining—when Gray took the inbounds pass and tried to throw a crosscourt pass that hit the Maryland basket. When James Tillman grabbed the loose ball and went up for a slam dunk, Gray thoughtlessly fouled him, allowing the Terps to tie the game with a three-point play and win in overtime.

Foster was about ready to cut his throat.

"I'm not sure if up to that moment in my life, I had ever felt worse," Foster told Feinstein. "All I could think of was, 'What Next?' One more disaster and I might have been done. I mean really done."

Instead of a disaster, Foster got a phone call from Banks, asking him to come to Philadelphia. "Coach, I've called a press conference," Banks said. "I'm going to announce I'm going to Duke."

It's difficult to recapture the excitement that Duke's pursuit of Banks created in the spring of 1977. At the time, there were three celebrated high school superstars: Albert King in New York, Earvin "Magic" Johnson in Michigan, and Banks in Philadelphia. Although all three had their regional partisans, Banks was probably the consensus pick as the best prospect of the three. A powerfully built 6-foot-7 forward, Banks combined strength and agility with a fundamental understanding of the game. He wasn't a great shooter, but he did everything else well and was generally acknowledged to be the best prospect to come out of Philadelphia in decades.

West Philadelphia coach Joey Goldenberg happened to be a counselor at the camp Foster and Litwack ran in the Poconos. That gave the Duke coach a head start toward landing a prospect that every top program in the country had targeted. It also helped that Banks liked the idea of attending a prestigious academic school. Duke, Banks said at his announcement, best combined the chance to play big-time basketball and get a big-time education.

"I feel like when the smoke clears, I'll make them a national power," he answered when asked why he'd choose such a downtrodden program.

His announcement touched off a firestorm in Durham. It was front-page news in the two Durham newspapers. Within forty-eight hours, Duke's ticket office sold out season tickets for the 1977–78 season.

On the morning of April 9, 1977 (the first day that national letters of intent could be signed), Banks rejected Phelps's appeal, signed the grant-in-aid letter from Duke, and walked outside and stuck it in his mailbox. Foster, who had used up his official visits, was sitting in his car down the street. As soon as Banks returned to his house, he drove by and pulled the precious document out of the mailbox.

Duke, the first team on Tobacco Road to integrate, had become the last to land a black star.

Banks found himself starting on the frontline along with Gminski and another freshman, the far less heralded Kenny Dennard from King (N.C.), the same little Tobacco Road town that had produced former Blue Devil guard Bobby Joe Harris. Spanarkel was back as a junior to anchor the backcourt, but the point guard position was expected to be a problem until midseason—when Indiana transfer Bob Bender (a former prep All-American who had won an NCAA championship ring with the 1976 Hoosiers) became eligible.

North Carolina was still regarded as the team to beat on Tobacco Road— with the fabulous Ford back for his senior season, O'Koren returning as a sophomore, and gifted freshman forward Al Wood from Georgia joining the lineup. Still, Duke was picked a surprising second in the ACC's preseason media poll.

"I expect Duke to make a run for the ACC championship and the national championship," UNC's Smith said of a team that had finished last or tied for last in the ACC for the four previous seasons.

The Blue Devils didn't look like championship contenders that December, getting off to a 7–2 start that included a lopsided loss to UNC in the Big Four Tournament and a controversial loss to Southern Cal in Los Angeles. The problem, clearly, was at the point. The team appeared to be marking time until Bender's arrival.

But another solution presented itself. On the night on January 2, 1978, Duke was playing Virginia Tech in Roanoke when Foster finally had enough of watching Gray struggle against the Hokies' press. In desperation, the Duke coach turned to walk-on John Harrell.

Harrell, who played at Durham's Hillside High School, had started as a freshman at North Carolina Central University, where his father taught math, before transferring to Duke. He had played a minor role off the bench in Duke's first nine games, but against Virginia Tech, he played thirty minutes and showed considerable poise in the face of a frenetic full-court press.

That was enough for Foster. Harrell was in the starting lineup when Duke went to College Park and upset Maryland forty-eight hours later. He stayed in the lineup even after Bender became eligible. The Indiana transfer became not the starter, but the team's sixth man. In that role, Bender contributed eleven points and four assists as Duke upset No. 2 North Carolina on January 14, moving into the AP poll at No. 17 the next week—which was Duke's first such appearance since 1971.

"That game established in our minds the idea that we were good enough to play with anyone," Dennard later told Feinstein. "I don't think we had thought in those terms before. After that, our feeling was that if somebody was going to beat us, they were going to have to be damn good."

The Blue Devils, as predicted by the media, did push UNC to the wire in the ACC regular season race, falling short only when Ford scored a career-high thirty-four points in his last home game to push the Tar Heels to a narrow 87–83 victory in Carmichael and the ACC regular season title.

"He was not only inspired . . . he was just taking it down and spinning it off his feet or under his legs or hooking it," Duke's Foster said of Ford. "We didn't have any defense for that."

But Ford's last game in Carmichael would prove to be his final moment of glory. The injury bug struck UNC again in postseason and this time the Tar Heels were not able to overcome it. The problem was a badly sprained ankle that Mike O'Koren suffered during a February trip to Providence. Although he returned to the lineup after suffering the injury, his taped-up ankle was never the same, and the Tar Heels couldn't replace his rebounding or his explosiveness.

UNC's troubles gave Foster's young Blue Devils a chance to seize the spotlight on Tobacco Road. By chance, the ACC Tournament championship was nationally televised for the first time, and a huge audience on ABC's *Wide World of Sports* watched Duke rally in the second half to defeat Wake Forest and earn its first NCAA bid since 1966.

"This is the greatest thing that's ever happened to me in basketball because I didn't know if we'd ever get here," Foster told the press.

Greater things were ahead for Foster and the Blue Devils. *Sports Illustrated* responded to the tournament triumph by putting Banks on its cover, although writer Kent Hannon dismissed Duke as, "a team of the future—too young to make a serious run this year."

He couldn't have been more wrong. The Blue Devils rolled through the East Regionals, then upset Notre Dame at the Final Four in St. Louis to earn a shot at powerful Kentucky in the national title game. The national media fell in love with the loosey-goosey young Devils, their exuberance in such stark contrast to the businesslike Wildcats, who labeled their spectacular 30–2 year as "the season without joy." It's hard to imagine Kyle Macy or Rick Robey disappearing on semifinal Saturday as Duke's Dennard did. When he finally returned to the dressing room, he was wearing a red plastic Arkansas hog hat that he had donned to cheer on the Razorbacks in their narrow semifinal loss.

Yet Duke's fun would come to the end in the title game as Kentucky senior Jack "Goose" Givens found a hole in the middle of the Duke zone and exploited it for twenty-three first-half points, including the Cats' last sixteen in a row. He would finish with forty-one points, hitting a remarkable eighteen of twenty-seven shots from the floor.

"I took one shot in the second half and it hit the side of the backboard and went in," Givens said. "That's the kind of night I was having."

Duke tried to fight back from a 66–50 deficit, getting twenty-two points from Banks, twenty-one from Spanarkel, and twenty from Gminski. The Blue Devils gained a small moral victory in the closing seconds, when Kentucky coach Joe Hall (a dead ringer for *King of the Hill*'s Hank Hill), who had cleared his bench, was forced to reinsert his starters to protect the Wildcats' 94–88 victory.

Duke fans chanted, "We'll be back" as their team accepted their second-place trophies. That seemed a reasonable boast for a team that started two freshmen, two sophomores, and a junior. But the Blue Devils were to discover just how fickle the basketball fates can be.

THE RIVALRY REBORN

As intense as Duke-Carolina games were in the first quarter century of the ACC, there were not many years when both were reaching for greatness at the same time. Only in 1961 and maybe in 1967 were both rivals rated contenders in the same year.

The three years from 1978 to 1980 would change that, as North Carolina and Duke battled for ACC and national supremacy while Tobacco Road rivals N.C. State and Wake Forest struggled to keep up.

Not surprisingly, Duke—with all five starters returning from its 1978 NCAA runnerups—started the 1978–79 season ranked as the nation's preseason No. 1 team. The Blue Devils held that ranking by sweeping N.C. State and North Carolina to claim its first Big Four Tournament title. But it would be a season of ups and downs for the Blue Devils, who were stunned by back-to-back losses to Ohio State and St. John's in the Holiday Festival in New York and by a decisive loss to UNC in Chapel Hill.

The Tar Heels, rebuilding after four years of riding Phil Ford's coattails, found a late-developing star in Dudley Bradley. A swing man from Maryland, Bradley had a disappointing career until suddenly blossoming as a defensive ace in his senior season. He moved into the starting lineup along with Dave Colescott, a former Indiana Mr. Basketball who had the unenviable job of replacing Ford at the point.

Bradley showed his promise early when he shut down Michigan State star Magic Johnson in an early season matchup in Chapel Hill. But his defining moment came in Raleigh after UNC had blown a big lead against the surging Wolfpack. He caught guard Clyde Austin looking the wrong way, picked his pocket, and scored the game-winning basket on a dunk with seven seconds left. Afterward, Raleigh reporter Caulton Tudor approached the distraught Austin and asked him what had happened.

"I'm not sure," Austin replied. "All I know is Dudley stole the ball, slammed it in my face, and Coach [Sloan] called me a son-of-a-bitch!"

The surprising contribution by Bradley helped UNC climb as high as No. 2 in the national rankings and battle Duke for the ACC regular season title. Just as in 1978, first place was up for grabs in the regular season finale—although this time the game was in Durham.

Dean Smith, looking to pull the Blue Devils out of their potent zone, elected to start the game in the Four Corners. Foster responded as Bubas had to Norm Sloan's stall tactics in the 1968 ACC Tournament: he stayed in his zone. The result was one of the most bizarre halves of basketball in ACC history. Duke won the opening tip and went up 2–0 when freshman Vince Taylor tipped in Gminski's missed shot. UNC then held the ball for over twelve minutes, until Chick Yonaker thought he had an open eight-footer from the left baseline.

He shot an air ball. Duke rebounded and scored a free throw to make it 3–0. After a Tar Heel turnover, the Devils scored to go up 5–0. UNC again held the ball until, with seconds left in the half, Yonaker fired again—and again missed everything. Duke's raucous student section, becoming nationally known as the Cameron Crazies, responded with a chant that would become famous: "Air ball! Air ball!"

More significantly, Duke converted at the other end. When Colescott's half-court heave at the buzzer came up short, the two teams left the court with Duke up 7–0. UNC was not only scoreless: they had failed to draw iron on their only three shots in the half. "If we'd just scored two points, I think we would have won the game," Smith said. "There was just something about that zero."

Smith elected to play normally in the second half, in which each team scored 40 points, and Duke emerged with a 47–40 victory and a share of the ACC title. But that merely set up a rematch exactly one week later in the ACC Tournament championship game in Greensboro. The Blue Devils had to survive a tough semifinal against N.C. State, but Bender turned in one of his best games with sixteen points and four assists in thirty-nine minutes of action to send Duke into the finals.

The next morning, the junior point guard woke up with a pain in his stomach and was rushed back to Duke Hospital where he was operated on for a case of acute appendicitis. He was unavailable for the championship game rematch with UNC. That shouldn't have been a problem with Harrell on hand to step into the role he filled so ably in 1978. But the young Durham native was disgruntled after losing his starting job—unfairly, he believed—in preseason practice. Disgusted by the turn of the events, the once happy-go-lucky Durham native turned sour. By the time he was called on to save Duke in Bender's absence, he was out of shape, both physically and psychologically.

The result was a frustrating night for the Blue Devils. UNC led most of the way and put the game away on a spectacular steal and dunk—right in Gminski's face—by Tournament MVP Dudley Bradley. "Coach Smith should get as much credit for this game as he got abuse for the [7–0 game]," UNC's O'Koren said.

As disappointing as the title game was for Duke, there was always a chance for redemption in the NCAA Tournament. For the first time, the NCAA field was seeded and observers were surprised when UNC and Duke were seeded 1–2 in the East Regionals. Both were scheduled to play one game in Raleigh's Reynolds Coliseum, followed by two games in Greensboro, when the Tar Heels and Blue Devils would almost certainly face each other in the tiebreaker fifth game, after going 2–2 head-to-head over the course of the season.

For once, the only time between 1975 and 1981, UNC was healthy for postseason play. Duke, on the other hand, had to endure a Carolina-like injury list. Not only was Bender missing from the NCAA opener against St. John's, but so was Kenny Dennard, who was sidelined by a sprained ankle suffered during a late-night scrimmage with a bunch of Blue Devil football players. As if that was not enough, Gminski suffered a case of food poisoning after eating a tainted pizza the night before a game day that was to become forever known on Tobacco Road as "Black Sunday."

The day began when Penn, getting twenty-five points from forward Tony Price and a strong floor game from veteran playmaker Bobby Willis, shocked the Tar Heels 72–71. Duke fans, thinking UNC's loss paved their way to the Final Four, were delighted as the Blue Devils took an early ten-point lead on the same St. John's team that had upset Duke in New York.

With a victory, the outlook would be bright for the Devils. Both Bender and Dennard were expected to be available for the regionals the next week in Greensboro. And Gminski, who twice pulled himself from the St. John's game to throw up into a bucket on the sidelines, would be 100% for the regional semifinals.

But Duke just didn't have enough healthy players to hold off the Redmen. St. John's took the lead late in the first half and maintained it most of the second half. Banks finally tied the game at 78-all with thirty seconds to play, but guard Reggie Carter hit a jumper over Harrell with five seconds left. When Gminski's desperation thirty-footer bounced off the rim, Duke's season was over.

Black Sunday was followed by Blue Monday as Clemson, Virginia, and Maryland all lost in the NIT, ending the worst forty-eight hours in ACC history. No one could believe it, especially not UNC's first-year assistant coach Roy Williams.

"That was the first experience I ever had with the swiftness, the suddenness that your season is over," the future Tar Heel head coach said. "It's not like golf, where you have a Mulligan. You lose and you go home and there's nothing you can do about it."

The missed chance would haunt Foster, who was growing increasing restless in Durham. And he wasn't the only coach on Tobacco Road who was thinking of leaving.

The first rumors about Norm Sloan surfaced in February, when officials at the University of Florida announced that they planned to pursue their former coach to replace former Dean Smith assistant John Lotz. At first the reports that N.C. State's fifty-three-year-old coach was negotiating with Florida didn't make sense. Why *would* Sloan return to the school he had left fourteen years earlier for his alma mater?

It turned out that Sloan's frustration, both with his own administration and what he perceived as the pro-UNC bias on Tobacco Road, had been festering for years. Sloan was angry that he and his assistants were the lowest-paid staff in the ACC. Florida, which had built a new basketball arena in his absence and at last seemed interested in promoting the winter sport, was offering Sloan a salary bump from $46,000 to $70,000, plus commensurate raises for his staff.

Sloan was also angry when the Pack lost in-state recruit after in-state recruit to his rival in Chapel Hill. Not even his national title—something Dean Smith had yet to win—could convince players such as Walter Davis and Phil Ford and James Worthy to play for the Pack. It didn't help his paranoia that the state's media was populated with graduates of the UNC School of Journalism and that many of the reporters on Tobacco Road appeared to worship his rival in Chapel Hill.

"If you're in a beauty contest, you want to win," Sloan said. "But when the same contestant always wins, it's time to find a new contest."

Sloan announced on the Monday before the 1980 ACC Tournament that he was resigning at the end of the season. The question was whether Duke would be looking too. While not as public as Florida's pursuit of Sloan, rumors were widespread that South Carolina was interested in luring Foster to Columbia. Publicly, the Blue Devil coach dodged the issue in the days leading up to the ACC Tournament; privately, he told his players that he was gone after the season.

Maybe that had something to do with Duke's performance in the tournament. The Blue Devils knocked off N.C. State in the first round and upset UNC in the semifinals. The victory marked a thirty-nine-point turnaround in six days against UNC, following a twenty-five-point loss in Chapel Hill with a 75–61 win. "What a difference a week makes," Smith said.

The Blue Devils continued to win for their lame-duck coach, edging regular season ACC champion Maryland in the championship game, giving Foster his second ACC title in three years. It also provided him with a stage to announce his resignation at Duke. Two days later, he appeared in Columbia, where he was introduced as the successor to the retiring Frank McGuire.

Like Sloan's departure, Foster's unexpected exit raised questions. Why would he leave a team that had spent most of the last three seasons in the top 10 for a dead-end position with a struggling independent that was being squeezed into insignificance between the ACC and the SEC?

There were no easy answers. Like Sloan, Foster was irritated by the way UNC's Smith was worshipped on Tobacco Road. At one point on his weekly radio show, he mumbled, "I thought Naismith invented basketball, not Deansmith."

Foster was leaving Duke with a 113–64 record after six seasons. He gave the Blue Devils two ACC titles, one trip to the Final Four, and another appearance in the Elite Eight (his 1980 team upset Kentucky in the Sweet 16 before losing to Purdue in the regional finals).

Sloan left an even greater legacy at N.C. State: a 266–127 record in fourteen seasons with three ACC titles and a national championship to his credit. His last recruiting class included Sidney Lowe, Thurl Bailey, and Dereck Whittenburg—three players who would serve as the foundation for one of the ACC's most memorable teams.

The twin departure of Foster and Sloan after the 1980 season would open the door for two young coaches to once again change the face of Tobacco Road. It would also leave Dean Smith more solidly entrenched than ever before as the King of Tobacco Road.

9

THE DEAN OF ACC COACHES

TECHNICALLY, DEAN SMITH BECAME THE "DEAN" OF ACC COACHES when Vic Bubas retired in 1969. But it was the dual departure of Duke's Bill Foster, who was exactly Smith's age, and N.C. State's Norm Sloan, who was two years older, that suddenly lifted the forty-nine-year-old Tar Heel coach to icon status. The coaches he had dueled in his early days were all long gone and now a second wave of Tobacco Road coaches had come and gone. Smith, who led UNC to six ACC titles and five Final Fours in his first eighteen seasons, had conquered all challengers. All that he lacked was a national title—and that was on the horizon.

The pieces of Smith's first national championship team began to fit into place during the 1980–81 season. It started with James Worthy, a 6-foot-8 forward from Gastonia, who had first impressed the Tar Heel coach as a gangly eighth-grader.

"He was one of the few young men I ever looked at as a high school player and felt certain he was going to be a college and pro player," Smith said. "It was a long wait. I once joked, 'We were hoping he'd go hardship and leave high school after his junior year, so he could come in and help us out.'"

Worthy possessed amazing quickness for a player his size, along with great strength and a good understanding of the game. He also did a dead-on imitation of Dean Smith—so good that he once used it to fool his own father on a telephone call. His freshman season was cut short when he slipped on a piece of ice at Carmichael and suffered a broken ankle, but he was back in action as a sophomore with three steel pins in his ankle. He joined senior All-American Al Wood to anchor what looked to be a formidable front line. It became even more formidable when Smith unveiled freshman prize Sam Perkins, a long, lanky big man from upstate New York.

Actually, Perkins grew up in Brooklyn, but he never played basketball in that hoop talent incubator. Raised by a grandmother who kept him close to home, Perkins didn't play for his high school team and he didn't inhabit the Brooklyn playgrounds. It wasn't until a social worker named Herb Crossman adopted the tall young man and moved him to Latham, New York, a suburb of Albany, that Perkins got a chance to play the game that he would end up playing for seventeen seasons in the NBA.

Perkins had great hands, great intelligence, and great agility. He also had a most unusual gift: "He had arms that seemed to unfold forever," Smith said. The Tar Heel coach began to lecture the media about the difference between a player's height, which he said was meaningless ("You don't play basketball with the top of your head"), and what he called "reaching height," the height a player could reach while standing flat-footed with his arms extended. In the case of the 6-foot-9 Perkins, his reaching height was 9-feet-4, well beyond most 7-footers.

UNC's backcourt was not as imposing, although Smith loved point guard Jimmy Black—a junior from New York City who didn't score much but was a fine ballhandler and an excellent defender. The backcourt weakness would occasionally be a problem as UNC tested itself against a tough schedule. The team emerged as one that was good enough to beat eventual national champion Indiana in December, but not quite good enough to handle Virginia—which swept two games from Carolina as sophomore center Ralph Sampson won the first of his three national player of the year awards.

Despite the twin losses to the Cavs, there was evidence that UNC was getting better. Worthy, his confidence in his rebuilt ankle growing, was averaging fourteen points and eight rebounds. Perkins had moved into the starting lineup, where he was playing with the poise and consistency that belied his freshman status. And fellow freshman Matt Doherty, a 6-foot-8 product of Long Island with a forward's body and a guard's skills, had established himself as a reliable sixth man.

North Carolina demonstrated its improvement during a March run that carried the Tar Heels all the way to the national title game. Carolina won the ACC Tournament in Landover, Maryland, without having to face Sampson and Virginia. But after winning the West Regionals in Salt Lake City, the Tar

Heels finally overcame the powerful Cavs in the Final Four in Philadelphia as Perkins neutralized Sampson and Al Wood scored a career-high thirty-nine points. "We got beat by a great player having a great day," disconsolate Virginia coach Terry Holland said.

Only Indiana, a team North Carolina had beaten at home in December, stood between the Tar Heels and Smith's first national title. Actually, the two teams came very close to being declared co-champions when President Ronald Reagan was shot by John Hinkley earlier that day. But when word came that Reagan was out of danger, the two coaches agreed to play the title game as scheduled. That proved unfortunate for the Tar Heels. Knight's pressure man-to-man defense broke down UNC's backcourt. Indiana, which forced nineteen UNC turnovers, blew the game open in the second half and pulled away for a 63–50 victory and the championship. "They just hound you," Worthy said. "I haven't seen a man-to-man defense like that all season."

The loss left Smith 0–6 in Final Four attempts, the longest such streak of futility in NCAA history. But the 1981 Tar Heels laid the groundwork for the team that would finally give the celebrated coach the one jewel missing from his crown.

"Our players went home disappointed and hungry," Smith said. "We went to the Final Four and finished in second place and were unhappy. It was really the mental thing that drove [the 1982] team."

Smith didn't know at the time that the final piece to UNC's championship puzzle would arrive on campus the next fall.

THE WILMINGTON LEGEND

In view of Michael Jordan's later ascension to god-like status, it's hard to keep his arrival at North Carolina in perspective. He was not yet the best basketball player on the planet in the fall of 1981, and nobody at that time could have expected him to achieve that status. But Jordan wasn't an unknown either.

UNC's Smith had first learned of the future superstar when Jordan was a junior at Wilmington Laney High School in the 1979–80 season. He sent assistant Bill Guthridge to scout the previously unknown prospect and was encouraged when Guthridge summed up "Mike" (as he was known in those days) Jordan with the words, "He's unmilked."

Smith invited Jordan to his basketball camp that summer and got his first look at the future legend. What he saw was a slender 6-foot-3 guard with superior quickness, great jumping ability, and an insatiable desire to get better. He still didn't realize how good Jordan could be at that point, so he called prep guru Howard Garfinkel and asked him to invite the young prospect to that summer's Five-Star Camp, where Jordan would get a chance to test himself against some of the nation's best prospects.

That turned out to be a recruiting mistake by the Tar Heel coach. Jordan dominated the camp and won MVP honors. Before Five-Star, Smith was the only major coach aware of Jordan's potential. After that week in Honesdale, Pennsylvania, every coach in the country knew about the Wilmington prodigy. Smith suddenly found himself recruiting against South Carolina, where Bill Foster took Jordan to meet the governor; N.C. State, where Jim Valvano turned on the charm and encouraged Jordan to follow in the footsteps of his childhood hero, David Thompson; and Maryland, where Lefty Driesell tried to convince Jordan's father that with the opening of the new Chesapeake Bay Bridge, College Park was as close to Wilmington as Chapel Hill.

Despite the sudden flurry of recruiting interest, Jordan elected to sign with the Tar Heels that fall. Identified as a future Tar Heel, Jordan's talent was finally on exhibition for curious fans and reporters. He earned a spot on the McDonald's All-America team, then set a scoring record in that fledging all-star game that would stand for more than twenty years.

By the time Jordan began workouts with UNC in October of 1981, it was widely assumed he'd join four returning regulars in the Tar Heel starting lineup. *Sports Illustrated*, which had decided to make North Carolina its preseason No. 1 team, wanted to put Jordan on the cover with Smith and four veterans: returning starters Worthy, Perkins, and Black, and 1981 sixth man Doherty. It would have been the first SI cover for the future superstar (who holds the *Sports Illustrated* cover record with fifty-one), but Smith vetoed the magazine's plan, despite a personal plea from editor Larry Keith, a UNC grad.

"In our program, freshmen learned that there was a hierarchy in which they earned their way upward," Smith said. "They don't star on national magazine covers before they so much as play a game."

Even with the unproven Jordan in the lineup, the Tar Heels clearly were head and shoulders above their Tobacco Road rivals. The only ACC threat would come from Virginia, where Sampson was back for his junior season and would win the second of his three straight national player of the year awards.

The Cavaliers started the season ranked No. 3, behind the top-ranked Heels and No. 2 Kentucky. On the day after Christmas, No. 1 UNC abused Kentucky 80–69 in the first college game ever played in the new Meadowlands Arena, cementing the team's status as the nation's best.

Jordan was in the starting lineup, and while he played well, the first month of the season demonstrated that the team's big improvement was due to the development of Worthy and Perkins. Worthy, a second-team All-ACC pick the year before, would end the season as a consensus first-team All-American and was the runner-up to Sampson in most of the national player of the year votes. Perkins, not even a second-team All-ACC pick as a freshman, was a consensus second-team All-American as a sophomore and the No. 3 vote-getter on the All-ACC team (behind Sampson and Worthy).

Jordan was the team's third scoring option. Sharing the lineup with Black and Doherty, who were reluctant outside shooters, Jordan was the team's primary perimeter option, even though he was not nearly the shooter that he was to become.

"The problem was that he had such huge hands," Smith said. "That made it harder for him to shoot. It was like you or I trying to shoot with a volleyball."

It was inevitable that No. 1-ranked UNC and No. 3 Virginia should meet for the ACC championship in Greensboro. For almost thirty-three minutes, the game lived up to the hype. North Carolina, getting sixteen points from Worthy, held a narrow 44–43 lead with 7:34 to play—then Smith ordered his team to pull the Cavaliers out of their zone.

"I thought we'd have a good chance to dictate the end of the game with our Four Corners because it might lure Sampson out from beneath the basket," Smith later explained.

Instead, the duel between two of the nation's best teams turned into another deep freeze game as Virginia coach Terry Holland refused to come out of his zone. For more than seven minutes, UNC held the ball as millions watched on TV, most of them fuming at the lack of action.

"It takes two to have a slower game," a defiant Smith said afterward. "If a 7-4 guy wants to stay under the basket, fine. A coach thinks about winning the game under the rules."

UNC would win, getting three free throws from Doherty in the final twenty-eight seconds and a key steal from Black. But the 47–45 Tar Heel victory would provoke a national outcry and fuel the growing demand for a shot clock to force the action in the college game. The ACC would respond almost immediately, adopting a bizarre set of experimental rules for the next season, including a thirty-second shot clock that was turned off in the game's final four minutes and a seventeen-foot three-point shot.

"That game gave the idea of a shot clock a lot of momentum," Virginia's Holland said. "The forty-five-second shot clock [adopted by the NCAA in 1985] is definitely a result of that game."

The 1982 title was Smith's eighth ACC championship, which was as many as Case and Bubas had won combined. More importantly in the short term, the game had the expected impact on the NCAA selection committee. The Tar Heels were seeded No. 1 in the East and sent to Charlotte. Virginia, seeded No. 1 in the Mideast, drew the unenviable task of playing a Sweet 16 game against Alabama-Birmingham on its home court in Birmingham. Virginia didn't handle that task as well as UNC had dealt with playing Utah in Salt Lake City the year before, falling to the Blazers despite nineteen points and twenty-one rebounds from Sampson.

North Carolina—its sights set squarely on the national championship—almost met the same fate, overlooking unheralded James Madison in a round of thirty-two games in Charlotte. The Tar Heels were a bit more businesslike the next weekend in Raleigh, eliminating Alabama and Villanova to earn another trip to the Final Four. It would be Smith's seventh career trip to the Final Four. In the moments after UNC celebrated its 70–60 victory over Villanova, the Tar Heel players made a symbolic statement that this would be unlike Smith's first six fruitless Final Four trips.

Maintenance workers had set up ladders under the basket to help the Tar Heel players cut down the nets—as championship teams had done ever since Everett Case brought the tradition to Tobacco Road. But Smith's players refused to cut down the Reynolds' nets. "The nets we want are hanging in the Superdome in New Orleans," Worthy explained to reporters.

Smith was surprised by his team's decision, but he felt good about UNC's chances as they prepared to visit the Big Easy. It was all coming together. All five Tar Heel starters had scored in double figures in both East Regional wins. And although Worthy won the regional MVP award, Smith was more impressed by the play of the unheralded Black, who hit ten of twelve shots in the regional doubleheader, passed out sixteen assists in the two games, and did a great job defending Alabama All-American Ennis Whatley.

Black would face another tough defensive assignment in New Orleans. UNC's semifinal opponent was Houston, which was led in scoring by All-American guard Rob Williams. However, after watching the Cougars on tape, Smith was more impressed by forward Clyde Drexler and by reserve center Akeem Olajuwon.

Almost 62,000 spectators got to watch North Carolina jump on Houston early, as the Tar Heels scored the first fourteen points of the game to take a lead that the Cougars could never quite overcome. Black shut down Williams, holding the All-American guard without a field goal. Perkins scored twenty-five points and Jordan added eighteen as UNC earned a 68–63 victory. When Georgetown knocked off Louisville (50–46) it set up a title game matchup between Smith and John Thompson, two of the closest friends in the coaching profession.

"It's not the coaches' game," the UNC coach said. "It's not Dean Smith vs. John Thompson. If it was, he'd take me inside and kill me."

Much of the pregame attention was on the nation's best freshman: it was not Jordan, but Georgetown's Patrick Ewing who arrived in New Orleans with something like the aura that Wilt Chamberlain had brought to the 1957 Final Four. Thompson decided to exploit Ewing's mystique with a psychological ploy that evoked memories of the mind games that Frank McGuire played with Chamberlain twenty-five years earlier. The Georgetown coach told his young big man to station himself under the basket and block everything the Tar Heels threw up, goaltending or not. He hoped the sight of his 7-foot wunderkind swatting away shots would intimidate the Heels.

Thompson's tactic might have worked, except for Worthy, who refused to be intimidated. Ewing blocked two shots and goaltended five more in the first ten minutes, but Worthy continued to attack the basket. He scored eighteen of UNC's thirty-one first-half points and kept the Heels close in a second half that saw the two teams trade the lead twelve times.

The Tar Heels needed everything to hold off the determined Hoyas. Worthy had back-to-back dunks with just over five minutes left to give the Heels a 57–56 lead, but Georgetown surged back in front. Jordan answered with a play that dazzled his coach: a left-handed layup that arched just over Ewing's outstretched fingertips, kissed off the glass, and dropped through.

Even so, a jumper by Sleepy Floyd, Worthy's prep rival from Gastonia, gave the Hoyas a 62–61 lead with less than a minute to play. Smith, wanting his team to attack without delay, was forced to call a time-out with thirty-two seconds left when his team looked hesitant and confused. "We're in great shape," he told his shaken players. "I'd rather be in our position now than Georgetown's."

Smith set up two plays: one in case the Hoyas came out of the time-out in the man-to-man, the other in case of a zone. In both instances, the first option was inside to Worthy, who already had twenty-eight points on the night. But as the team broke the huddle, some instinct told Smith that his precocious freshman would end up with the shot. "If it comes to you, Michael," he said, grabbing Jordan as he left the huddle, "knock it down."

That's just what Jordan did. With Georgetown packing its zone in tight on Worthy and Perkins, Black floated a cross-court pass to the wide-open freshman, who elevated right in front of the Tar Heel bench and swished the eighteen-footer.

"Coming over tonight on the bus, I had a feeling I'd be in position to take that last shot," Jordan said. "I've never had a thought like that before. It just struck me. All I could think about was whether I'd hit it or miss it."

There was still time for Georgetown to answer. The Hoyas did exactly what Smith wanted his team to do on the previous possession—push the ball downcourt without calling a time-out. All was confusion as Georgetown point guard Freddie Brown pulled up at the top of the key and faked a pass to his right.

Worthy gambled on the steal and lunged out of position. Then Brown did an amazing thing, throwing the ball behind him, right to the startled Carolina star.

"I think Brown made the mistake because we were wearing white and as the No. 1 seed, Georgetown had worn white throughout the tournament," Smith said. "James must have looked like an ally."

Brown's mistake sealed UNC's 63–62 victory and finally gave Smith the national title to cap his stellar career.

"It would have bothered me if we'd lost this one," he said. "But only because this is the first time [in the Final Four] that I thought we had the best team."

North Carolina would have been the clear-cut favorite to repeat as national champion—with Worthy returning for his senior year to join Perkins, Jordan, and Doherty. But after talking to Jerry West of the Lakers, Smith determined that Worthy would be the first player taken in the NBA draft.

"I didn't see how he had a choice," Smith said. "It certainly adds perspective when a player suffers a serious injury as James did during his freshman season. James loved going to school, but his father agreed with me—he should turn pro."

Worthy did become the No. 1 pick in the draft, joining Magic Johnson and Kareem Abdul-Jabbar with the Lakers, where he would become a seven-time all-star and play on three NBA title teams. He was given the nickname "Big Game James" in Los Angeles, but in reality that was a nickname he started earning in the 1982 NCAA championship game, when he gave Smith his first national title.

JORDAN TAKES FLIGHT

Worthy's departure didn't exactly leave the Tar Heels depleted. Smith still retained three starters from his title team, including All-American Sam Perkins. His recruiting class included two of the top five prospects in the nation, both from Tobacco Road. But it didn't take Smith long to realize that UNC's chances of repeating as champions would hinge on the incredible changes in Michael Jordan's game.

"The first time I felt there was something truly unprecedented about Michael Jordan as a player was in the summer between his freshman and sophomore year," Smith wrote in his autobiography. "I have never seen that kind of improvement in anyone . . . ever."

Some of it was physical. Jordan shot up from 6-foot-3½ as a freshman to 6-foot-6 at the start of his sophomore year. His 40-yard dash time improved from 4.55 in October of 1981 to 4.39 (which would be an exceptional time for an NFL cornerback) in October of 1982. He was stronger and faster and had spent the summer improving his ballhandling skills and his mid-range shooting.

Former Tar Heel star Billy Cunningham, then the general manager of the 76ers, watched the new Jordan scrimmage that fall against a group of UNC pros and told Smith, "He's going to be the greatest player who ever came out of here."

It wouldn't take long for the rest of the nation to see what Cunningham had seen in that scrimmage. Jordan broke out of the gate quickly, despite playing the first month with a soft cast on his injured left wrist. In the third game of the season, he made a miraculous play to prevent a homecourt loss to Tulane, stealing an inbounds pass and hitting a last-second shot to force overtime. He blocked a last-second layup by Chuck Driesell (the son of coach Lefty Driesell) to preserve a one-point victory over Maryland. And he sparked a remarkable comeback from a sixteen-point deficit against Sampson and Virginia, winning the game with his steal from future pro Rick Carlisle.

"Michael was tremendous, but that's getting routine for him," teammate Matt Doherty said. "There are a lot of players on the playgrounds of New York who have the moves and ability. Michael has all of those things and the smarts to go with it. That's the key to him always being in the right place at the right time."

Jordan's emergence as a college star of the first order was finally complete. He was a unanimous first-team All-American and even challenged two-time defending national player of the year Ralph Sampson in the POY voting. Indeed, *The Sporting News* actually picked Jordan ahead of Sampson.

And the Tar Heel star was still getting better. As soon as UNC returned to campus after suffering a disappointing loss to Georgia in the NCAA East title game, Jordan headed straight from the team bus to Carmichael Auditorium, where he shot alone late into the night. It was a symbol of the dedication that would make him the greatest pro of his generation, and maybe of all time.

But Jordan still had a long way to go to challenge David Thompson as the greatest college player in Tobacco Road history. And he mounted that challenge as a junior in 1983–84 when he was, without challenge, the finest player in college basketball.

He averaged a modest 19.6 points a game, but he shot an eye-popping 55.4% from the floor. He rebounded well, distributed the ball, and was the best defensive player in the game. Although he led a remarkably talented Tar Heel team to a 26–1 regular season record and a No. 1 ranking in the final AP poll, Jordan's final season at Carolina came to an ignominious end against Indiana in the East Regional semifinals in Atlanta. The Tar Heel superstar, benched by Smith in the first half after picking up two quick fouls, played just twenty-six minutes and scored just thirteen points, defended by a slow, unathletic junior, Dan Dakich.

"Dakich did a job, sure, but I had the shots I normally take," Jordan said, adding, "I was trying not to think about it, but I just don't shoot well in the Omni."

Although Jordan swept every national player of the year award after his junior season, North Carolina's disappointing finishes in 1983 and 1984 point to a stunning irony: the greatest clutch player in NBA history often failed to rise to the occasion as a college star. True, he hit the game-winner against Georgetown to give Dean Smith his first NCAA title. But that was Worthy's team and the freshman from Wilmington had the luxury of playing in the shadow of his talented teammate. When Jordan became UNC's star player in the next two years, he could not elevate the Tar Heels to any postseason success.

Jordan's indisputable greatness in the NBA makes it difficult to view his collegiate career objectively. He was unquestionably a great player at Carolina. But taken as a whole, it's hard to argue that his college career stacks up even to UNC stars such as Larry Miller or Charlie Scott, much less to ACC icon David Thompson.

10

THE CARDIAC PACK

IT WASN'T FUN COACHING IN THE SHADOW OF DEAN SMITH'S juggernaut. N.C. State's Jim Valvano tried to maintain his sense of humor, but as the losses to the powerful Tar Heels piled up in his early years in Raleigh, his frustration grew. On the night of March 6, 1982, the Wolfpack coach had to meet the press after suffering another loss to his team's primary rival—this one in the semifinals of the ACC Tournament in Greensboro. It was his sixth loss without a win to Smith and the Tar Heels.

"I don't know when we're going to beat him, but I know I'm going to outlive him," Valvano, still a week away from his thirty-fifth birthday, joked.

Of course, we now know that Valvano didn't outlive his rival. On the night he made that poignant joke, "Jimmy V" was just twelve years away from his tragic death. He was to succumb to cancer in April of 1993, just weeks after the indestructible Smith won his second national championship in New Orleans. At least Valvano's frustration with North Carolina didn't last that much longer either. He was on the verge of not only beating Smith, but also matching his greatest achievement.

But it didn't come easy.

In hindsight, Jim Valvano seemed like the perfect choice to replace Norman Sloan at N.C. State. In one of those weird, convoluted connections that crop up so often on Tobacco Road, Valvano was a protégé of departing Duke coach Bill Foster. The son of a high school coach, Valvano had walked on for Foster at Rutgers and starred in the backcourt there beside All-American Bob Lloyd.

As a young coach, first at Johns Hopkins and then at Iona, Valvano developed his own style—a street-smart New York version of the kind of off-the-cuff humor that Bones McKinney once dished out on Tobacco Road.

"I once asked a ref if he could give me a technical for what I was thinking about him," Valvano said. "He said, 'Of course not.' So I told him, 'Well, I think you stink!'"

He told reporters about the time he had introduced himself to the mother of a prospect as, "Jim Valvano, Iona College," and claimed her response was, "Aren't you a little young to own a college?"

Behind the humor was a sharp basketball mind. Valvano was not an innovative X-and-O technician such as UNC's Smith, but a coach with the same kind of gut instincts that had made Al McGuire so successful at Marquette.

"In all my years of teaching and working with young people, I've only made this statement about two people: they were born to coach," UCLA's John Wooden said. "One was Denny Crum, when he played for me. The other was Jimmy Valvano, who was a freshman at Rutgers when I first met him at a basketball camp in the Poconos."

Valvano was introduced as Sloan's successor on March 27 to the same reporters who had attended Mike Krzyzewski's press conference at Duke exactly one week earlier.

"I had an unbelievable job at Iona," Valvano told the North Carolina media, "but my dream was to come here—to the ACC. I just can't believe I can't get it done."

Even though Krzyzewski beat Valvano to Tobacco Road by a week, Jimmy V would find success at his new school far faster than Coach K did at Duke. Of course, Valvano inherited a slightly stronger talent base than his rival. He inherited a trio of sophomores who would make magic two years in the future. But he also had holes to fill after the graduation of four-year starters Hawkeye Whitney and Clyde "The Glide" Austin. For the time being, the postgame press conferences in Raleigh would be more entertaining than the product on the court.

Valvano's first season in Raleigh was a 14–13 disappointment, highlighted mainly by back-to-back wins in Madison Square Garden over his old Iona team and over St. John's to win the Holiday Classic.

If Valvano was going to win more than fourteen games in a season, he was going to need to find help for the three quality players he inherited from Sloan:

slender forward Thurl Bailey from Bladensburg (Md.) and guards Dereck Whittenburg and Sidney Lowe, prep teammates from DeMatha High School in Hyattsville (Md.).

Lowe and Whittenburg had actually been together much longer than that, sharing a backcourt in junior high school and on the Washington, D.C. playgrounds where they first met. Both were stocky, 6-foot-1 guards, but while they were built alike, they possessed very different games. Lowe was the consummate point guard—a terrific defender and playmaker with only an average jump shot. Whittenburg was an explosive scorer, with astonishing range on his deadly, high-arching jumper and the strength to post up most backcourt defenders. Bailey, who joined the two DeMatha stars as a freshman at N.C. State, was a slender 6-foot-11 forward with a sweet baseline jumper. He functioned as a small forward on offense but was able to defend in the post.

As Valvano embarked on his first real recruiting effort, he was looking for strength up front and backcourt depth. He was to find both, but not where he was looking for it. At the time, Valvano's big get appeared to be prep All-American Walter "Dinky" Proctor, a strong 6-foot-8 forward from New York. But Proctor's game turned out to be dinky indeed as he averaged 1.1 points in the thirty-nine games he played at N.C. State. Less celebrated, but eventually far more useful, were three unheralded recruits: Lorenzo Charles, a bullish 6-foot-7 forward from New York City; Terry Gannon, a 6-foot sharp-shooter from Joliet (Ill.); and Cozell McQueen, a gawky 6-foot-11 center from Bennettsville (S.C.), who delighted reporters with his declaration that he had signed with N.C. State "to get out of the South." It was a toss-up as to who was more geographically challenged: McQueen or Lefty Driesell.

None of Valvano's three recruits were good enough to start as freshmen, but the growing maturity of the Bailey-Lowe-Whittenburg trio helped the Pack improve to 22–10 in Valvano's second season, a jump from seventh to fourth place in the ACC standings. The season even included a bid to the NCAA Tournament, although that resulted in an embarrassing 58–51 flameout against UT-Chattanooga in the first round.

Despite the disappointing finish, Valvano was remarkably upbeat heading into his third season. In the first place, he thought the ACC's experimental rules (the short three-point shot, the thirty-second shot clock) would help his guards, especially Whittenburg and Gannon. In the second place, he had added another prep All-American from New York, explosive scorer Ernie Myers.

Outsiders were surprised when Myers failed to crack Valvano's starting lineup. Instead, sophomores McQueen and Charles, who both averaged 2.2 points in very limited roles as freshmen, joined State's senior triumvirate on the floor as the Pack opened 7–2 against a strong schedule. It got even stronger when No. 2 Virginia and senior center Ralph Sampson visited Reynolds on January 12. The fired-up Pack led the heavily favored Cavs throughout the first half and seemed to be in control early in the second half when Whittenburg (who had scored twenty-seven points in the game's first twenty-five minutes) went up for a jumper in front of the Wolfpack bench. He came down on the foot of Virginia defender Othell Wilson—and crumpled to the floor in pain.

Whittenburg had broken the fifth metatarsal bone in his right foot. The first prognosis was that he'd miss the rest of his senior season. The crushing news was followed by a Wolfpack collapse as Virginia rallied for an 88–80 victory. The next day before practice, Valvano gathered his distraught team around him and delivered a crucial message.

"Now, a lot of people are writing us off," he told them. "They are saying our season is over. I'm telling you, I believe something good is going to happen to us. I'm telling you, it's too soon to quit."

Those last four words would become the motto of the miracle that was to follow. A decade later, the philosophy behind them would morph into the inspirational message that a dying Jim Valvano would use to inspire the world.

N.C. State's 1983 fight for survival began slowly enough. Myers, whose freshman season had been a disappointment to that point, stepped into Whittenburg's starting spot and began to play to his potential. McQueen and Charles also began to take on a bigger role in Whittenburg's absence and Gannon emerged as an offensive sparkplug off the bench, hitting an astonishing 58.9% of his attempts from the ACC's short three-point line.

The first hint that N.C. State might do more than merely survive in Whittenburg's absence came on February 19, when Valvano finally got his first career victory over Dean Smith. The losing streak that bothered him so much had reached seven straight with a lopsided loss in Chapel Hill soon after Whittenburg's injury. But the rematch in Raleigh was a different story.

The combination of Bailey's short baseline jumpers and Gannon's three-point bombs helped the Pack grab a narrow 37–36 lead at the break. The game stayed close throughout the second half as the lights on the phony noise meter hanging from the Reynolds rafters stayed on the top peg. Valvano threw a bewildering variety of defenses at the powerful Heels: zones; man-to-man; a box-and-one on Michael Jordan (with the tiny Gannon matched against the UNC superstar); a triangle-and-two on Jordan and Sam Perkins; and Jimmy V's favorite piece of junk, a 1-3-1 alignment that used Lowe at the bottom of the zone, running the baseline.

Valvano's schemes and the frenzy of the crowd carried N.C. State into the final seconds with the lead. And when Lowe finished a fast break with eight seconds left by passing the ball through his legs behind him to the trailing Bailey for the clinching dunk, Valvano finally had his signature victory over the great Dean Smith.

"I don't think anything can top this feeling," Bailey told reporters in the locker room, with tears streaming down his face. "Even if we went to the NCAA, even to the Final Four, even if we won it all—at this point, at this moment, I don't think anything could feel better than this."

Could anyone have believed that, six weeks later, Bailey and the Pack would get to experience the type of success Bailey had thrown out as an impossible comparison to the drama of beating North Carolina?

Valvano didn't expect it, even after he learned that Whittenburg might be coming back after all. Despite what the doctors said, the senior guard had experienced exactly the same injury in high school and always believed that he could return before the end of the season.

"I understood what it took to come back," Whittenburg told writer Tim Peeler. "I knew I was coming back. The great thing was, the team grew up while I was out and they were an even better team when I came back."

That was obvious in the final regular season game. N.C. State simply massacred a very good Wake Forest team in Raleigh. The Pack, getting twenty-five points from both Whittenburg and Gannon, scored fifty-six first-half points against the Deacons, then added an incredible seventy-four more points in the second half. State's 130–89 victory over the team that finished 7–7 in the ACC should have served warning that there was something special about the Wolfpack.

DESTINY'S DARLINGS

When the 1983 ACC Tournament opened in Atlanta's Omni, most of the attention was focused on No. 2 Virginia and No. 5 North Carolina—the two superpowers expected to repeat their 1982 battle for the title. However, there was a considerable interest in the first-round matchup between fourth-seeded N.C. State (17–10) and fifth-seeded Wake Forest (17–10). There was speculation that both teams needed a strong tournament run to earn an at-large NCAA Tournament bid.

Whether true or not (and the fact that first-round loser Wake Forest ended up in the NIT indicates that it probably was), the Pack started postseason play with the approach that every game was life or death. Although the Pack had routed the Deacons just six days earlier in Raleigh, State had to fight for its life in the rematch, only pulling out a 71–70 victory on a free throw by Lorenzo Charles with three seconds to play.

N.C. State was still not assured of an NCAA bid as the Pack prepared to face North Carolina in the semifinals. It was widely assumed that the greatly superior Tar Heels would take revenge for that once-in-a-lifetime Wolfpack upset in Raleigh two weeks earlier. Only it didn't happen. Jordan and Perkins were once again bamboozled by Valvano's shifting defenses. The two All-Americans missed twenty-four of thirty-seven shots, including a twenty-five-foot jumper by Perkins at the end of regulation that would have eliminated the Pack and probably sent them to the NIT. Instead, Lowe, en route to a career-high twenty-six-point performance, dominated the extra period to send State into the finals—and probably into the NCAA Tournament as well.

The next afternoon against the second-ranked Cavs, the Pack took the "probably" out of the equation. N.C. State was nursing a 71–66 lead when Virginia assistant coach Jim Larranaga was whistled for a technical foul for coming off the bench to protest a call. Whittenburg hit both free throws, then followed with a driving shot over Sampson to put the game out of reach.

"We lost it," a very disappointed Sampson said. "I don't think they beat us."

Virginia was still a No. 1 seed in the NCAA Tournament, as it turned out in the same West Regional where N.C. State was assigned. The Wolfpack, seeded No. 6 in the region, drew a first-round game against Pepperdine in Corvallis, Oregon.

Valvano was worried that the emotion of winning the ACC Tournament and achieving the team's goal of earning an NCAA bid might leave his team drained for the late-night game with the little-known team from Southern California.

"We might lose tomorrow night to Pepperdine," Valvano told reporters at his team's Thursday press conference. "It wouldn't surprise me if we do. We're going to be flat at hell. We're going to get caught up in a street brawl with a team that's a lot better than our guys believe and then we'll get scared and start making stupid mistakes."

Then Valvano added something that sounded crazy at the time, but would prove to be as prophetic as the first part of his statement. "If we do somehow or another win this game, watch out," he warned. "I think we'll win it all."

In those days, the new all-sports network ESPN carried the majority of the early round NCAA games. But CBS, which had just purchased the primary tournament contract, picked up late-night games on the first Thursday and Friday nights of the tournament for a national feed. When the network picked State-Pepperdine for its Friday night game, it meant the whole nation would be watching as the Pack's miracle began to unfold.

The State-Pepperdine game started at 11:40 p.m. Eastern Standard Time and seemed to last forever. As Valvano predicted, State was absolutely horrible —shooting 42% from the floor and getting outrebounded by the smaller Waves. With the Corvallis crowd pulling loudly for the underdog team from the West Coast, Pepperdine forged a six-point lead with a minute left in overtime and had CBS commentator Dick Stockton already focusing on the network's weekend lineup of games. But it was still "too soon to quit."

Improbably, Dane Suttle, the nation's No. 3 free throw shooter, twice missed the front end of a one-and-one in the final thirty seconds and State was able to tie the game on an even more improbable follow shot by McQueen. It was his only basket of the game, a left-handed jumper that surprised everybody except the sophomore big man. "I knew I'd make that shot when I took it," he said.

With Lowe out with five fouls, Whittenburg moved to the point in the final five minutes and directed the Pack to a 69–67 victory, making eight of ten free throws in the final five minutes. It was nearly 3 a.m. in Raleigh when the game ended, but the Raleigh newspaper stopped the presses and managed to get the final score in a few hundred final editions.

In Corvallis, Valvano told his team, "Hey, we may be destined to win this thing." But out on the court, UNLV All-American Sidney Green was assuring Rebel fans they had nothing to worry about in Sunday afternoon's second-round matchup. "We're going to kick their butts," he boasted. As for Bailey, the player Green would match up against, he said, "He didn't show me much. We're not worried about Bailey."

Bailey showed him more in the second round, pouring in twenty-five points, including the game-winning follow shot. The Pack was down twelve midway through the second half and still trailed by three points with forty seconds left, but Bailey hit a baseline jumper to make it 70–69; then Gannon fouled Eldridge Hudson, who naturally missed the first of the 1-and-1. Whittenburg missed a jumper at the other end and Bailey's tip also rolled out. But the lanky senior grabbed the rebound again and this time finished with a strong move to beat the No. 6 ranked Rebels, 71–70.

"Has anybody interviewed Sidney Green yet?" Bailey asked reporters in the State locker room. Then he added, "You keep hearing that word, destiny, don't you?"

The Thursday night West Regional semifinal turned out to be almost devoid of drama. State, which had traveled directly to Ogden, Utah, after beating UNLV in Corvallis (without returning to Raleigh), actually took the lead at the half after shooting 59% from the floor.

"Don't worry," Utah coach Jerry Pimm told his team. "They can't keep shooting like that." He was right: State shot 79% in the second half to blitz the Utes 75–56 in front of another hostile crowd.

State was one game from the Final Four, but standing in the way was Virginia—a team that had dominated Valvano's teams before the ACC Tournament championship game. It was the worst-possible matchup for Valvano's miracle workers. The Cavs were still angry about the loss in Atlanta, blaming the officiating for their defeat. And State didn't have the advantage of the ACC's short three-point line that it had used so well to neutralize the imposing Sampson.

"With a day off and an old ACC rival we've played three times, we'll be alright," a very confident Terry Holland told reporters before the game.

Sampson, his collegiate career on the line, was magnificent. The 7-foot-4 senior had twenty-three points on eight of ten shooting and eleven rebounds. The Cavs led by seven points and seemed in control of the game. But the Cardiac Pack, as it did so often that month, fought back to take a one-point lead on two free throws by Charles. After Holland called a time-out to set up his final play with seventeen seconds left, Valvano assigned one man to guard Othell Wilson and set up a three-man triangle around Sampson. "We had Sampson surrounded," Valvano said.

Unable to find the national player of the year down low, guard Tim Mullen launched a long jumper from the top of the key. Wilson, who had broken Whittenburg's foot two months earlier, rebounded and threw the ball up toward the basket—whether a desperation shot or a lob for the MIA Sampson has never been quite determined. Whatever it was, the ball came up short and the buzzer sounded just before the rebound was tipped back to Sampson. With the pressure off, the Virginia All-American finally put up a shot that didn't matter.

"At least now they know we can beat them," the always quotable Bailey said.

N.C. State returned to Raleigh before the Final Four, "because we had run out of underwear," Valvano said. But he found that his team couldn't get anything done with the excitement that gripped the N.C. State campus. Crowds from four to six thousand people attended his practices in Reynolds, interrupting his lessons with their cheers. As a result, he elected to take his team to Albuquerque a day early.

The State-Georgia semifinal, which Valvano called "the jayvee game," was seen at the time as a preliminary to the real championship game—a semifinal match between powerful Louisville, which had climbed to No. 2 in the rankings after the Pack beat Virginia in the ACC Tournament, and No. 1 Houston, led by All-American center Akeem Olajuwon and future all-pro swing man Clyde Drexler. Many of the faces were familiar to writers who had seen UNC beat the Cougars in the 1982 semifinals; but this was a better team, with Williams replaced by talented freshman Alvin Franklin and Olajuwon blossoming into a superstar.

Houston demonstrated its power against Louisville as the two teams staged a spectacular dunkathon early in the second half—a ten-minute blitz that left courtside observers in awe of both teams. It was so impressive that when the Cougars pulled away for their 91–84 victory, many in the crowd were ready to hand the championship trophy to Guy Lewis's team. "It was like we didn't have a chance," Lowe said.

Certainly, N.C. State didn't appear to be much of a threat, not even after slopping its way to a 67–60 victory over Georgia. On the eve of the championship game, *Washington Post* columnist David Kindred summed up the feeling of many when he wrote: "Trees will tap dance, elephants will ride in the Indianapolis 500 and Orson Welles will skip breakfast, lunch and dinner before N.C. State finds a way to beat Houston."

About the only person outside the Wolfpack family that gave Jim Valvano's crew a ghost of a chance was UNC's Dean Smith, who picked the Pack in an interview with an Albuquerque TV reporter.

Valvano amused the media in his off-day press conference, suggesting, "We may hold the ball until Tuesday." But when he closed the door to the locker room, he was deadly serious.

"We're going to control tempo," he told his team, according to an account he later wrote in a book titled *Too Soon to Quit.* "We'll run when we want to run. We'll stop when we want to stop and all I ask is to be in position to win the game at the end," he told them.

Once again, Valvano proved to be as astute a prognosticator as he was a coach. N.C. State did control tempo, frustrating the Cougar racehorses. The Wolfpack seized a 33–25 lead with what Valvano called "a perfect half" and had the crowd at New Mexico's Pit buzzing during the break. Was the unthinkable possible?

It didn't seem that way when Houston outscored State 17–2 to start the second half, turning its eight-point deficit into a 42–35 lead with ten minutes to play. At that point, Lewis saved the Pack with a coaching decision that echoed back to the one Dick Harp made to save North Carolina in the 1957 NCAA title game.

Lewis ordered his fastbreaking team into a stall, breaking his team's momentum and allowing the Pack players to catch their breath. Valvano allowed the clock to run down until he could employ the strategy that he'd used to such good effect against Pepperdine: the intentional foul.

Michael Young went 0-for-4 from the line and Houston supersub Benny Anders was 2-of-5 as State clawed back to tie the game at 52-all. With just over a minute left, Valvano put the freshman Franklin, an 80% foul shooter on the season, at the line. When he missed the front end of the one-and-one, the State players found themselves with the ball and a chance to complete a miracle.

Valvano borrowed Dean Smith's Four Corners set for his final play. He wanted Lowe to drive the middle and set up either Bailey or Whittenburg or Gannon for the game-winning jump shot. But Lowe started his drive too early. He got the ball to Bailey on his left, and the 6-foot-11 senior was momentarily open from his favorite spot on the floor. But just as Mo Howard did nine years earlier in a similar situation (and from almost the same spot on the court), Bailey passed up the shot. All of Valvano's careful plans broke down as the big forward whipped the ball back outside to Whittenburg, who, like Lucas in 1974, was forced to launch an impossible shot.

Whittenburg's thirty-five-foot heave was an air ball. Olajuwon, stationed under the basket, turned and blocked out, looking for a carom off the rim. But Charles, coming in from the right corner, could see that the shot was going to fall short. With Olajuwon out of the way, the 6-foot-7 Wolfpack forward found himself in perfect position to grab the miss almost as if it were a lob from Tim Stoddard to David Thompson and, without coming down, slam it home to give N.C. State a 54–52 victory. On the Wolfpack radio network, play-by-play man Wally Ausley screamed, "The glass slipper fits!"

On the court, the TV cameras followed Valvano as he looked for somebody, anybody, to hug. But his players were all busy hugging each other and Jimmy V ended up in the arms of Wolfpack athletic director Willis Casey.

"He hugged me and that wasn't so bad," Valvano told reporters. "But then he kissed me right on the lips too. I could just see some guy out in Kansas watching this on television and saying, 'Martha, come here. You've got to see this.'"

N.C. State's improbable triumph made Valvano a national hero—a headliner whose popularity even challenged the status of Smith on Tobacco Road. After all, it had taken the Tar Heel coach twenty years of struggle and the presence of three future all-pros to finally claim his first national title. Then a year later, the fast-talking Valvano matched his achievement with a squad that wasn't nearly as talented as at least a dozen of Smith's best teams.

N.C. State finally returned to Raleigh for a tumultuous celebration in Reynolds Coliseum. But it was ten years later, when the dying Valvano returned to Reynolds to honor the Pack's second national championship team on its tenth anniversary, that the true meaning of the 1983 miracle became clear.

"The '83 team taught us about dreaming and the importance of dreaming," Valvano told the crowd in Reynolds. "That team taught me persistence, the idea of never, ever quitting."

11

THE RISE OF MIKE KRZYZEWSKI

M<small>IKE WHO?</small>

In the days after Bill Foster announced his resignation at Duke, the first name linked to the vacant job was former Blue Devil assistant Chuck Daly, who was working at that time as an assistant coach for the NBA's Philadelphia 76ers. Later, Boston College coach Tom Davis would attract the media's attention. Finally, the Durham newspaper proclaimed with some confidence that the three finalists for the job were Foster assistant Bob Wenzel, Old Dominion head coach Paul Webb, and Mississippi head coach Bob Weltlich.

"It will be a coach whose last name starts with a *W*," the *Durham Morning Herald* confidently reported.

It turned out that no media outlet had any idea what Duke Athletics Director Tom Butters was up to. The Ohio native, a former relief pitcher for the Pittsburgh Pirates, had high expectations for the Duke basketball program, so his first pitch was not to the little- known (at the time) Daly, but to the man he perceived as the best college basketball coach in the country. Butters called Indiana's Bobby Knight and offered him the Duke job. Knight declined, but suggested a couple of his protégés as possibilities, including Southern Methodist University's Dave Bliss and Weltlich

Butters discussed his options with Steve Vacendak, the former Duke guard who was about to become an associate athletic director at his alma mater. It was Vacendak who first brought up the Army coach with the unpronounceable name. Since the Army coach was also a Knight protégé, Butters called the Indiana coach again and asked him what he thought about Mike Krzyzewski.

"Knight's comment was, 'If you like me as a basketball coach, here's a man who has all my good qualities and none of my bad ones,'" Butters said.

After hearing that endorsement, Duke's athletic director met secretly with the young Army coach and talked to him about the job. In the end, Butters sent him home, concerned about his youth (Krzyzewski had just turned thirty-three) and his 9–17 record in his most recent season at Army. "But I couldn't get him out of my mind," Butters said.

Krzyzewski, a product of a tough Polish neighborhood in Chicago, had played four years for Knight at Army, where he excelled as a defender and ball-handler. One of his best games was when the Cadets knocked off South Carolina in the NIT and Krzyzewski outplayed Gamecock guard Bobby Cremins.

After five years of military service, Captain Krzyzewski resigned his commission and joined Knight's staff at Indiana, where he served one year as a graduate assistant coach. He returned to West Point as head coach in 1975, leading the U.S. Military Academy to back-to-back records of 20–8 in 1977 and 19–9 in 1978.

Butters agonized about giving the job to a young coach with such an undistinguished record, but in the end, he gave in to his gut instincts and made the controversial hire. Duke introduced its new coach on March 20 to three dozen reporters who hadn't heard of the Army coach, never suspected he was a candidate for the job, and couldn't even pronounce his name.

"It's *sha-CHEFF-skee*," the new coach explained. "That's K-r-z-y-z-e-w-s-k-i. And if you think that's bad, you should have heard it before I changed it. For those of you who can't pronounce it, you can just call me Coach K."

It would be many years before that initial would become shorthand for the most powerful coach in college basketball and the assembled reporters would understand just how big Butters's gamble had paid off.

COACH K

If it was tough for Valvano, building a winner in the shadow of Dean Smith's juggernaut, just imagine what it was like for Mike Krzyzewski when his contemporary in Raleigh won the 1983 title and he had to contend with not one, but two national championship rivals in his own neighborhood.

"I was not aware of how good the conference was until I got in it," Krzyzewski told author Bill Brill. "Everything was harder than I thought—recruiting, playing, everything. I knew about the top guys, but I wasn't aware of the talent from three through eight. And the coaching was so good."

Krzyzewski was building slowly, just as Smith did in his early days at North Carolina. And while the young Duke coach was never hung in effigy as Smith was, he did endure his share of discontent from impatient Blue Devil fans.

Nobody complained when Krzyzewski went 17–13 in 1981 with the left-overs of Foster's three straight nationally ranked teams. He got about as much out of Gene Banks, Kenny Dennard, and Vince Taylor—Duke's only three legitimate ACC players—as possible.

That included a memorable upset of No. 11 North Carolina in the final home game for Banks and Dennard. The former Philadelphia schoolboy star, once rated a prospect on the level of Wilt Chamberlain and Magic Johnson, made the All-ACC first team for the first time as a senior under Krzyzewski. He had not become the superstar that most expected. But it was also hard to dismiss his career as a disappointment after his role in Duke's 1978 title run. And certainly nobody ever went out with more flair. During pregame introductions, Banks threw roses to the Cameron Crazies—then, with one second left and Duke down two to their hated rivals, he took an inbounds pass from Dennard and turned and launched an eighteen-footer just over the outstretched fingers of UNC's Sam Perkins. The buzzer sounded as the ball dropped through the net. Appropriately, Banks scored the game-winner in overtime.

Unfortunately, his career ended when he suffered a broken arm in practice after a quick ACC Tournament exit. Duke still managed to win two NIT games without its star forward, but for the second straight year, Purdue sent the Blue Devils home—disappointed, but hardly dismayed after Krzyzewski's first season.

The real dismay occurred on the recruiting trail, where Krzyzewski's inexperience as a big-time recruiter became evident. Time and again, he'd go to the wire with a key recruiting target—and time and again, he'd finish second.

Krzyzewski's best recruit proved to be rough-and-tumble Canadian forward Dan Meagher, but he would provide little immediate help for what was shaping up as a dreadful team (senior Vince Taylor was the only ACC-quality player on the roster). When Duke started 1–4 in 1981–82, the same season UNC was making its run to the national title, the Blue Devil faithful began to grumble about their young coach.

Ironically, as Krzyzewski's second Duke team collapsed on the court, the young coach finally began to score on the recruiting trail. His first get was an early commitment from Weldon Williams, a highly regarded small forward from Illinois who was a major target for several Big Ten teams. A few weeks later, Coach K beat out most of the Big 8 to land 6-foot-9 Bill Jackman from tiny Grant (Neb.), who was touted as "the next Larry Bird." Just before Christmas, Krzyzewski stole 6-foot-8 Californian Jay Bilas from the Pac-10 Conference.

Krzyzewski's well-publicized recruiting success was taking some of the heat off him as his second team stumbled to a 10–17 finish, edging the 1974 Blue Devils as the worst Duke team since 1927. What nobody knew at the time was that his early recruiting success was an illusion. Of his first three recruits, only Bilas would become a significant contributor. Jackman, overawed by the competition he found in the ACC, would flee back to Nebraska after one season in Durham. Williams would stick around for four years, but his degree in microbiology was a lot more impressive than anything he ever did on the floor. But Krzyzewski was still recruiting hard—and in the spring on 1982, he was to land the three players who would finally get his program off the ground.

The first was Mark Alarie, a versatile 6-foot-8 forward from Scottsdale, Arizona, who possessed the inside-outside skills that Krzyzewski coveted for his motion offense. The second was Washington, D.C. guard Johnny Dawkins. Coach K loved the athleticism and the competitiveness of the slender (let's be honest, the skinny) playground product.

"I believed in him," Dawkins said, explaining his choice many years later. "I didn't know where we were going. I knew we were going to recruit like crazy. I saw him assembling a great team. I knew he had the passion and desire."

Krzyzewski's passion made him greedy. He wanted 6-foot-4 prep All-American Curtis Hunter from Durham's Southern High School. So did almost everybody else in the country, including Valvano at State and UNC's Dean Smith. As usual, Smith got what he wanted, and at a press conference attended by more than a dozen reporters, Hunter announced he was going to North Carolina. Instead of Hunter, Krzyzewski signed 6-foot-5 David Henderson from the tiny farming community of Drewry (N.C.), about forty-five minutes north of Durham. Ironically, Henderson would turn out to be a far better college player than the more heralded Hunter.

Krzyzewski almost didn't last long enough to reap his 1982 recruiting success. His freshman-dominated 1983 team—with Dawkins, Alarie, Bilas, and

Henderson all in the starting lineup—was just one game better at 11–17 than the 1982 team. The harsh criticism of the young coach, somewhat muted by his recruiting success the year before, exploded as the heralded freshmen proved incapable of beating Wagner at home.

"You heard the rumbling," Dawkins said. "People were always coming up and asking questions: 'What do you think? Can he do this? Can he coach? Why aren't you guys playing zone?'"

The 1983 season ended with a horrendous 109–66 loss to Virginia in the first-round of the ACC Tournament in Atlanta. Two days before Valvano was to enjoy his moment of glory by upsetting the Cavs in the ACC title game, Duke endured its worst loss in tournament history.

Even worse, Krzyzewski learned that Virginia's Sampson, who had picked up a foul for elbowing Bilas eleven seconds into the game, had complained to reporters that Duke was a dirty team. Coach K was still fuming as the team's coaches and a handful of administrators gathered at Denny's for a late-night dinner. Sports Information Director Johnny Moore raised his glass of water and offered a toast: "Here's to forgetting tonight," he said. Krzyzewski stopped him. "No, here's to never forgetting tonight," he said.

The next fall, when the Duke players gathered for the first day of practice, they saw the Virginia score, 109–66, lit up on the scoreboard.

The 1983–84 Duke team had one important addition. Tommy Amaker, a 6-foot, 150-pound freshman from Fairfax, Virginia, was the new starting point guard. Dawkins was allowed to move to his natural position at wing guard, while Alarie, Bilas, and the maturing Meagher started up front. Henderson bought into the idea of being the team's sixth man. After winning just ten and eleven games in the two previous seasons, the Blue Devils won fourteen of their first fifteen in 1983–84, including a sweet 78–72 victory at Virginia, which was the first of sixteen straight victories over the team that had embarrassed Krzyzewski in Atlanta. Despite the fast start, Duke was still not ranked and Krzyzewski was still not secure in his job. In fact, he was to face his greatest crisis in January as the young Devils lost four ACC games in a row.

The first was at home against Maryland and was somewhat overshadowed by the behavior of the Cameron Crazies. Herman Veal—a senior forward for the Terps—had been accused of assaulting a coed, and Driesell had reportedly intervened and tried to prevent her from filing charges against him. That was grist for the nation's most creative (sometimes) and abusive (always) fan base.

Veal was showered by condoms during pregame introductions. During the game, he was subjected to the chant, "Rape . . . rape . . . rape." The closest thing to a clever taunt that afternoon was a sign that asked, "Hey, Herman, did you send her flowers?"

Not coincidentally, Veal played a terrific game as the Terps broke Duke's six-game winning streak with an 81–75 victory. Worse, from Krzyzewski's point of view, was the lambasting Duke took in the national media for the horrid conduct of its crowd. The young coach responded by meeting privately with Duke student groups in an effort to get them to clean up their act. They were on their best behavior when No. 1 North Carolina came to Cameron exactly one week after the Maryland debacle. The Crazies wore halos fashioned out of coat hangers covered with aluminum foil and greeted the hated Tar Heels with signs that said, "Welcome honored guests" and chanted, "We beg to differ" at the refs, in place of their normal, "Bullshit!"

But the good feelings didn't last long beyond tipoff.

Krzyzewski had not had much luck against the powerful Tar Heels since Banks's final home game in 1981. But his sophomore-dominated team gave the unbeaten visitors everything they could handle. Henderson, with twenty points, actually outplayed the mighty Jordan (eighteen points), and Alarie held his own with Perkins.

Duke took a 40–39 halftime lead as UNC assistant Bill Guthridge chased the refs off the floor, screaming at the men in striped shirts. Krzyzewski, also frustrated by the officiating, called a time-out early in the second half and spent the entire break staring at young ref Mike Moser. But nothing topped the spectacle of Dean Smith interrupting the game with a tirade in front of the scorer's table. The Tar Heel coach, angry that a sub wasn't buzzed into the game quickly enough, demanded that Tommy Hunt, the man working the scoreboard, sound the buzzer. Hunt tried to explain that he couldn't do that with the ball in play. Smith's response was to reach over and try and sound the buzzer himself—but he pushed the wrong button and gave his team a quick twenty-point boost on the scoreboard instead.

Somehow, Smith avoided a technical foul, and with Jordan finally beating Henderson for back-to-back baskets, the Tar Heels pulled out a 78–73 victory. The Duke coach was fuming when he stormed into the media room and delivered a withering tirade.

"I want to tell you something," he told the assembled reporters. "When you come in here and start talking about how Duke has no class, you'd better start getting your stories straight—because our students had class and our team had class. There was not one person on our bench who was pointing a finger at the officials or banging on the scorer's table. So let's get some things straight around here and quit the double standard that exits in this league!"

Amazingly, there were Duke fans who couldn't see how quickly Krzyzewski was closing the gap on UNC's program. Butters, who was the school's top fund-raiser in addition to his duties as athletic director, was getting pressure from boosters who wanted him to fire the young coach. He even received a death threat from one anonymous fan who didn't like Coach K.

Butters's response was to call Krzyzewski into his office. "He came in and sat down," Butters told Dick Weiss. "I told him, 'We've got a public who doesn't know how good you are. We've got press who are too stupid to tell them how good you are. And the biggest problem right now is I'm not sure you know how good you are.' With that, I opened up my desk and tossed a new five-year contract to him."

The new contract, which included a substantial raise in pay, was an amazing vote of confidence for an unproven coach. But like Butters's initial gamble to hire an unknown coach, it was to pay huge dividends . . . but not right away.

Duke blew another chance to upset the Tar Heels when future coach Matt Doherty hit a running jumper to force overtime in Chapel Hill. Doherty added two clutch free throws to force a second extra period and Carolina finally beat off the Krzyzewski's hungry young Devils.

"Having played that game, we knew we could beat Carolina," Dawkins said. "The groundwork was laid. We had an opportunity and it slipped away. All the while, we were learning. We had two tough lessons in how to close games out."

The Blue Devils cashed in that knowledge in the ACC Tournament semifinals. Duke built a ten-point first-half lead, then bounced back after North Carolina rallied to take the lead. Late in the game, Krzyzewski prepared his team for the victory.

"I remember being in the huddle," Alarie told Dick Weiss, "and Coach K said, 'Okay, when we beat these guys, let's pretend like we've been there before.' He told us to be calm because we were going to win."

And Duke did win, a 77–75 victory over the team that was the gold standard on Tobacco Road.

"The horn sounded and I'm thinking, as excited as we are, let's pretend that we've been there before," Alarie said. "And then I look over at Coach K—and he's jumping all around like a little kid."

Krzyzewski still had a ways to go to get Duke where he wanted it to be. The Blue Devils, emotionally drained and physically exhausted by their triumph over Carolina, had nothing left for Maryland in the ACC championship game. And Krzyzewski's first NCAA experience proved to be a short one as Duke lost to Washington in Pullman, Washington.

Krzyzewski's 1984 accomplishment wasn't as dramatic as Jimmy Valvano's 1983 breakthrough, but it would prove to be more lasting. Never again would Duke fans question Coach K's fitness for the job. Butters would get no more death threats. And freed of concerns from his rear, the Army-trained coach would take Duke basketball to places that even their most demanding fans never dreamed of.

THE BIRTH OF ANOTHER DYNASTY

Coach K did not immediately capitalize on his 1984 success. His junior-based team did win twenty-three games in 1985—including a momentous win in Carmichael Auditorium, where Dawkins scored thirty-four points and added eight rebounds, four assists, and four steals to lead the Blue Devils to their first win on UNC's home court since 1965. But a hip injury slowed Alarie late in the season and Georgia Tech knocked off Duke in the first round of the ACC Tournament. Duke flamed out in the second round of the NCAA Tournament again, blowing a big lead to Boston College after Henderson went down with a sprained ankle.

That spring, Duke's hard-working young coach scored a significant recruiting victory, landing the nation's No. 1 prospect out of DeMatha High School in Hyattsville, Maryland. Danny Ferry, the son of Bob Ferry, the general manager of the Washington Bullets, picked Duke over entreaties from Maryland's Lefty Driesell and North Carolina's Dean Smith.

"I just sensed something special in Coach K," Ferry said. "I sensed a guy who was a really good coach, a guy I really wanted to play for. I saw greatness."

Krzyzewski's great 1982 recruiting class—Dawkins, Alarie, Henderson, and Bilas—would provide the cornerstone for his first great team in 1986.

Ferry would be limited to a supporting role that year. But the multi-talented big man from Maryland turned out to be the foundation for the teams that would follow. He guaranteed that Krzyzewski's career would not mirror Mc-Kinney's or Foster's: one great team, then obscurity.

Duke was picked third in the media's 1986 preseason ACC poll, well behind Georgia Tech and North Carolina. The first hint that Duke might be better than expectations came in late November in New York. Reaching the final four of the inaugural preseason NIT, the Blue Devils found themselves part of a spectacular field, beating St. John's and Kansas to claim the title.

The wins continued to pile up as Duke climbed to No. 3 in the national rankings—still behind No. 1 North Carolina and No. 2 Georgia Tech, which had flip-flopped in the rankings after UNC started so impressively with victories over UCLA, Missouri, Purdue, and UNLV. The Blue Devils' equally strong play set a perfect stage for January 18, 1986, when North Carolina would open the doors to its spectacular new basketball arena.

The Tar Heels, cramped by tiny Carmichael Auditorium, had been scheming for a new facility since the mid-1970s. Remembering the legislative interference that had built so many compromises into Carmichael, UNC officials were determined to raise the entire $34 million cost of the new facility from private sources. Unfortunately, by opting for private financing, UNC had to make some different compromises. By trading prime seat locations for major contributions, students and middle-class boosters (usually the loudest and most enthusiastic fans) were pushed far from the floor. The sedate fat-cat boosters who did surround the court insulated the play from the kind of fan mania that gave Duke and N.C. State such a huge homecourt advantage.

Of course, that wasn't evident on that first beautiful winter afternoon (even the weather cooperated for the grand opening!) when 21,800 fans filed into the building to watch No. 1 North Carolina (17–0) take on No. 3 Duke (16–0).

Duke's Mark Alarie would score the first basket in the building that had been renamed the Dean E. Smith Student Activities Center at a gala dedication party the night before. But North Carolina soon seized control of the game and—to the delight of the first-day crowd—built a sixteen-point second-half lead, exploiting Duke's pressure man-to-man defense with countless backdoor cuts. Although Duke fought back in the last two minutes to cut the final margin to 96–93, the issue was never really in doubt and the Tar Heel faithful celebrated the glorious victory by their glorious team in their glorious new building.

But it would not be a glorious season for the Tar Heels. Carolina seemed on its way to its twenty-fifth victory in twenty-six games when Len Bias rallied unranked Maryland to an overtime victory in Chapel Hill—handing UNC its first-ever loss in its new building. More importantly for UNC, guard Steve Hale took an elbow to the chest from Bias in the overtime and suffered a collapsed lung. His departure from the lineup appeared to discombobulate the Tar Heels. UNC still had plenty of talent, but without the steady senior in the backcourt, the Tar Heels promptly lost four of five games and gave up their No. 1 ranking.

Waiting to inherit the top spot in the polls was Duke, which had regained its momentum after the back-to-back losses at UNC and at Georgia Tech. The Blue Devils reeled off thirteen straight wins to close the regular season. The whole nation got to see the Duke-Carolina rematch in Cameron. The Tar Heels were still without the Hale, who sat on the Tar Heel bench in street clothes, his arm in a sling to take the pressure off his damaged lung. The always sympathetic Cameron Crazies serenaded him with the chant, "In-Hale, Ex-Hale!" UNC shot 64% from the floor without him, but Duke was never threatened en route to an 82–74 victory that clinched Krzyzewski's first ACC regular season title.

He added his first ACC Tournament title the next weekend in Greensboro, beating Wake Forest, Virginia, and Georgia Tech.

"One by one, we've accomplished our goals this season," Bilas told reporters after the title game.

But there was one more goal left: the NCAA Tournament. Duke, the top seed in the East, would get to open play on the same Greensboro Court that had just hosted the ACC title game. The top-seeded Blue Devils were matched against Mississippi Valley State, an all-black school from the Mississippi Delta known mainly for producing wide receiver Jerry Rice, who was starring at the time for the San Francisco 49ers.

The NCAA had expanded from forty-eight to sixty-four teams just the year before, creating the No. 1 versus No. 16 matchup. Over the next twenty-one years no No. 1 would ever be upset by the No. 16 team. But the format was only in its second year in 1986 and no one knew that. So when Mississippi Valley State raced to an eleven-point second-half lead in Greensboro, the top-seeded Blue Devils appeared to be in big trouble. "We weren't prepared for their quickness," Krzyzewski said.

The Delta Devils pressed Duke all over the court, forcing twenty-three turnovers and taking the Blue Devils to the brink of panic before Dawkins brought them back. Abandoning Krzyzewski's motion offense and going one-on-one against the Mississippi team's press, he scored sixteen points in a five-minute span to save the nation's No. 1 ranked team.

"You want to know what pressure is?" Dawkins asked. "That's pressure. We were down. It's late and they have momentum. I can remember being on that floor and thinking to myself, 'We are not losing this game.' In the huddles, that was the theme: 'We are not losing this game.' You have to will it."

Duke did rally to beat Mississippi Valley State, 85–78, thanks to twenty-seven points by Dawkins. And after easy victories over Old Dominion, DePaul, and David Robinson's surprising Navy Midshipmen, Krzyzewski found himself in the Final Four for the first time, matched up against Kansas.

Dean Smith disciple, and former Art Heyman assailant, Larry Brown had guided the Jayhawks to a 35–3 record and the Big Eight Championship. The semifinal matchup in Dallas between No. 1 Duke and No. 2 Kansas was another of those semifinal duels touted as the "real championship game." Indeed, it proved to be a thriller. All the Dukies except Dawkins shot poorly, but the Devils hung in the game with some ferocious man-to-man defense, finally winning on a follow shot by Ferry.

In many ways, Duke's return to the title game was reminiscent of the scene in St. Louis eight years earlier, where the national media gloried in the team's loose, articulate kids. With all five seniors on the podium beside Krzyzewski, a reporter asked them all to try to pronounce their coach's still-new-to-the-public name. Four players answered correctly, then Alarie broke up the room by deadpanning, "Coach K."

Duke was once again the media darling. But Krzyzewski was worried about his team's condition going into the championship game. The long season had worn down several players. Alarie and Henderson were particularly bothered by tired legs and neither had shot well in the NCAA Tournament. The inexperienced young coach couldn't figure out how to deal with the problem.

"If I had known then what I know now, I could have helped my team," Krzyzewski said several years later. "But we were very weary, except for Dawkins and Amaker, who never got tired. We had no legs."

That problem was disguised early in the championship game as Dawkins and Amaker frazzled Louisville guards Milt Wagner and Jeff Hall with their first-half pressure. Amaker set a Final Four record with seven steals and Dawkins poured in twenty-four points as Duke took a narrow lead and held it for most of the game.

But when Louisville's Denny Crum switched to a diamond-and-one defense in an effort to shut down Dawkins, no other Blue Devil stepped up. Henderson and Alarie missed seventeen of twenty-six shots. When Louisville finally took the lead on a jumper by Billy Thompson, Henderson, who so often hit the clutch shot in his career, missed an open jumper. Dawkins grabbed the rebound and put up a follow that he thought was in, but the ball rolled out. Louisville freshman Pervis "Never Nervous" Ellison clinched the 72–69 victory when he slammed home Jeff Hall's ensuing air ball—very much like the play N.C. State's Lorenzo Charles made to beat Houston in 1983.

"We played well and extremely hard, but we didn't shoot well," Krzyzewski said. But he pointed out that Duke finished 37–3, a record for total victories that would be matched, but has still has not been broken.

"I don't want our guys hanging their heads," the Duke coach said. "They've had an excellent season and it's been an excellent four years for the seniors."

Indeed, Duke's Class of 1986 ended its four-year run by transforming the program from an ACC also-ran into a national power. Along the way, the six players brought in by Krzyzewski in the fall of 1982 combined to score 7,494 points—the most by any single recruiting class in college basketball history.

"They will go down as the greatest not-great team ever," N.C. State's Jim Valvano said of the '86 Devils.

THE DUEL

North Carolina was not about to take Duke's emergence lightly. Dean Smith had fought off similar challenges in the past, overcoming Frank McGuire's great Roche-Riker teams; surviving Norm Sloan's David Thompson–Tommy Burleson juggernaut; outlasting Bill Foster's Banks-Gminski-Spanarkel challenge; even triumphing over Ralph Sampson's threat at Virginia.

The Tar Heel coach added the weapon that he thought he needed to quash the Krzyzewski challenge in the spring of 1986.

A year after Duke landed Ferry, the top-rated player in his class, Smith beat out his old friend John Thompson at Georgetown for J.R. Reid, the top-rated player in his class. The Virginia Beach, Virginia, big man replaced Brad

Daugherty, the NBA's top draft pick, in the middle of the Tar Heel lineup and the imposing freshman became an immediate sensation. Not only did Reid play well, averaging 14.7 points and shooting 58% from the floor as a freshman: he had a charisma that made him a fan favorite.

Reid was a star from the first moment he stepped on the court at Carolina. It took Danny Ferry two years to realize his prep potential. Just as Michael Jordan made the leap from solid supporting player to superstar in between in freshmen and sophomore seasons, Ferry made a very similar leap before his junior year in 1987–88.

The 6-foot-10 DeMatha product began opening up facets of his game that he had only hinted at before. Always a tough, bruising inside player, Ferry began to play more and more on the perimeter where his perimeter jumper (38 three-pointers) and his extraordinary passing skills (139 assists) made him a matchup problem for opposing defenses. He anchored what was essentially a positionless team that also featured 6-foot-5 center Robert Brickey and 6-foot-6 defensive ace Billy King.

The Tar Heels answered with the powerful post tandem of Reid and 6-foot-10 Californian Scott Williams. With Jeff Lebo handling the point and a number of talented wings available, Smith had a deep, balanced team. His shooting guard was a hometown product from Chapel Hill who demonstrated how deeply basketball had penetrated Tobacco Road culture, with African-American guard Ranzino Smith being named for white N.C. State All-American Sammy Ranzino.

The Tar Heels showed off their depth by beating No. 1 Syracuse in the Hall of Fame Tip-Off Classic, despite the one-game suspension of Reid and Englishman Steve Bucknall for an off-season confrontation with an N.C. State student at a Raleigh nightclub. Redshirt freshman Pete Chilcutt, an Alabama product who had picked UNC over Duke, and true freshman Rick Fox, a Bahama native who had played high school basketball in Indiana, started in their places and helped UNC to beat the team that had eliminated the Tar Heels from the 1987 NCAA Tournament.

It was on that afternoon in Springfield, Massachusetts, when ESPN commentator Dick Vitale first dubbed Dean Smith, "the Michelangelo of college basketball coaches."

"Michelangelo" appeared to be painting another masterpiece in 1988, leading his team to thirteen wins in fourteen games and a No. 2 national ranking.

That's when Duke rolled into Chapel Hill and the Reid-Ferry duel began to dominate Tobacco Road.

Statistically, the UNC big man played one of his best games against the Blue Devils. He outscored Ferry 27–19 and outrebounded him 13–10. But Ferry also contributed seven assists and hit a free throw with fifty-two seconds left to give Duke a 70–69 lead. In that final, interminable fifty-two seconds, Ferry's defense kept Reid from touching the ball as the Tar Heels missed three shots and a tip-in. Finally, Brickey rushed to the corner and tipped away Lebo's potential game-winner to give Duke just its second victory on UNC's home court in twenty-two years.

A month later, Ferry clearly outplayed Reid in Cameron as the Devils broke open a close game at the half and coasted to a 96–81 victory, giving Krzyzewski his first-ever regular season sweep over Smith—the first for any Duke coach since Bubas swept the Heels in 1966.

But it was to get better for the Blue Devils.

North Carolina cruised into the ACC Tournament title game a week later in Greensboro, while Duke needed a late jumper by Ferry to edge N.C. State 75–73 in the semifinals. The media, pulling out all the old quotes from Case and McGuire about how hard it is to beat a good team three times in a season, generally predicted a UNC victory in the championship game.

Smith expected one too. The Tar Heel coach sensed that there was more riding on the 1988 ACC title game than mere pride. North Carolina had offered its home court as a site for NCAA Tournament play. At that time, teams that hosted NCAA events usually got to play at home, although there was growing criticism of the practice. Smith couldn't know that the NCAA selection committee had penciled in the ACC Tournament champion for Chapel Hill and the ACC runner-up for Salt Lake City and the West Regionals—but he had to suspect that it was possible.

To clinch the home court for the first two rounds of the NCAA Tournament, Smith and the Tar Heels needed to beat a Duke team that was beginning to turn up the defensive pressure.

"They are awesome," Georgia Tech's Bobby Cremins said after a February loss to the Devils. "Duke's defense is the best I've seen in years."

That defense was on display in the ACC title game, limiting UNC to 33.3% shooting while forcing twenty turnovers. King, who would be named the national defensive player of the year, shuffled from Lebo to Bucknall to

Kevin Madden, harassing them all. Ferry once again shut down Reid—limiting the Tar Heel star to seven points in thirty-three minutes, while scoring nineteen himself.

Duke was ahead 61–59 when Ferry rebounded a missed free throw and scored to push the lead to four points. Carolina got back within two points and appeared to be on the verge of a tie when freshman guard King Rice broke ahead of the pack and raced toward the basket for an uncontested layup. But Duke's Quin Snyder caught him from behind and blocked Rice's shot, protecting the lead and allowing the Devils to hold on for a 65–61 victory.

Duke students were quick to don T-shirts proclaiming a "Triple Crown," celebrating three victories over the Tar Heels in a single season. What made it even sweeter was getting the No. 2 seed in the East and the chance to play two NCAA games on UNC's home court. That would provide the Blue Devils with a relatively easy path to the regional finals. Duke coasted past Boston University and SMU in the Smith Center, then knocked off Rhode Island in the Meadowlands to set up a game with No. 1 Temple, the top seed in the East. John Chaney's Owls featured a tenacious matchup zone defense and relied on spectacular freshman guard Mark Macon to key the offense. Krzyzewski asked King to take on the Temple star.

"I watched film . . . I had a lot of tapes," King told Dick Weiss. "I knew that whenever he looked to score, he always dribbled left. If he went right, he always came back to his left to shoot that stop-and-pop jumper. I tried to push him out of his range. I wanted to contest everything. I was just so focused."

Macon launched twenty-nine shots against King. He hit six as Duke won 63–53 and returned to the Final Four for the second time in three years.

North Carolina—which matched Duke's early NCAA success with wins over North Texas State, high-scoring Loyola Marymount, and tenth-ranked Michigan—couldn't keep up with No. 2 Arizona in the West Regional finals in Seattle. The Tar Heels led the favored Wildcats by two at the half, but foul trouble to Reid, Williams, and Bucknall proved fatal in the second half as Arizona pulled away for a 70–52 victory.

Duke, so lucky in the early NCAA pairings, drew some bad luck in the Final Four and fell to "Danny and the Miracles"—the Danny Manning–led Kansas Jayhawks in front of a hostile crowd in Kansas City. Still, even the team's disappointment in Kansas City couldn't spoil a surprisingly successful season. Ferry, who beat out Reid for ACC Player of the Year honors and added the Case Award as the ACC Tournament MVP, had finished with a narrow, but clear edge on his rival. But their duel wasn't over.

Both big men returned for the 1988–89 season and they picked up where they left off. Ferry started especially hot. His twenty-three points led Duke past Kentucky in the Tip-Off Classic. In early December, he exploded for an ACC record fifty-eight points in a 117–102 victory in Miami. Duke won its first thirteen games and climbed to No. 1 in the national rankings. A loss to Missouri in the preseason NIT and upsets at the hands of Iowa and Virginia left No. 13 UNC regarded as a big underdog when the Tar Heels traveled to Duke to take on the top-ranked Blue Devils in the middle of January.

UNC's chances of ending its three-game losing streak to its rivals seemed slim when Smith announced that starting point guard Jeff Lebo would miss the game with a pulled muscle. In his place, the Tar Heels started disappointing sophomore King Rice. The powerfully built guard from Binghamton (N.Y.) had arrived in Chapel Hill the year before and was touted as the nation's best point guard prospect. But ACC opponents soon learned that while Rice was quick and strong with the ball, he was a terrible shooter. Defenders backed off of him, taking away his driving lanes and turning him into an ineffectual player.

Krzyzewski refused to change his in-your-face pressure defense for anyone, even Rice. As a result, he turned the Tar Heel backup into the star he was once projected to be. Rice played thirty-four minutes and scored fourteen points and passed out seven assists, mostly to Scott Williams, who led all scorers with twenty-two points. Reid (thirteen points, ten rebounds) and Ferry (fourteen points, six rebounds, six assists) cancelled each other out, but the Tar Heel big man had his first victory over his rival in two years.

Ferry was far more effective in the rematch in Chapel Hill with twenty-four points, seven rebounds, and six assists; but it was the return of Lebo to the point that helped Duke pull out an 88–86 victory. While Lebo, the son of a prep coach and an excellent shooter, was a better all-around player than Rice, he was the wrong point guard to play against Duke. He lacked the quickness to beat the Blue Devil pressure and lost for the fourth straight time as UNC's starting point guard against Duke.

The Duke–North Carolina duel had so mesmerized the ACC that few noticed that N.C. State had actually edged both for the regular season title. That seemed a fluke, especially after the Wolfpack flamed out in the first round of the ACC Tournament in Atlanta, becoming the first No. 1 seed to lose to a No. 8. Maryland stunned the Pack 71–49, a lopsided upset that was so surprising that it almost seemed appropriate that Terrapin coach Bob Wade was carried off the court after suffering a mild heart attack.

North Carolina disposed of the Terps twenty-four hours later, setting up the championship game rematch that everyone wanted to see: Duke vs. UNC, Ferry vs. Reid.

Three days before the championship game, Dean Smith threw gasoline on the flaming rivalry. And Reid and Ferry were once again at the center of the controversy.

Smith's ire was raised during UNC's visit to Duke earlier that year. In the stands, he spied signs that said, "J.R. Can't Reid." It was not the most original work by the Cameron Crazies, for similar signs had been in evidence at a variety of places since Reid's arrival two years earlier. But somehow the sight of those not-so-clever signs at Duke fired the anger of the Tar Heel coach. "I felt the sign was a racial slur," Smith said. "They were suggesting that J.R. couldn't read because he was black."

To illustrate his point that the racial stereotypes were wrong, Smith told reporters that the combined SAT scores for his black big men, Reid and Scott Williams, were higher than the combined SAT scores of Duke's white post players, Ferry and freshman Christian Laettner.

"We had tried hard to recruit Ferry and Laettner, so I knew their scores, which were very good," he said.

Smith later claimed that he used two players on each side so no one would accuse him of singling out one player. Cynics suggested that the old math major was playing with the numbers: Reid actually had the lowest test scores of the four, but Scott Williams had the highest score, thus Smith had to combine numbers to find a formula that would put Reid on the winning side.

Naturally, Duke fans reacted with outrage that Smith would reveal the supposedly private academic information about two of their players. Krzyzewski bit his lip in public, jokingly responding that, "My math scores were better than my verbal. That's because I'm Polish and from Chicago and I still say, 'Youse guys.'" Privately, he was infuriated by his rival's comments. The controversy helped lift the championship game to a level of ferocity not seen since the Art Heyman–Larry Brown duel in the early 1960s. Only now it was Ferry vs. Reid.

Ferry, who raised his scoring average to 22.6 points a game as a senior, had claimed his second straight ACC player of the year award, while Reid was left off both the first and second team All-ACC squads. In hindsight, it's hard to understand the perception that his game had dropped that drastically. True, his scoring average had fallen from 18.0 the year before to 16.9 in 1989, but he still shot an astonishing 61.4% from the floor and rebounded well.

Although Ferry appeared to have won his duel with Reid in a decisive manner, the Tar Heel big man had the one last chance to build his case. Before Sunday's championship game, the Tar Heels got together for a player-only meeting and ironed out their differences.

"What was said is private," Bucknall told reporters. "But no one let anything stay on their chest. There was a lot of stuff said that probably didn't sit well. But everybody took in it stride. Nobody cared about scoring or awards or any of the individual stuff."

The Ferry-Reid rivalry, the Duke-Carolina rivalry, Lebo's struggles against the Devils, Smith's controversial remarks: they all helped create one of the most intense, brutally contested matchups ever seen in the ACC. And although it was played in Atlanta, it very much belonged to Tobacco Road.

North Carolina took an early lead as Reid and Williams dominated down low. Krzyzewski took exception to that domination, screaming at UNC's Williams after what he perceived as unnecessary elbow. Smith, who had engaged in a similar verbal exchange with Kentucky's Rick Robey twelve years earlier, responded by leaping off the bench and screaming at Krzyzewski, "Don't talk to my players!" Coach K answered, "Fuck you!"

If anything, the intensity increased as the game went on. Reid was not at the top of his game, scoring fourteen points on 5-of-11 shooting. But Ferry, who missed fourteen of twenty shots from the floor, struggled even more. Duke freshman Christian Laettner brought the Devils back with one of his best games, but UNC was nursing a 77–74 lead when Williams missed a clinching free throw with one second left. Ferry grabbed the rebound and threw a baseball pass at the basket, seventy-five feet away.

For just an instant, it looked like his desperation heave was on line. Smith, watching from the sideline, was afraid it would drop for a game-tying three-pointer. Instead, the ball hit the back of the rim and bounced away.

"The old man could have had a heart attack if Danny Ferry's shot had gone in," Smith said.

The tournament victory was Smith's ninth ACC championship, but his first since 1982. More importantly, it was his way of saying that UNC would not give up supremacy on Tobacco Road without a fight. But Smith got a nasty shock later that Sunday night as he waited with his team in the Atlanta airport for the return trip to Chapel Hill. Sports Information Director Steve Kirschner was watching the NCAA selection show in an airport bar and he jotted down the pairings on a cocktail napkin.

To Smith's surprise, Duke was given the favorable seed in the East, while UNC was seeded No. 2 in the Southeast Region. The Blue Devils would get to play two games in Greensboro, while UNC would have to return to Atlanta for first- and second-round games.

"It's ironic that last year Duke beat us in the ACC championship game and played in our building, while we were sent to Utah," Smith said. "This year we beat them in the title game and again they stay in North Carolina and we get shipped out. The idea in the past has been if you are the best, you stay in your natural region."

Privately, Smith believed that Duke Athletic Director Tom Butters, a member of the selection committee, had pulled strings to help the Blue Devils. Committee members explained they were trying to balance the field; they didn't want to put UNC, rated the strongest No. 2 seed in the field, in the same region with Georgetown, rated the strongest No. 1 seed. Instead, UNC was put in a region with Oklahoma, rated the weakest No. 1. However, the Tar Heels were also in the same region as No. 3 seed Michigan, a team Carolina had faced, and beaten, in both the 1987 and 1988 NCAA Tournaments.

"That was unfair," Smith complained. "Their seniors, especially Glen Rice, remembered the two previous years."

Michigan got thirty-four points from Rice and eliminated the Tar Heels in a Sweet 16 game in Rupp Arena in Lexington (Ky.). A bitter Smith stood outside the UNC dressing room and complained to two North Carolina reporters, "I'd have rather played Minnesota."

His bitter comment was a jibe at the easy path Duke had to the regional finals. The Blue Devils got past South Carolina State and West Virginia in Greensboro to earn another trip to the Meadowlands, where they drew not No. 3 seed Stanford, but No. 11 seed Minnesota in the regional semifinals.

Georgetown proved to be a paper tiger in the regional finals. Duke handled the Hoyas with surprising ease. The key was the freshman Laettner, who laid the foundations of his legendary NCAA status by dominating the much-hyped Alonzo Mourning in the post. Laettner's twenty-four points, coupled with twenty-three by guard Phil Henderson and twenty-one by Ferry, carried Duke to an 85–77 victory and a second straight trip to the Final Four.

Unfortunately, Duke's visit to Seattle would turn into a nightmare for the Devils in the semifinals against Seton Hall. Krzyzewski's team got off to a 26–8 lead before Brickey went down with a sprained ankle. Laettner, who was playing well, got into foul trouble and was limited to thirteen points in twenty-one minutes. Ferry did his best (thirty-four points and ten rebounds in forty minutes of action), but a five-point halftime lead slipped away early in the second half—and with Australian import Andrew Gaze on fire, the Pirates pulled away for a lopsided 95–78 victory.

Although the departure of Ferry and Reid, who was advised by Smith to turn pro after his junior season, would signal a new phase in the Duke-Carolina rivalry, the twin departures were not about to change the balance of power on Tobacco Road. In fact, the next four years were going to produce the most spectacular run of success the region had ever seen.

12

THE FALL OF JIM VALVANO

Jimmy V lost a little of his coaching luster in the years following his 1983 NCAA triumph. Valvano's State teams still won at a good rate—winning between nineteen and twenty-three games in eight straight seasons. He reached the NCAA Elite Eight twice and salvaged his worst season in 1987 with another miracle championship, stunning regular season ACC champion UNC in the ACC Tournament title game in Landover, Maryland. He assembled one of the greatest backcourts in ACC history—the celebrated "Fire and Ice" tandem of point guard Chris Corchiani and shooting guard Rodney Monroe—and used them to claim the 1989 ACC regular season title.

Valvano remained as entertaining as ever—but he was starting to draw critics who questioned the quality of the kids he brought in and his own burgeoning off-court activites. ACC coaches had long exploited their celebrity for financial gain (Everett Case made himself rich by running a chain of fast-food joints in Indiana), but even some of Valvano's colleagues wondered if he was taking on too much when he became athletic director at State and also signed up to do TV and radio commentary in-season, often flying out of town to cover a game while his assistants stayed and ran practice.

The questions surrounded his program exploded on January 7, 1989, when the Raleigh *News & Observer* broke the news of Peter Golenbock's "exposé" of the Wolfpack basketball program, a book entitled *Personal Fouls.*

The story was front-page news and played ahead of a story about the inauguration of new North Carolina governor Jim Martin. According to a copy of the book's dust jacket obtained by the paper, Golenbock claimed to have un-covered a long list of sins beneath the façade of Jim Valvano's basketball pro-gram—drug-use, illegal inducements, grade-fixing, but most of all an uncaring coach who used and discarded players with little regard to their well-being.

"To protect his million and a half dollar annual income," the book jacket proclaimed, "Valvano had to keep winning—and that meant having his best players taken care of by whatever means necessary."

Golenbock's still-unseen charges touched off a firestorm in Raleigh, fueled by *News & Observer* managing editor Claude Sitton, who kept the story on the paper's front page day after day. Wolfpack officials challenged many of Golen-bock's outrageous claims, sending a letter detailing mistakes in the manuscript to Simon & Schuster, which was scheduled to publish *Personal Fouls* in Janu-ary. The publisher, confronted by evidence of the author's sloppy research, withdrew the book from its publication list. Golenbock soon found a new pub-lisher in Carroll & Graf and his book was released on July 28, 1989. By that time his charges, and the relentless coverage by State's hometown newspaper, had touched off investigations—by the NCAA and the state legislature, which appointed its own committee to probe the alleged sins of the N.C. State bas-ketball program, and even by the FBI, which investigated point-shaving claims.

"I'm convinced that Golenbock's book did not cause me to lose my job at N.C. State," Valvano later wrote. "It did serve as a catalyst for the investigations that followed."

The NCAA investigation it provoked found no evidence of major viola-tions at N.C. State. The organization's thorough study of the program turned up two secondary rule violations: Wolfpack players often sold their compli-mentary tickets; the players were also found to have traded in free sneakers for other athletic wear. Although neither violation was deemed major in itself, the NCAA ruled that together they demonstrated "a lack of institutional control." N.C. State received a two-year probation and a one-year NCAA Tournament ban for the problems. Chief NCAA investigator David Didion wrote Valvano a letter in which he praised Valvano's character and his performance at State. Part of the letter reads:

> I consider myself a good judge of character and I have come to believe
> that you are one of the best people I've ever met in intercollegiate athletics

and one of the best people I have met, period . . . Anyway, what all this leads up to is: you're good for intercollegiate athletics, good for N.C. State and good for the NCAA. I hope you stay at N.C. State and continue to do as you've always done and not change anything about your methods or personality. If I had a son, I would feel comfortable with you as his coach.

The legislature's probe of the Wolfpack athletic program also found problems: not the grade-changing or outright cheating charged by Golenbock, but a long history of academic shortcuts that involved the entire Wolfpack athletic program. The *Charlotte Observer* reported the release of the legislature's investigative commission report with the headline: "UNC Probe Exonerates Valvano."

But the committee did report academic abuse in the Wolfpack athletic program. The overall picture that emerged was of a school more concerned about keeping athletes eligible than steering them toward degrees. It was North Carolina's Dean Smith, a paragon long praised for the academic success of his players, who pointed out the flaw in using the committee findings to attack Valvano. "He was hired to win basketball games, not to graduate players," Smith said. "He did what he was hired to do."

Smith understood that Valvano had come to an athletic program that had long displayed little concern for the graduation of its athletes. Everett Case and Norm Sloan had poor graduation rates. Neither football coach Lou Holtz nor Bo Rein had paid much attention to academics either. Valvano became the scapegoat for decades of academic disregard by the Wolfpack athletic program. The irony is that he was probably the best-educated coach on Tobacco Road, an insatiable reader with a Master's Degree in English who could quote Shakespeare or poetry with equal ease.

Valvano couldn't survive the cloud that gathered over his program after the controversy generated by Golenbock's book exploded. He resigned his job as athletic director in 1989 but hoped to remain as head basketball coach. He had guided the 1990 Wolfpack team to eighteen wins in twenty-six games when a story broke on ABC News quoting an unnamed N.C. State player as claiming that several Wolfpack players were involved in point-shaving during the 1987 season.

Valvano knew that whether true or not (investigations by both the FBI and State Bureau of Investigation never uncovered any evidence of point-shaving), the new controversy was the final blow for his troubled program. Valvano called interim athletic director Hal Hopfenberg and offered to resign "for the good of the university."

Valvano left N.C. State with a ten-year record of 209–114. More importantly, he left the school a national championship banner and two ACC titles.

In one way, Jimmy V got out just in time. Just as President William Friday's self-imposed sanctions set back the programs at State and Carolina in the wake of the point-shaving scandal in the early 1960s, a new set of draconian academic requirements imposed on the program would bury the Pack for most of the 1990s.

The Pack's Tobacco Road neighbors were rocketing upward to glory, but with the departure of Valvano after the 1990 season, N.C. State would miss the ride.

NEVER GIVE UP

Jimmy V borrowed a quote from Bones McKinney for his autobiography, which was subtitled, *They Gave Me a Lifetime Contract and Then They Declared Me Dead.* The book ends with a poignant description of how Valvano planned to spend the rest of his life. Near the end were the lines: "Once I thought I'd coach at N.C. State forever," he wrote, "[but] I've figured out that it's not wise to predict the future."

Not long after those words were written, Valvano began experiencing back pains. On June 12, 1992, a little more than two years after his ouster from N.C. State, the ebullient ex-coach was diagnosed with cancer. He was given less than a year to live. Valanvo's response to his death sentence would transform him from a successful, popular, but controversial coach into a national icon. Although weakened by the disease and in constant pain, he fought back with a courage that even evoked admiration from his harshest detractors.

Duke's Mike Krzyzewski had never been a Valvano-basher, but he had never been a close friend either. In a way that's odd, since both had ridden such similar career tracks. They had come to Tobacco Road within a week of each other and each had built his program in the shadow of Dean Smith's powerhouse in Chapel Hill. Both won national titles: Valvano in 1983; Krzyzewski in 1991–92.

But the intense rivalry between Duke and N.C. State had kept them apart. It wasn't until Valvano stepped down and began his battle with cancer that the

Future Duke coach Vic Bubas, left center, learns at the shoulder of N.C. State's Everett Case, right center.
(PHOTO COURTESY OF THE UNIVERSITY OF NORTH CAROLINA)

Frank McGuire poses in his sweats. He would have been more familiar to UNC fans in one of his hand-tailored suits.
(PHOTO COURTESY OF THE UNIVERSITY OF NORTH CAROLINA)

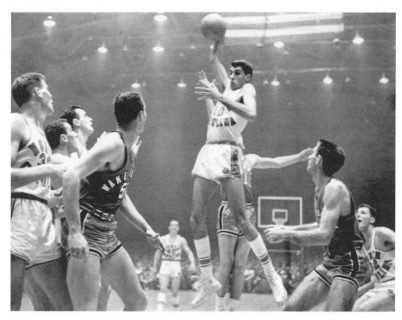

Lennie Rosenbluth snares a rebound against Wake Forest in the 1957 ACC Tournament semifinals. (PHOTO COURTESY OF THE UNIVERSITY OF NORTH CAROLINA)

Len Chappell drives on Ohio State's Jerry Lucas during a 1962 loss to the No. 1 Buckeyes in Winston-Salem. (PHOTO COURTESY OF WAKE FOREST UNIVERSITY)

'Ol Bones'—McKinney stalks the sidelines as Wake Forest's coach. (PHOTO COURTESY OF WAKE FOREST UNIVERSITY)

Art Heyman bullies Clemson as Duke bullies the ACC in the early 1960s. (PHOTO COURTESY OF DUKE UNIVERSITY)

Jeff Mullins escaped Lexington, Kentucky, to star for the Blue Devils. (PHOTO COURTESY OF DUKE UNIVERSITY)

Larry Miller accepts the first of his two Case Awards as the MVP of the ACC Tournament. (PHOTO COURTESY OF THE UNIVERSITY OF NORTH CAROLINA)

Charlie Scott changed the face of basketball on Tobacco Road. (PHOTO COURTESY OF THE UNIVERSITY OF NORTH CAROLINA)

"Stormin' Norman" Sloan keeps his temper under control as he works the sideline. (PHOTO COURTESY OF N.C. STATE UNIVERSITY)

The incomparable David Thompson celebrates the Pack's 1974 NCAA championship. (PHOTO COURTESY OF N.C. STATE UNIVERSITY)

Tommy Burleson—the Newland Needle—towered over the ACC. (PHOTO COURTESY OF N.C. STATE UNIVERSITY)

Phil Ford, left, proved to be an extension of Coach Dean Smith on the floor.
(PHOTO COURTESY OF THE UNIVERSITY OF NORTH CAROLINA)

Bill Foster dueled Dean Smith for Tobacco Road supremacy in the late 1970s.
(PHOTO COURTESY OF DUKE UNIVERSITY)

Freshman Gene Banks revived the Devils and led them to the 1978 NCAA title game. (PHOTO COURTESY OF DUKE UNIVERSITY)

"Big Game" James Worthy slams one home against Kentucky. (PHOTO COURTESY OF THE UNIVERSITY OF NORTH CAROLINA)

Michael Jordan—the future NBA superstar—first took flight in Chapel Hill. (PHOTO COURTESY OF THE UNIVERSITY OF NORTH CAROLINA)

Happy days! Jim Valvano, left, shares a laugh with ESPN's Dick Vitale. (PHOTO COURTESY OF N.C. STATE UNIVERSITY)

*Johnny Dawkins
drives Mike
Krzyzewski's
program to the top
for the first time.*
(PHOTO COURTESY OF
DUKE UNIVERSITY)

*J.R. Reid shows off the power
that made him the focal point
of a duel with Duke's Danny
Ferry.* (PHOTO COURTESY OF THE
UNIVERSITY OF NORTH CAROLINA)

*Danny Ferry helps Coach K
sustain his program after the
1986 Final Four.* (PHOTO
COURTESY OF BOB DONNAN)

*Christian Laettner—love him
or hate him—is Tobacco Road's
consummate winner.* (PHOTO
COURTESY OF BOB DONNAN)

Mike Krzyzewski celebrates his second straight national championship. (PHOTO COURTESY OF BOB DONNAN)

Dave Odom led Wake Forest back to national prominence. (PHOTO COURTESY OF WAKE FOREST UNIVERSITY)

Tim Duncan soars to swat away a shot by Duke's Erik Meek. (PHOTO COURTESY OF WAKE FOREST UNIVERSITY)

Dean Smith cuts down the nets after winning his record thirteenth ACC title. (PHOTO COURTESY OF THE UNIVERSITY OF NORTH CAROLINA)

Bill Guthridge guides UNC into the post-Dean Smith era. (PHOTO COURTESY OF BOB DONNAN)

Tourney MVP Jason Williams celebrates 2000 ACC championship. (PHOTO COURTESY OF BOB DONNAN)

Wake Forest's Skip Prosser mounted a twenty-first-century challenge to the Duke–UNC dominance on Tobacco Road. (PHOTO COURTESY OF WAKE FOREST UNIVERSITY)

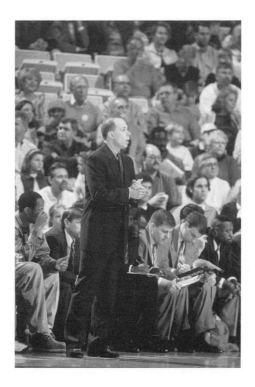

Herb Sendek revived N.C. State after a decade of mediocrity. (PHOTO COURTESY OF BOB DONNAN)

Roy Williams returned home to lead UNC to its fourth NCAA title. (PHOTO COURTESY OF THE UNIVERSITY OF NORTH CAROLINA)

Sean May led North Carolina back to the top of the college basketball world. (PHOTO COURTESY OF BOB DONNAN)

two men really got to know each other. The ailing coach underwent treatment for his disease at Duke Hospital and it was there that Krzyzewski's courtesy visit turned into friendship.

"I don't know if you can become that close when you are competing against each other, but I always respected him," Krzyzewski said. "I got to know Jimmy better when he went into broadcasting. I think our relationship grew closer after that. After he was diagnosed with cancer, we had a special relationship."

Krzyzewski became Valvano's most frequent visitor outside the coach's own family. In between visits to Duke Hospital, Valvano continued his duties as an ESPN and ABC basketball commentator. An amazing transformation would take place when he was in front of the cameras. Observers would see him sitting there, in obvious pain, then the lights would come on and he'd appear to be as bright and chipper as the Jimmy V of '83.

Valvano had decided to use his celebrity as a weapon to fight cancer. He established the V Foundation to raise money for cancer research, turning himself into a symbol of resistance to the terrible disease. He used the tenth anniversary celebration for the 1983 N.C. State national championship team to try out his message on a receptive audience.

Valvano, assigned to broadcast Duke's February 21 visit to Raleigh for ABC, made his first visit to Reynolds Coliseum since resigning almost three years earlier. Reporters who saw him shuffling along the old arena's narrow corridors, using a small device to pump morphine into his body, were shocked at his appearance. But when the dying coach walked to midcourt to greet the returnees from his 1983 team, he was as bright and energetic as the Valvano they all remembered.

"Cancer has taken away my physical ability," Valvano told the crowd. "But what cancer cannot touch is my mind, my heart and my soul. Those three things will carry on forever."

He used the 1983 team as a metaphor for the battle he was fighting. "They are special, not just because they put the banner up there, but because they taught me and the world so many important lessons. No. 1, hope. Things can get better in spite of adversity. The '83 team taught us about dreaming and the importance of dreaming. That nothing can happen, if not first the dream . . . That team taught me about persistence, the idea of never, ever quitting."

Two weeks later, Valvano used a refined version of the speech at the nationally televised ESPY Awards, where he received the Arthur Ashe Award for courage. His final words became his legacy: "Don't give up . . . Don't ever give up."

On the morning of April 28, 1993—barely six weeks after his appearance at the ESPYs and three weeks after UNC's national championship victory in New Orleans—he died at Duke Hospital. He was forty-seven years old.

"He was a remarkable guy," said Mike Krzyzewski, who was with him at the end. "He had a lot to give. He gave a lot and he had a lot more to give. He was an amazing guy and I loved him."

13

BACK TO BACK

In many ways, 1990 was the worst season in Tobacco Road history. As Valvano was being squeezed out in Raleigh, the schools outside North Carolina appeared to be taking control of the ACC. Clemson won the league's regular season race and Georgia Tech won the ACC Tournament title. It was the first (and still the only) time that a Tobacco Road team hasn't won one or the other.

But Tobacco Road's two powers would take significant steps in 1990 to lay the groundwork for success in the new decade.

North Carolina also looked to the future while enduring its worst season since 1969. Even as the Heels struggled on the court in 1990, Smith was enjoying great success on the recruiting trail. Helped by the contributions of new assistant coach Phil Ford, who proved to be as dynamic a recruiter as he had been a point guard, the Tar Heels pulled in a five-man recruiting class hailed as the best of all time. It included five prep All-Americans: 7-foot center Eric Montross from Indianapolis, 6-foot-10 forward Clifford Rozier from Florida, 6-foot-3 point guard Derrick Phelps and 6-foot-6 forward Brian Reese from New York, and 6-foot-8 forward Pat Sullivan from New Jersey.

Smith beat his new rival Krzyzewski out for Montross, the son of a former Michigan standout, and Sullivan, who grew up playing on the same playgrounds that produced Mike O'Koren and Jim Spanarkel. But the Duke coach wasn't entirely shut out, beating Smith for the year's single top-recruiting prize. Grant Hill, the 6-foot-8 son of former NFL running back Calvin Hill, was a top target for both schools. And the academically inclined young star whose father graduated from Yale and whose mother was a suitemate of Hillary Rodham's (later Clinton) at Wellesley liked both schools.

"It came down to Duke and North Carolina," Hill told Dick Weiss. "From the outside looking in, you think the programs are just alike. But as I got to know both coaches and both situations, I realized there were a lot of differences. I'm not saying one is better than the other but I just felt more comfortable at Duke." Hill would join a Duke program that had suffered its ups and downs with a freshman point guard in 1990.

Bobby Hurley very easily could have played at North Carolina. In fact, that was his first choice coming out of St. Anthony's High School in Jersey City, New Jersey. But when he learned that UNC's Smith was targeting New York City sensation Kenny Anderson as its primary point guard target, the disappointed Hurley reacted much as Billy Packer had done thirty years earlier when rejected by Duke, opting to sign with his favorite's biggest rival. It turned into a double disaster for the Tar Heel coach as Anderson ended up signing with Bobby Cremins at Georgia Tech and Hurley proved to be a key piece in Duke's back-to-back national title teams.

Krzyzewski's new point guard proved to be a tenacious on-the-ball defender and a genius as a playmaker. But he was also an emotional train wreck, an immature kid who whined at officials and screamed at opponents and generally made himself one of the most disliked players in the ACC.

"I couldn't turn it around my freshman year," Hurley told Barry Jacobs. "If I had a couple of bad plays in a game, I wasn't able to turn it around and do some positive things. It would just turn out to be a totally bad game for me."

The quality of Hurley's play varied widely. He was excellent in early season losses to No. 1 Syracuse and No. 8 Michigan and, in early January, he outplayed Anderson in a victory at Georgia Tech. But less than a week later, Duke traveled to Chapel Hill and Hurley was abused by the stronger, more experienced Rice.

"King Rice was tremendous," Hurley admitted. "I was impressed with his resolve and his toughness. He just kicked the crap out of us tonight."

The low point for the Devils came after Duke's 83–72 loss to Georgia Tech in the ACC Tournament semifinals at the new Charlotte Coliseum. As reporters gathered in the losing locker room, they were treated to an angry tirade from senior guard Phil Henderson.

"We've got a bunch of fuckin' babies on this team," Henderson finally blurted. "We've got to get tougher or we're not going anywhere this year."

Maybe Henderson's remarks were needed: the Blue Devils responded to the tongue-lashing by rolling past Richmond, St. John's, and UCLA to reach the East Regional title game in the Meadowlands for the fourth time in five years. And there, once again, Krzyzewski's team made the New Jersey arena their own.

The victim this time was top-seeded Connecticut, enjoying the greatest season in its history under coach Jim Calhoun. The Huskies were ranked third in the nation and were a heavy favorite to give the school its first Final Four. Instead, with Duke down one and 2.6 seconds left in overtime, Laettner would make his second stab at NCAA immortality. He inbounded the ball in front of the Duke bench, took a return pass from roommate Brian Davis, and launched a double-pumped fifteen-footer at the buzzer.

The shot swished, setting off a wild celebration and sending Duke back to the Final Four for the third time in a row and the fourth time in three years. It was probably the trip that certified Krzyzewski's status as a national figure and something of an NCAA Tournament specialist; although he had reached the 1986 Final Four in Dallas with the nation's No. 1 team, his next three Final Four teams were all longshots.

"Those three years, we shouldn't have gotten there," Krzyzewski told author Bill Brill. "In 1988, we weren't an awesome team. In 1989, we couldn't influence games. And in '90, I don't know how we made it."

Duke upset Arkansas in the national semifinals in Denver. The only negative note to the easy 97–83 victory was the poor play of Hurley, who was plagued by an intestinal disorder that sent him racing from the bench to the locker room midway through the first half. Hurley's condition proved to be an insurmountable problem two nights later, when Duke faced UNLV in the national title game. The freshman's shaky play was mirrored by a team that looked slow and physically intimidated by Jerry Tarkanian's powerful Rebels. Krzyzewski's young team was never in the game: their 103–73 loss replaced UNC's 1968 loss to UCLA as the most lopsided score in championship game history.

"I don't know how much of it was us," Krzyzewski said. "They were just totally in control. I think it was the best that a team has ever played against me as a coach."

It wasn't understood at the time, but in hindsight it's easy to see that the pieces were in place for what was to follow. Laettner was maturing into a star and Hurley lacked only consistency to be a great player at the point. The addition of the multi-talented Grant Hill a year later would finally bring Krzyzewski the ultimate prize.

TOBACCO ROAD STRETCHES TO INDY

Duke did not get off to a particularly impressive start the next season. The Blue Devils won ten out of twelve games before the ACC season, but only a victory at Oklahoma was in the least bit impressive. And after the Devils opened ACC play with a lopsided 84–61 loss at Virginia, Duke dropped out of the top 10.

Krzyzewski was so angry about his team's pitiful performance in Charlottesville that when the team got back to Durham at 2 a.m. that Sunday morning after a four-hour bus ride, he put them through a brutal ninety-minute practice. During the course of the scrimmage, freshman Grant Hill took an elbow from Christian Laettner and suffered a broken nose. He would miss two games, then play the next month with a hockey mask on his face.

Eight miles away, Dean Smith's North Carolina Tar Heels appeared to have regained their status as the kings of Tobacco Road after welcoming their highly touted freshman class. Dubbed "The New Kids on the Block" (after a popular boy-band), the newcomers were able to blend smoothly with veterans: seniors King Rice, Rick Fox, and Pete Chilcutt; junior Hubert Davis (a nephew of former UNC star Walter Davis); promising sophomore forward George Lynch. "The freshmen gave us as much depth as we ever had," Smith noted.

The Tar Heels won thirteen of fourteen games to open the season, and they vaulted past Duke in the polls after beating Connecticut, Kentucky, and Purdue in successive games. UNC's streak ended when Carolina traveled to Duke, where Hurley finally overcame Rice in a 74–60 victory. A month later, the Blue Devil point guard again outplayed his rival as Duke swept UNC with a victory in the Smith Center.

"Hurley was the reason they came out on top," Rice said. "Last year, I'm not sure he understood the rivalry and I did a lot of talking and it seemed to get to him. But I've never had anything against Bobby."

It was a reflection of the back-and-forth nature of the rivalry that when the two powers met in the ACC title game a week later, North Carolina destroyed the team that had swept it in the regular season. The highlight of UNC's 97–74 rout for the reporters in the front press row of the Charlotte Coliseum was a - little scene played out after a time-out before a UNC inbounds pass. Referee

Gerald Donaghy was waiting to hand the ball to UNC's Rice when, within easy hearing of about a dozen reporters, a frustrated Laettner blistered Donaghy with an obscenity-laced tirade. But the official acted as if he couldn't hear the out-of-control Duke star, despite prompting from the Tar Heel point guard.

"Did you hear that?" Rice kept asking. "Can he say that?" The incident illustrated the competitive nature of a player who would dominate the NCAA Tournament as no player had since Lew Alcindor in the 1960s.

Laettner was often dismissed as a "pretty boy" for his good looks (so much like Luke Perry from the then-popular TV show, *Beverly Hills, 90210*) and for his prep school background. But he was, in reality, a tough, blue-collar kid from the lower-middle-class Buffalo suburb of Angola. Laettner attended the Nichols School on scholarship, rising every morning at 6 a.m. to make the forty-five-minute commute from his home.

Duke, Virginia, and North Carolina waged an intense recruiting battle for the 6-foot-11 prep All-American. During Laettner's official visit to Chapel Hill, Smith invited his family to visit Granville Towers, the dorm where most of his players lived. On the way, Laettner's mother asked Smith about the Duke-Carolina rivalry. She said that Smith pooh-poohed the rivalry as a media invention.

"At that point, the elevator door opened and there was the door to J.R. Reid's room—covered with 'Fuck Duke' and 'Duke Sucks' posters," she said.

Laettner would prove to be a thorn in UNC's side for four years. But Dean wasn't the only one the Buffalo big man tormented. Sometimes his own teammates felt his competitive fire. (According to one persistent rumor, which was denied by everybody involved, Hill's broken nose after the Virginia game came not in practice—but as the result of a punch from Laettner on the bus ride home.) "He was cocky," Grant Hill said. "He was arrogant. He thought he was the best thing in the world."

Laettner's competitive nature could go too far—as it did in the 1991 ACC title game, when he cursed out Donaghy, or in the 1992 Kentucky game, when he "stomped" on Aminu Timberlake. But it could also carry Laettner to unimaginable heights, far beyond his talent. It helped him humiliate LSU's Shaquille O'Neal in a 1991 game in Cameron. The next year, he matched up with O'Neal in Baton Rouge and while "Shaq" played well, Laettner nailed back-to-back three-point shots to deal the LSU big man another bitter defeat.

"Christian had a fire," Krzyzewski said. "It's like I'm the landlord of an apartment building and I could either use that fire to heat the building or to burn it down. Christian's fire heated our building to the highest level."

Laettner's fire proved to be the driving force behind Duke's recovery from its ACC Tournament humiliation at the hands of North Carolina. The Blue Devils, sent to the Midwest as the No. 2 seed, breezed by Louisiana-Monroe, Iowa, UConn, and St. John's to give Krzyzewski his fourth straight Final Four appearance.

North Carolina would join the Blue Devils in Indianapolis after rolling through the East without trouble until the regional title game, when the Heels had to survive a last-second, three-point try from senior Mark Macon to get past Temple. Macon, shut down by Duke's Billy King in the 1988 East title game, scored thirty-one points this time—but he didn't get enough help to overcome Carolina's balance.

The arrival of two teams from Tobacco Road in Indianapolis thrilled the state's basketball fans; but the reaction was somewhat muted by the widespread perception that the weekend would be a coronation for unbeaten No. 1 ranked UNLV. Tarkanian's Runnin' Rebels team was being touted as the greatest team of all time: like Houston in 1983, the team was being handed the title before the games were played. Certainly nothing that happened in Denver the year before did anything to change that perception. UNLV's 103-72 victory over the Blue Devils had replaced UCLA's 1968 victory over UNC as the most lopsided title game in history.

"Bring on the Rebels and send out the clowns," one columnist wrote to describe the 1991 Final Four. "There's no way this year to beat them," CBS commentator Mike Francesa said.

Duke and UNC were in opposite brackets, but that didn't prevent a confrontation as students from the two schools lined up side by side at the will-call windows of the Hoosier Dome on the morning of the semifinals. Tar Heel students started chanting "0-for-4," to taunt the Dukies for their Final Four futility under Krzyzewski. The Duke students answered with the chant, "Long time no see"—to emphasize that it had been nine years since UNC last reached the Final Four.

The Tar Heels were matched against Kansas in the semifinals, coached by former UNC assistant Roy Williams.

The Jayhawks' coach had grown up on Tobacco Road in Asheville (N.C.) and had joined Smith's staff in 1979 as a part-time coach. ("Part-time pay, full-time work," Williams liked to joke.) He was sitting beside Smith in New Orleans when Jordan had hit the shot that gave the Tar Heel coach his title. When another Smith disciple, Larry Brown, left Kansas with probation looming after winning the 1988 national title, UNC's Smith turned down a chance to return to his alma mater, but he convinced his good friend Bob Frederick, the KU athletic director, to gamble on the unknown Williams.

It proved to be almost as good a gamble for Kansas as Tom Butters's gamble on the unknown Army coach had proven to be for Duke.

The student schooled the master in the first semifinal game in 1991. Carolina was plagued by a problem that would spoil five of their six Final Four trips over the next decade: abysmal shooting. The normally deadly Tar Heels missed forty-five of seventy-three shots from the floor. The Tar Heels, finding one reliable scorer in junior guard Hubert Davis, closed to within one point twice in the second half; but the team couldn't get the stop or hit the shot to regain command. Instead, Kansas pulled away in the final minutes.

The game took an unfortunate turn in the final seconds when Smith was ejected by official Pete Pavia. The Tar Heel coach, who had picked up a technical foul earlier in the game, was walking a sub to the scorer's table after Rick Fox fouled out. He had his hand on Brian Reese's shoulder as he kept asking Pavia, "How much time have I got?" The official ignored Smith until the coach wandered out of the coaches' box, still asking, "How much time have I got?"

Pavia's whistle and the ensuing T wrote a bizarre ending to a gut-wrenching loss for the Tar Heels. Smith appeared to be almost in a daze as he left the court, wearing a crooked smile as he walked past the Kansas bench so he could hug his protégé and shake hands with the Jayhawk subs. A few minutes later when the final buzzer sounded on Kansas's 79–73 victory, UNC assistant Bill Guthridge made a quite different exit—chasing Pavia off the court, screaming, "That's bush! That's bull!" until he was slammed against a wall by a security guard.

"Coach Smith did not lose control," Rick Fox complained. "I wonder if this official had a vendetta against him?"

The day would get much worse for the Tar Heel nation. After their team lost to Kansas, most UNC fans clung to the consolation that Duke was also destined to lose in the semifinals. Almost everybody expected powerful UNLV to repeat its 1990 whipping of Duke: everybody except Krzyzewski. "Last year's loss helped prepare me for this game," the Duke coach said.

To help prepare them for the rematch, he showed his players a tape of the previous year's title game. Krzyzewski used it to convince them that despite the lopsided final margin, the 1990 game actually turned on a handful of uncharacteristic mistakes that his players could correct. He also convinced them that Vegas would enter the game cocky and overconfident and that Duke would have the psychological advantage.

"It was not a gameplan and it was no Xs and Os," Laettner said. "It was what was inside of us. The heart of every one on this team. It was how hard we were going to play."

Duke showed its resolve in the opening moments, when Laettner tipped the opening toss to Grant Hill, who surprised the Rebels by streaking to the basket for a layup. Hurley, healthy this time, handled the Vegas pressure without problem, committing just three turnovers and passing out seven assists in forty minutes of action. Even out-matched senior Greg Koubek, getting a lot of help from Laettner, was giving the far-more-talented Larry Johnson fits: the UNLV superstar managed just ten shots in the game and scored just thirteen points.

At the other end of the floor, Laettner proved to be a weapon that Vegas couldn't match. He scored nine points as Duke seized a quick 15–6 lead. He had twenty at the half, then took a feed from Hurley and scored on the first possession of the second half to tie the game at 43. Laettner would finish with twenty-eight points, helping the Devils stay close. That was the key, Krzyzewski kept telling his players: stay close. "If it's close, they won't know how to handle it because they haven't been in a close game all year," Krzyzewski said.

Yet, with guard Anderson Hunt scoring nineteen of his game-high twenty-nine points in the second half, the Rebels were able to build a five-point lead. There were just over two minutes left when Duke brought the ball downcourt and CBS commentator Billy Packer noted that UNLV had gone to its "Amoeba Zone."

"Duke doesn't need a three here . . ." Packer was saying, just as Hurley went up with a three-point shot from the left of the key. As the shot swished, cutting the deficit to two points, Packer smoothly recovered and continued: ". . . unless it comes out of the offense, like that one did."

Vegas, as Krzyzewski predicted, showed signs of panic. The Rebels couldn't get off a shot and committed a shot-clock violation. At the other end, freshman

Grant Hill, looking like a 6-foot-8 point guard, sliced through the Vegas zone and fed the ball to Laettner's roommate, Brian Davis, who slashed in from the left to score and draw a foul. His old-fashioned three-point play gave Duke a one-point lead with 1:02 left.

Larry Johnson made a free throw at the other end to tie the score, but the tie didn't last long. Guard Thomas Hill (no relation to Grant Hill) attempted a short jumper with sixteen seconds left. It missed, but Laettner pulled down the rebound. Before he could go back up with the follow, he was fouled. Tarkanian called time-out with 12.7 seconds left.

Two years earlier, freshman Christian Laettner had missed a potential game-tying free throw in a regular season game against Arizona in the Meadowlands. Afterward, he was consoled by ex-President Richard Nixon, a graduate of Duke's Law School. Laettner told Nixon that he would never miss a free throw in the clutch again.

"He wanted to shoot those free throws," Krzyzewski said. "There was no way in the world that he was going to miss."

He didn't—and when the game ended with Anderson Hunt's wild shot clanging off the rim and into the arms of Bobby Hurley, the Duke players grabbed each other in a wild celebration. Hurley jumped on the back of little-used backup center Clay Buckley—the son of former Duke standout Jay Buckley and the nephew of Bruce Buckley, whose crucial layup was blocked in UNC's 1977 title game loss to Marquette.

As his players celebrated, Krzyzewski walked off the court with his palms up, making a "settle down" motion. He knew that Duke was still one win from the championship.

"Immediately, I was thinking of the next game," he said. "Because we didn't come here to beat Vegas. We came to Indianapolis to win a championship."

Krzyzewski remembered what happened in 1986, when No. 1 Duke had seemingly clinched the title with a hard-fought semifinal victory over No. 2 Kansas. That was his first Final Four, and he often bemoaned his inability to help his team recover in time for Monday night's title game. He was more experienced in 1991 and used every bit of that experience to help his team get by the Jayhawks in the Hoosier Dome. Krzyzewski first put that experience to use on Sunday, when before the off-day of practice he staged a temper tantrum to wake up his self-satisfied team and remind them they still had another game to win.

On Monday night, Krzyzewski subbed judiciously to help his tired players get through the game. Laettner, who went the full forty against Vegas, played just thirty-two minutes against Kansas, usually getting a minute or so rest before each TV time-out.

Koubek, the only senior in the lineup, hit just one shot in the title game—a three-pointer on Duke's first possession, which gave the Devils a lead they would never surrender. Moments later, Hurley threw a half-court pass on the break that soared toward the roof of the Hoosier Dome. Grant Hill reached his right arm into the stratosphere, got one hand on the ball, and slammed it into the basket.

"That was a David Thompson–type dunk from yesteryear," Billy Packer screamed after watching the replay. Of course, Thompson would have had to guide it in without dunking, but the reference was still apt—although it might have baffled a new generation of fans who had forgotten Skywalker.

In many ways, Duke's 1991 title game victory over Kansas resembled the game David Thompson and N.C. State won over Marquette after their emotional semifinal victory over UCLA. In both cases, the title game was something of a letdown; but in both cases, the Tobacco Road representative managed an efficient workmanlike win. Kansas stayed close to the Devils all night but could never regain the lead. Laettner, going twelve for twelve from the foul line, scored eighteen and added ten rebounds, while Hurley, going the full forty minutes for the second game in a row, passed out nine assists and hit a pair of timely three-pointers. Sophomore guard Billy McCaffrey scored twelve of his sixteen off the bench in the second half, and that was just enough to get Duke home with a 72–65 victory.

"It took an emotional, physical investment for eighty minutes [in the Final Four]," Krzyzewski said. "I just love the fact my kids could do that. Even when we got the trophy, the thought came, 'I'm happy for this team and I'm happy for the teams that helped prepare me for this. I hope they shared in it.'"

It was the first championship for the school and the first for Krzyzewski, who finally won it all in his fifth Final Four trip.

It would not be the last title—either for Duke or Coach K.

REPEAT

A large, enthusiastic crowd gathered in Cameron Indoor Stadium to greet Duke's 1991 champs on their return from Indianapolis. During the ceremony, Krzyzewski jokingly asked the students to decide where the banner should hang. When they pointed to a spot in one end zone, the coach told the cheering crowd, "I probably shouldn't say this, but there's room up there for another banner just like it."

Both Frank McGuire in 1958 and Norm Sloan in 1975 had made similar boasts about their post-championship seasons. Duke also lost one starter off its title team, but senior forward Greg Koubek, while a solid player, was hardly in a class with Lennie Rosenbluth or Tommy Burleson or James Worthy, the major loss off UNC's 1982 champs. Krzyzewski's roster was still loaded. The big three—Laettner, Hurley, and Grant Hill—were all back, along with veterans Thomas Hill, Brian Davis, and Antonio Lang. They were joined by freshman big man Cherokee Parks, a prep All-American from California who seemed to have many of the inside/outside skills that had made Ferry and Laettner so formidable. In fact, Krzyzewski had thought all along that 1992, and not 1991, would be his year.

"Winning in 1991 was a tremendous achievement, but we were always building for 1992," he told Bill Brill. "We knew we would have a great team then."

Not surprisingly, Duke was the preseason pick as the nation's No. 1 team. The Duke coach welcomed the challenge of being No.1.

"We're not defending our title," he told reporters on the first day of practice. "We're pursuing a new title."

Duke's pursuit of a title would be handicapped by a long string of injuries to key players, but the Blue Devils were at full strength just before Christmas, when the team visited Ann Arbor and dueled Michigan in a game that would launch the "Fab Five" to national prominence. Top-ranked Duke took a twelve-point lead on the Wolverines, but with freshmen Chris Webber, Jalen Rose, and Juwan Howard showing off their incredible talent, Steve Fisher's young team rallied to take a five-point lead with 1:28 to play. Hurley scored six points in the final eighty-eight seconds to force overtime. The junior point guard, who finished with twenty-six points, carried the team after Laettner fouled out and Duke escaped with an 88–85 victory over a team that they would see again.

That was just about the only early test for the Devils, who carried a 17–0 record into Chapel Hill for the first meeting with the Tar Heels.

Smith's team had taken a step back with the graduation loss of Rice, Fox, and Chilcutt. In addition, talented big man Clifford Rozier, unhappy with Smith's demands that he play defense and work hard in practice, decided to transfer. The Florida native had wanted to go to Florida State; but with the Seminoles joining the ACC as a ninth member for the 1991–92 season, Smith refused to release Rozier to a team he'd have to play twice each season. Instead, Rozier wound up at Louisville, where he became an All-American.

Smith's concerns about Florida State proved prescient when FSU played its first-ever ACC game in the Smith Center and stunned the Tar Heels 86–74. Seminole guard Sam Cassell added insult to injury, when he told reporters that he and his teammates weren't concerned about UNC's homecourt edge because they knew they were facing "a cheese and wine crowd."

That line, which soon morphed into the more familiar "wine and cheese crowd," would haunt the UNC program for more than a decade. Indeed, because of the compromises made to pay for the mammoth structure, the Smith Center usually lacked the passion that marked Cameron Indoor Stadium or Reynolds Coliseum.

"Usually" is the operative word. On occasion, even the fat cats surrounding the court would get excited and the Smith Center would be as loud and raucous as Carmichael had ever been. That usually happened when Duke came to town—and the Blue Devils' visit on February 5, 1992 was one of those moments.

Smith still boasted Montross in the middle, the dependable Lynch at one forward, the athletic Reese at the other, and a solid backcourt with Phelps and Hubert Davis. The Heels were 15–3 and ranked No. 9 in the nation. That might have been good enough for the Tar Heel faithful most seasons, but not in a year when the hated Blue Devils were anointed as the best team in the nation. "I'm tired of hearing about Duke," Montross complained to reporters.

The Tar Heels got to play out their emotions in a brutal game that approached the 1989 ACC title clash in intensity. Midway through the first half, Hurley hurt his foot. It turned out that he had broken a metatarsal bone and would miss the next five games, but he stayed on the floor against the Tar Heels and limped through thirty-seven painful minutes. On the other side, Montross caught an elbow from Laettner and his subsequent trip to the foul line, with blood streaming from the cut over his eye, would come to symbolize the game. The Tar Heels nursed a narrow lead into the final seconds and won 75–73 when Laettner missed two potential tying shots in the final thirty seconds.

But the loss to UNC, and the temporary loss of Hurley, barely slowed Duke's express. Krzyzewski moved Grant Hill to the point and with the 6-foot-8 soph at the controls, Duke went on the road and won at LSU, Georgia Tech, and N.C. State. The Devils remained No. 1 as they headed to Winston-Salem for a matchup with Dave Odom's improving Deacons.

New coach Dave Odom was rebuilding the Wake program to respectability, and his inspired Deacons took a two-point lead into the final seconds of their game with the Blue Devils. Needing a basket in a hurry, Krzyzewski set up a play that Duke had worked on in practice: Grant Hill on the baseline would throw a baseball pass to Laettner at the opponent's foul line. The senior center was supposed to catch it, turn, and shoot. Unfortunately, Hill's pass hooked right-to-left and in an attempt to run it down, Laettner stepped out of bounds. The missed connection went almost unnoticed at the time but would soon achieve major significance.

That was the last slip for Duke, which closed out the regular season with four straight wins—including a surprisingly easy victory over the Tar Heels in the rematch in Durham. And one year after getting blown out by UNC in the 1991 title game, the Blue Devils returned the favor in the 1992 title game, routing the Tar Heels 94–74, which was almost an exact reversal of the previous year's 96–74 UNC win. There were no obscene tirades from Laettner this time, but merely a twenty-five-point, ten-rebound effort that earned him the Case Award as the tourney's MVP.

"I didn't think they could play better than they did against us in Durham," UNC's Dean Smith said. "But they did."

North Carolina and Wake Forest also followed top-seeded Duke into the NCAA Tournament. The Deacs didn't last long, losing to Louisville in the first round. North Carolina did a little better, knocking off Miami of Ohio and Alabama in Cincinnati to extend Smith's streak of Sweet 16 appearances to a record twelve straight. The Heels went out to No. 1 seed Ohio State in Rupp Arena in Lexington, Kentucky, but not before setting up a scene that would become memorable in ACC annals.

It involved Duke—which had cruised past Campbell and Iowa in Greensboro, as expected, to reach the East Regional semifinals. The stage was not the familiar Meadowlands Arena outside New York, but the Philadelphia Spectrum, a cramped and aging facility graced by a bronze statue of Rocky outside the main entrance.

The fictional boxing hero, the ultimate underdog, was an appropriate symbol for the 1992 East Regionals. Duke was Apollo Creed, the unbeatable favorite. Kentucky, rebuilding under charismatic coach Rick Pitino, would play the role of Rocky, the loveable underdog. And just as in the movie, Creed would win—but Rocky would go the distance.

Even so, no one expected Kentucky to push Duke to the limit in the regional championship game. Even the hundreds of Kentucky fans who packed Pitino's, the Italian restaurant in Lexington owned by the Wildcats' coach, to watch the game together at the bar seemed apprehensive as their overachieving team tipped it off against the top-ranked Blue Devils. Above them, a dozen North Carolina writers in town to cover UNC watched the show from a private room with a glassed-in view of the bar area below.

Duke had enjoyed the underdog role against mighty UNLV the year before. Now they had a chance to find out how the Rebels felt. Kentucky was an extraordinarily close-knit group that featured just one true star, sophomore forward Jamal Mashburn. At the heart of the team were four lightly regarded seniors who had decided to stick it out at Kentucky when scandal ripped the program under former coach Eddie Sutton.

Forever known in Kentucky lore as "The Unforgettables," they dueled Duke in what ESPN voted as the greatest college basketball game in the last quarter century. Both teams were superb: Duke shot 65.4% from the floor and converted twenty-eight of thirty-four free throws; Kentucky shot 56.9% and forced twenty turnovers.

The game surged back and fourth. On a number of occasions, Duke seemed to be on the verge of breaking it open, but on each occasion, Mashburn or point guard Sean Woods or senior John Pelphrey would make a shot and bring the Wildcats back. With the score tied at 93 in the end of regulation, Hurley's driving shot missed and forced the game into overtime.

The game kept getting better and better. Kentucky took the lead in overtime, but Hurley's three-pointer brought Duke back. In the final thirty-two seconds of the extra period, the two teams traded amazing plays with dizzying rapidity.

"Every single play, it seemed like they'd rise to the occasion and make it greater than the play before," said future UNC coach Roy Williams, who watched on TV.

With the score tied at 98, Laettner converted an acrobatic double-pump shot between two defenders as the shot clock expired. With 19 seconds left, Mashburn converted a three-point play and the 'Cats were up one. Duke seemed back in command as Mashburn fouled out and Laettner converted two free throws with 7.8 seconds left. But Kentucky—trying to get the ball to Pelphrey or Richie Farmer on the wing—instead got an unbelievable shot from

Woods, who drove the lane and threw up a rainbow over Laettner. The ball banked in to give Kentucky a 103–102 lead with 2.1 seconds left. "To be honest, I thought we had lost," Grant Hill said later.

As the Duke players huddled around Krzyzewski to try to set up a game-winning play, the party of North Carolina reporters in Lexington watched as the Kentucky fans below celebrated their apparent victory. In the adjoining parking garage, South Carolina coach Eddie Fogler, the former backcourt mate of Charlie Scott at North Carolina, had been sitting in his car, listening to Cawood Ledford's call of the game. When Wood hit his shot, Fogler turned off his engine and headed for Pitino's Restaurant, where he was supposed to meet former teammate Jim Delany, the commissioner of the Big Ten.

In Philadelphia, Krzyzewski greeted his despondent players with the words, "We're going to win this game and here's how we're going to do it."

It turned out that his plan was to use the same play that had failed at Wake Forest—a long pass from Grant Hill to Laettner at the foul line. "The Wake Forest moment came into my mind for a hot second," Hill said. "I thought, Grant, just don't throw a curve."

Pitino made the forever-debated decision not to challenge Hill on the baseline. That gave the Duke forward room to pick his spot and make his football-like pass. Hill moved slightly to his right and let his Hail Mary go—right on line this time to where Laettner was waiting. Two Kentucky players defended Laettner at the foul line, but Pitino had warned them not to foul the deadly free throw shooter. So neither Pelphrey nor Deron Feldhaus challenged Laettner for the ball. He went up alone and caught it cleanly.

Then he did something that took Krzyzewski's breath away. He calmly dribbled once to his right, spun left, and launched an eighteen-footer. He capped his perfect day with the most memorable single shot in NCAA history. Laettner's buzzer-beater swished through, giving Duke the 104–103 victory.

"It took a while to sink in," Grant Hill said. "After we won, I still couldn't believe we won. Kentucky played a great game. I was just happy I had the big guy on my side."

In the pandemonium that followed Laettner's shot, Krzyzewski found Kentucky's Farmer lying on the floor. He helped the fallen Kentucky senior to his feet and hugged him.

"He told me, 'You guys are not losers,'" Farmer said. "He said, 'Keep your heads up. Tonight, there are no losers.'"

The Duke coach made his way to the Kentucky radio broadcast crew, where he asked for a chance to address the Kentucky audience. He used the opportunity to honor the legendary Ledford, broadcasting his final game, and to praise the Kentucky kids who had come so close, but lost so cruelly.

"I'll always marvel at how many great plays so many players made on both sides," the Duke coach told the media. "I think we've all been a part of one of the great games ever. I'm a little bit stunned. As a guy who loves the game itself, I've been standing around trying to figure out what a lucky son of a gun I am to be involved."

In Pitino's restaurant in Lexington, it was as if a bomb had gone off. Fogler entered the bar area and was surprised to find the place quiet and empty.

"What happened?" he asked one of the North Carolina reporters on hand. "I thought they'd be celebrating all night."

Fogler was stunned to learn that the basketball world has turned upside down in the few seconds he'd taken to walk from his car to the restaurant.

Duke, so lucky to avoid defeat in Philiadelphia, still had to win two more games in the Final Four in Minneapolis to assure its place in history. And it wouldn't be easy with Indiana and Bobby Knight waiting in the semifinals.

It was a difficult emotional matchup for Krzyzewski. Earlier in his career, he seemed proud to be labeled a Knight disciple. Knight appeared to take paternal pride in Krzyzewski's success. The Duke coach even had his mentor speak to his team before the 1986 title game and Knight wore a big Duke button all around Dallas that weekend. The next year, when title-bound Indiana eliminated Duke in the Sweet 16, the pregame and postgame interviews were almost a love-fest between the two opposing coaches.

"It's hard for me to enjoy this very much thinking about Mike," Knight said after beating the Blue Devils.

But in the weeks before the 1992 Final Four, something changed. It was a very different game than the Knight-Krzyzewski matchup in 1987 or the Dean Smith–Roy Williams duel in 1991. This one was Darth Vader vs. Obi-Wan Kenobi.

The game itself turned into a wild affair. With Laettner struggling, Hurley saved Duke in the first half, hitting four three-pointers to trim a twelve-point deficit late in the period to just five points at the break. Then the Blue Devils opened the second half with a 21–3 spurt, helped by a technical foul on

Knight, who screamed at ref John Clougherty, "You're not going to let the punks win, are you?"

Duke suffered a blow when senior starter Brian Davis, who had played such a huge role in the Vegas win a year earlier, went down with a sprained ankle. When Grant Hill fouled out, little-used reserve Marty Clark came off the bench as the Hoosiers scrambled to rally. Clark hit five of six free throws down the stretch—just enough to help the Devils survive three straight three-pointers in the final minute from equally obscure Indiana sub Todd Leary.

Krzyzewski was surprised by Knight's perfunctory postgame handshake, then stunned when he was snubbed by his mentor in a hallway en route to the NCAA interview area. For the next decade, the two coaches would be estranged, each blaming the other for betraying their friendship.

But Krzyzewski didn't have time to dwell on Knight's behavior that weekend. He still had to nurse his team to one more win. And he was disturbed by the lackluster play of his star Laettner. It almost seemed as if his incredible performance against Kentucky had drained all the emotion from him. There was no question that the hero of Duke's 81–78 victory was Hurley, who hit six three-pointers and scored a career-high twenty-six points.

"I don't think we win without Hurley," Krzyzewski said. "He had one of those magnificent games. He was playing at a much higher level than any of our other players."

Duke found Michigan's Fab Five waiting for a rematch in the title game. A lot had changed since Duke's overtime win at Michigan just before Christmas. Fisher's "Fab Five" freshmen starters were national sensations, impressing an entire generation of young basketball players with their cocky attitudes and their baggy shorts. The title game was widely perceived as a duel between the old school Blue Devils and college basketball's new wave.

For a half, it looked like the new would sweep away the old. Michigan, playing with passion and flair, took a one-point halftime lead on a late shot by Jalen Rose. The signature play of the half was Chris Webber's spinning behind-the-back pass to Rob Pelinka for a fast-break layup. Hurley once again kept the team together with help from senior guard Thomas Hill. At halftime, the Blue Devil players were expecting a tongue-lashing from Krzyzewski. They got one alright, but not from the Duke coach: Hurley blistered his teammates and led them back on the floor in fury.

"He showed his leadership," teammate Antonio Lang said. "He did something at halftime that really impressed me. He said vocally, 'What are we doing? Why aren't we playing hard? Do we want to play hard? Do we want to win?' If it weren't for Bobby, it would have been tough for us to win this thing."

For the second straight game, Duke spurted after the break. Hurley got Laettner started with a behind-the-back feed for a layup on a fast break, then found his teammate open on the wing for a three-pointer. The Blue Devils stretched their lead to seven points with ten minutes left—but for just an instant, it looked like the younger, fresher Wolverines had the legs for a successful charge. As Michigan closed to within 48–45, Duke appeared tired and vulnerable. The injured Davis had tried to play, but couldn't. Laettner appeared done. Even the indestructible Hurley looked worn down. That's when Grant Hill took his game to the next level.

The 6-foot-8 sophomore simply took control. His baseline drive and reverse layup stopped the Michigan momentum. A few moments later, he repeated his baseline drive, finishing this time with a reverse slam dunk that seemed to take the heart out of the Wolverines. Instead of fading, Duke dominated the final seven minutes, outscoring Michigan 23–6 down the stretch to post a deceptively lopsided 71–51 victory.

"To go wire to wire number one and have four really tough games in a row to end the NCAAs, that was not something that was given to us," Krzyzewski said. "We had to earn it."

The Duke players had a statement of their own to make. After listening to Michigan's trash-talk all week without responding, they answered by donning T-shirts that had been hidden under their bench. "You can talk the game . . . Can you play the game?" the front of the shirts said. On the backs were: "Duke . . . We can play."

At that moment, nobody in college basketball played any better.

14

THE EMPIRE STRIKES BACK

Duke's ascension to the top of the college basketball world was hard to take in Chapel Hill. While North Carolina hadn't always had the best team every single season in the 1970s and 1980s, it had been at least a quarter century since anybody else on Tobacco Road could claim to have a better program.

But in 1992, there was no doubt who ruled the region. After six Final Four trips in seven years, capped by back-to-back national titles, Mike Krzyzewski was the King of Tobacco Road and Duke was the state's premier program. Chris Collins, the son of former NBA star and coach Doug Collins, saw it when he arrived on campus as a freshman that fall.

"I came in on the heels of the back-to-back championships," he said. "For me, it was like joining the Beatles. Duke was on top. It was nuts. That was kind of the start of Duke becoming that team, you know—you love 'em or you hate 'em."

That status had always belonged to Smith's Tar Heels. The old ABC Brigade was joined by the ABD (Anybody But Duke) Club. The fans of N.C. State and Wake Forest were charter members of both organizations and it was hard to tell which rival they hated more. But neither the Wolfpack nor the Deacons appeared to be in position to challenge the mighty Devils as the 1992–93 season opened. The Deacons were closing the gap, but in Raleigh, Les Robinson's program was in a shambles—symbolized by an opening night loss at home to UNC Wilmington.

North Carolina opened the same night with a lopsided victory over Old Dominion. The big news in Chapel Hill was the performance of sophomore Donald Williams, who scored twenty-one points in twenty-five minutes.

Williams had been a focus of controversy in Chapel Hill for more than a year. Celebrated as the best shooter in high school basketball as a senior at nearby Garner (N.C.) High School, he was expected to be an immediate star when he picked UNC after a frantic recruiting push by Les Robinson at N.C. State. However, Williams's stardom did not come. He languished on the bench even as the 1991–92 Tar Heels struggled to find a shooter to complement senior Hubert Davis.

The graduation of Davis opened up a hole that Williams was quick to fill. The sophomore from Garner still came off the bench, but he played enough to win MVP honors in the Tournament of Champions in Charlotte—scoring twenty-three points in twenty-two minutes against South Carolina and adding nineteen points in sixteen minutes against Texas.

The Tar Heels were proving to be a deep, balanced team. The core consisted of the four juniors who remained from "The New Kids on the Block" group. But Williams, first off the bench and later as a starter, provided the perimeter firepower the team needed and senior George Lynch proved to be the team's inspirational leader. "He has the heart of a lion," Smith said of his 6-foot-7, 215-pound forward.

Lynch was born two months premature in Roanoke (Va.). Weighing three pounds at birth, he had to fight for life. He continued that fight as he grew older and stronger, becoming one of the nation's top basketball prospects as a senior at Flint Hill Academy. He disappointed his hometown fans when he elected to play for Smith at UNC, rather than attend either Virginia or Virginia Tech, both within easy driving distance of his hometown.

Unlike Williams, Lynch made an immediate impact when he joined the Tar Heels as a freshman. A powerful inside player, he was a starter on the 1991 Final Four team and had established himself as one of the best rebounders in the ACC. Although he was the quintessential college power forward, Lynch—looking to his future in the NBA—always wanted to play small forward. To his credit, he never let his desire to play small forward detract from his performance in the role Smith asked him to play. His teammates recognized his sacrifice, which was one of the reasons he became the heart and soul of a team that began to climb in the polls.

Still, Duke—even without Laettner and Brian Davis—appeared to be the ACC's dominant team through December. The Blue Devils upset No. 1 Michigan in early December, then won ten straight games and routed UNC 81–67 in Cameron.

"K's got two [NCAA titles] . . . Dean's got one!" the Cameron Crazies taunted Smith before, during, and after the Blue Devil win.

Duke was 19–3 and ranked No. 3 in the nation when disaster struck. Mike Krzyzewski was celebrating his forty-sixth birthday on the day Duke took on Wake Forest in Cameron. The Blue Devils had routed the Deacons 86–59 a month earlier in Winston-Salem. With Wake's starting point guard Charlie Harrison out with an injury, the Blue Devils appeared poised to claim victory number twenty. Duke opened up an early nine-point lead as Grant Hill hit his first four shots from the floor.

"I thought it would be a career night," Hill said. But midway through the first half, Hill came out of a scramble for a loose ball limping. The 6-foot-8 junior, his left foot obviously hurting, tried to play on; but with just over sixteen minutes left in the game, he went to the bench for good. In his absence, Wake's Rodney Rogers—who grew up in the Durham projects across town from the Duke campus—took over the game. His thirty-five points (on 16-of-18 shooting) lead Odom's Deacons to a stunning 98–86 upset.

Or maybe it was not so stunning. Without Grant Hill—who would miss the final six games of the regular season with a broken toe—Duke was no longer a dominant team, going 5–5 in the team's final ten games.

"We were having a great year . . . We really had a good thing going," Collins recalled. "Then Grant breaks his toe. We tried to hold it together, but he could never get healthy. Even when he came back [for the ACC and NCAA Tournaments], it was never the same. Once he went down with the foot, it was a huge piece because he was the versatile player [who] was the mismatch no one had an answer for."

When Duke declined after Grant Hill's injury, North Carolina was ready to step into the power vacuum at the top of the ACC. The Tar Heels had lost for the first time when they faced the Fab Five in the semifinals of the Rainbow Classic in Honolulu. Facing another loss at home to Florida State, the Tar Heels rallied from a twenty-one-point, second-half deficit to edge the Seminoles. UNC finished the regular season with nine straight wins, climbing to

No. 1 in the nation just before decisively beating short-handed Duke 83–69 on Lynch's Senior Day in Chapel Hill.

An unexpected snowfall hit Charlotte during the ACC Tournament semifinals on Saturday, March 13—the day after Georgia Tech bounced struggling Duke from the tourney. The snow didn't appear to be a lucky omen for the Tar Heels. Point guard Derrick Phelps took a nasty fall in the second half against Virginia and was carted off on a stretcher. He lay outside the Coliseum for almost twenty minutes, with snow falling on top of him, as paramedics waited for an ambulance to negotiate the tournament traffic and the slippery roads. "I was scared," Phelps later told reporters. "I didn't know what the injury was. I was hurt and my legs were numb."

The injury was diagnosed as a bruised tailbone, and although Phelps would miss the ACC title game the next day, he was able to return for the next week's NCAA Tournament. Georgia Tech exploited his absence to upset the Heels 77–75 in the championship game.

"We can't replace Derrick," Henrik Rodl said. "He sets the tone of the defense and does all sorts of stuff for us."

Phelps's absence seemed to bother Donald Williams the most. Forced to revert to the point guard role, the sophomore guard missed fourteen of eighteen shots against the Cavaliers. It was not a good omen for the Tar Heels entering NCAA play. Neither was the tournament loss itself: in each of Dean Smith's previous eight Final Four trips, his teams had won the ACC Tournament.

Despite the loss to Georgia Tech, North Carolina was still seeded No. 1 in the East and given two easy games in Winston-Salem against East Carolina and Rhode Island. The path got a bit tougher when UNC moved on to the Meadowlands to take on No. 12 Arkansas and No. 7 Cincinnati. But the combination of strong play from Lynch down low and some late three-point shooting by Williams in both games punched UNC's ticket to New Orleans.

"I seem to concentrate more when the game is on the line," Williams said. "As soon as the ball came to me, I could hear Coach Smith yell, 'Knock it down!' That gave me a lot of confidence."

The Tar Heel players celebrated the regional win by donning Final Four T-shirts and hats. But taking a cue from the 1982 team, they refused to cut down the nets.

There was another parallel to 1982, the year of UNC's last title. The Final Four was back in the New Orleans Superdome, where James Worthy's spectacular play and Michael Jordan's clutch shot had beaten Georgetown in the title game. And the semifinal opponent was an echo of UNC's last Final Four trip in 1991. For the second time in two years, Smith had to get past his protégé Roy Williams to reach the title game.

The difference between the 1991 UNC-Kansas game and the 1993 re-match came down to one player: Donald Williams. The sophomore shooting guard, his head shaved in Jordanesque fashion after the regional victory, came out on fire and provided the outside threat that the Tar Heels lacked in Indianapolis. Williams hit seven of eleven shots, including five of seven three-point tries, to score twenty-five points.

His success opened things up inside for 7-footer Eric Montross, who abused Kansas big men Eric Pauley and Greg Ostertag for twenty-three points. Lynch added fourteen points and ten rebounds as UNC coasted to a 78–68 victory. Back in Chapel Hill, thousands of students poured onto Franklin Street to celebrate the victory. One sign contained the message: "We're here . . . Where's Dook?"

Ironically, to claim the title North Carolina would have to get past the same Michigan Fab Five that Duke had disposed of a year earlier. The five Wolverines—now older, more experienced, and more famous than ever—presented a formidable challenge, especially with the confidence that came from beating the Tar Heels in Hawaii. In the title game, Williams would almost exactly duplicate his Kansas effort: he hit eight of twelve shots this time, five of seven three-pointers, and again scored twenty-five points. The Tar Heels would need every one of them. With just under seven minutes left, UNC trailed by a point when Smith was confronted with a decision that tested his entire coaching philosophy.

In his very first year as a head coach, Smith had devised what he called "the tired signal"—a raised fist to indicate that a player was winded and needed to come out of the game. He told his players that if they pulled themselves for fatigue, they could reinsert themselves in the game when rested. "Tired players make mental errors and they tend to rest on defense," Smith once explained. "I'd rather have fresh subs in the game than tired starters."

The Tar Heel coach used to joke that he was so nervous in that first game that when Larry Brown flashed him the tired signal, Smith said he jumped up, raised his fist in the air, and shouted, "Atta boy, Larry, go get 'em!"

But with the 1993 national title game on the line, Smith knew exactly what it meant when he saw that four of his starters were raising their fists, asking for relief. Down a point with just 6:50 left, could he afford to clear his bench?

That moment, down one to Michigan with 6:50 to play, was the test of Smith's commitment to his system. And in the crisis he stuck with what he believed in, calling a time-out to get his tired starters out and insert four subs, including little-used guard Scott Cherry. Despite the criticism showered on Smith by CBS commentator Billy Packer, the veteran coach defended his decision.

"What kind of message would it have sent to change our rules now?" he wrote in his autobiography. "It would be telling them that we didn't have the courage to do the things in the NCAA Tournament that we practiced daily."

UNC's subs committed a shot-clock violation, but in the next few minutes, Smith's rested starters returned and regained the lead while Michigan's weary regulars faltered. Lynch gave UNC a brief five-point lead with a basket and an assist to Montross, but Michigan fought back to within one point when Pat Sullivan went to the line with twenty seconds to play. The junior forward hit his first free throw but missed his second. Michigan's Webber rebounded, setting the stage for a wild ending that would take its place in NCAA lore beside Freddie Brown's bizarre pass to James Worthy eleven years earlier.

It started when Webber turned and started to throw a pass to Jalen Rose in front of the Tar Heel bench. But just before he released the ball, Lynch jumped in the passing lane and the Michigan senior had to pull the ball back. In the process, Webber took two clear steps as Packer screamed on the CBS telecast, "He walked!"

But official Ed Hightower, who appeared to be looking right at the play, didn't call it. His blown call actually turned out to be a bad break for Michigan (which still would have had time to salvage the game at that point). Webber, realizing that time was running out, dribbled the ball upcourt and came to a stop right in front of the Michigan bench. Phelps and Lynch trapped him there and the desperate Webber put the ball under his arm and called time-out. Only Michigan didn't have a time-out left, earning a technical foul.

Williams converted the two ensuing free throws, then took an inbounds pass and was fouled; he hit two more free throws to wrap up the 77–71 victory for the Heels. The sophomore from Garner was named the Final Four Most Outstanding Player. On accepting the trophy, he dedicated the award to Jim Valvano, who was at that moment just weeks away from dying of cancer. "He was the first coach to recruit me," Williams said. "He's a great guy."

Williams's gesture got little attention from reporters, who were obsessed with Webber's snafu. "It's all part of the game," Smith told reporters, when asked about Webber's error on the same end of the Superdome floor where Freddie Brown had blundered in Smith's last title game. "Neither one necessarily meant we would win. I've often said, you've got to be lucky and good."

North Carolina was both very lucky and very good in 1993. And the sweetest part of winning the title? That had to be when Duke Athletic Director Tom Butters, the chairman of the NCAA men's basketball committee, handed Smith the championship trophy. It was his second championship, tying Krzyzewski, and restoring the natural order of things on Tobacco Road.

At least for the time being.

15

KRZYZEWSKI'S "BACK"

As MUCH AS GRANT HILL'S INJURY SPOILED DUKE'S 1993 SEASON, IT may have been a blessing in disguise for the Blue Devils. "If he didn't break his foot, he might have gone pro," Chris Collins suggested.

Instead, Hill elected to return to Duke for his senior season, anchoring a team that started the year in North Carolina's shadow. But 1994 would prove to be almost an exact reversal of the previous season. As internal dissent rocked the No. 1 Tar Heels, Krzyzewski put together a team that, while not quite as talented, played together and maximized its strengths.

"That was a close-knit team," Collins recalled. "It was a real fun team to play on. The expectations weren't great. It was really rewarding to accomplish what we did."

Collins, a sophomore with almost unlimited range on his jump shot, started in the backcourt with freshman Jeff Capel, a big, physical point guard whose father was the head coach at North Carolina A&T (and later Old Dominion). But Hill often ran the offense from his "point forward" position. He responded with one of the great all-around seasons in ACC history. Averaging just under thirty-six minutes a game, he gave the Devils 17.4 points, 6.9 rebounds, 5.2 assists, more than two steals, and just over a blocked shot a game. In addition, he was voted the national defensive player of the year.

Duke edged North Carolina, the nation's preseason No. 1 team, for the regular season title and represented Tobacco Road at the Final Four in Charlotte— where the Blue Devils came excruciatingly close to winning a third national title in four years. Krzyzewski's team led Arkansas by twelve points early in the second half of the title game, but a seven-minute dry spell allowed the Razorbacks to regain the lead. The score was tied and the shot clock was about to expire when Arkansas All-American Scotty Thurman launched a desperation three-point try from the right key—his shot just clearing the outstretched fingers of Duke's Antonio Lang. "Scotty made a tough shot," Lang said. "I was right over him. I don't know how he made it."

Thurman's rainbow connected, giving Arkansas a three-point lead with less than a minute to play. Duke rushed the ball downcourt and Collins launched a long three-point try of his own, which seemed to go halfway down before rimming out. Arkansas rebounded and converted its free throws to clinch a 76–72 victory.

"It was disappointing not to win it at the end," Collins said. "I know we weren't supposed to get that far, but when you do and you're one bounce either way from winning the whole thing . . . that's tough."

Duke's near-miss was painful, but it appeared to be an effective response to UNC's 1993 title. The rivalry between the two Tobacco Road neighbors was being played out at unimaginable levels. Between 1986 and 1994, UNC and Duke had combined for three national titles and made nine Final Four appearances. Each had won three ACC titles in that span and one or the other had finished No. 1 in the regular season standings seven times in the nine seasons.

Who could have guessed that one of the two juggernauts was headed for disaster?

THE BACK INJURY

Krzyzewski, his empire seemingly secure, went about rebuilding his team after the departure of the last of the three superstars from his back-to-back title teams. He had to replace All-American Grant Hill and forward Antonio Lang after the 1994 near-miss, but he added three prominent prep guards—including sharpshooter Trajan Langdon, the first notable prospect ever produced by the state of Alaska, and the tough little point guard from Baltimore, Steve Wojciechowski, who was perhaps the only player in Duke history with a more convoluted name than the Blue Devil coach.

Krzyzewski sounded upbeat as he met with the media just before the opening of fall practice. But there was one obvious problem. The Duke coach was suffering such back pain that he could neither sit nor stand up straight for the thirty-minute press conference. Instead, he leaned on a podium as he talked to reporters about his plans for the season. Coach K's doctors wanted him to have back surgery to repair what they called "a degenerative disc." At first, he resisted their advice, planning to tough it out; but the pain was so persistent that he finally agreed to undergo surgery in late October, a week after the start of practice. The doctors pronounced the operation a success and told Krzyzewski that he needed six weeks of rest to recover.

He was back at practice in ten days.

"You could tell he was struggling physically," Collins said. "We didn't know the emotional toll it was taking on him."

Krzyzewski felt like his presence was needed. The 1995 Blue Devils were a painfully young team. Aside from senior center Cherokee Parks (and his backup Erik Meek), the only veteran presence on the team was Collins. But the junior guard broke his foot on the first day of practice, leaving the backcourt to three freshmen and the sophomore Capel. There was talent there, but Krzyzewski believed he needed to be there as a rock for his young players. At first, it seemed to work: Krzyzewski guided the young Devils to six victories in seven games, including a win over No. 16 Illinois in the first college game ever played in the United Center and a win at No. 23 Michigan.

"You still didn't see any signs of us having problems," Collins said. "We started the season strong. It was in Hawaii that we first started to see signs that coach was struggling."

The long airplane trip aggravated Krzyzewski's back problems. Even as Duke won two of three games in the Rainbow Classic, the coach was in obvious pain. He spent most of the flight back to Durham lying in the aisle. "I honestly believed that it was mind over matter," Krzyzewski later explained. "If I believed that I could handle the pain, I could handle the pain."

Duke was 9–2 and ranked No. 11 in the AP poll when Clemson visited Cameron for the ACC opener for both teams. The Tigers, in their first season under Rick Barnes, were unbeaten against a weak schedule. That didn't impress anybody: Clemson was projected to finish dead last in the nine-team ACC. Instead, the Tigers opened ACC play by stunning Duke in Durham.

"We were horrible . . . terrible," Collins said. "We couldn't have felt worse. We came to practice the next day and Coach K wasn't there."

Krzyzewski was at Duke Hospital, finally giving up the fight to block out the pain after his wife had threatened to leave him if he didn't seek help. He visited his team one last time before checking into a hospital bed. He told them that he wouldn't be going with them to Georgia Tech for that Saturday night's game.

"I can clearly remember the meeting when he told us he wasn't going with us to Georgia Tech," Collins said. "I can't even begin to describe the color of his face. It was kind of a gray-green. This guy was always our rock. If we were struggling, he'd get us back on track. Now all of a sudden, he's breaking down. It showed his human side."

Originally, Krzyzewski was hoping to resume his duties after a few days of rest—maybe a week or two. When it became clear that his condition would not permit his return that season, he went to Athletic Director Tom Butters, the man who had hired him, and offered to resign. Butters wouldn't hear of it.

"Mike, this is your job whenever you're ready to come back," Butters told him. "I don't care if it's tomorrow or six weeks from now or six months from now. It's your job. I don't want anybody else as my basketball coach."

Less than a week later, Duke announced that Krzyzewski would miss the rest of the season and that assistant coach Pete Gaudet, who had succeeded Coach K at Army before coming to Duke, would serve as interim head coach. It was Gaudet who had to bear the brunt of the frustration that would follow. The decline started at Georgia Tech, a team Duke had beaten ten days earlier in Hawaii. This time, the Jackets won by seven. After a loss on the road at No. 14 Wake Forest, disaster struck in a home game with Virginia. The Blue Devils frittered away a twenty-six-point, second-half lead and lost in double overtime.

"There must have been eight to ten games that followed where the game was tied or we led in the last two minutes," Collins said. "We lost them all. Those were the kind of games we always seemed to win when Coach K was there."

The most painful—and thrilling—of the close losses was No. 2 North Carolina's visit to Cameron on February 2, 1995. The Blue Devils overcame a seventeen-point, second-half deficit, rallying to force overtime against a Tar Heel team that boasted superstars Jerry Stackhouse and Rasheed Wallace. Down eight points with seventeen seconds left in the first overtime, Duke rallied to tie the game on a mid-court prayer by Jeff Capel.

"That was as loud as I've ever heard Cameron," Collins said. "But what gets lost is that we lost. People remember the comeback we made and that Jeff hit the shot . . . they forget we lost the game."

Indeed, UNC handed Duke its ninth loss in ten games when Wojciechowski missed a potential tying jumper at the end of the second overtime.

Although the game is viewed as a classic in the rivalry, for the downtrodden Blue Devils, it was just another episode in their interminable season of disaster. But even though the regular season ended with a disheartening loss in Chapel Hill, the Blue Devils saw their first ray of light: Krzyzewski returned to practice.

"We were allowed just very limited access to him [during the season]," Collins said. "Nobody knew how he was doing. It was a hard situation. Then the week before we went to the ACC Tournament, he was allowed to come back and conduct practice. I saw the fire in his eyes and I knew that week that he was going to be back."

16

GOLDSBORO AND ST. CROIX

IF ANYBODY WAS DESTINED TO COACH ON TOBACCO ROAD, IT WAS Dave Odom.

Born in Goldsboro, North Carolina, a blue-collar tobacco town just to the southeast of Raleigh, George David Odom grew up listening to Ray Reeve, Add Penfield, and Bill Currie broadcast the glories of Everett Case, Frank McGuire, and Bones McKinney. As a three-sport star at Goldsboro High, Odom was labeled "Little Davey" Odom, a nickname he hated. But it followed him to Guilford College just outside Greensboro, where he was recruited off the football team to play point guard for Coach Jerry Steele.

Steele was himself a protégé of Bones McKinney, regarded as Wake Forest's enforcer in his three seasons as a backup to Dave Budd and Len Chappell. He fueled Odom's love affair with basketball and helped guide him into high school coaching. Odom started in his hometown of Goldsboro, but soon moved to Durham High School, where he coached in a gym named for Paul Sykes, the man who had nurtured Bones McKinney decades earlier.

It was at Durham High that Odom first found notoriety. Odom used a box-and-one defense to stifle Rocky Mount's Phil Ford as he engineered a monumental upset at the Sykes Gym. He also became a noted summer camp instructor, working at Howard Garfinkel's Five-Star Camp in Pennsylvania. He attracted the attention of Carl Tacy, who hired the young high school coach as an assistant at Wake Forest.

A decade later, after a brief stint as head coach at East Carolina and six years on Terry Holland's staff at Virginia, Odom returned to Winston-Salem as head coach, trying to revive a program that hadn't finished better than 3–11 in the ACC in Bob Staak's four seasons. But Odom had a couple of advantages as he started his rebuilding effort. One was the completion of Lawrence Joel Coliseum, a beautiful 14,407-seat arena built on the site of the old Memorial Auditorium where Chappell and Packer had starred. No longer would Wake Forest have to play its home games in Greensboro, more than half an hour's drive from campus.

Odom's other big edge was his intimate knowledge of the highways and byways of Tobacco Road. Like Carl Tacy before him, he would prove adept at discovering unheralded prospects from around the state. Unlike Tacy, his background at Five-Star Camp would give him entry into the competition for some of the nation's best prospects.

Odom used his connections to score an immediate triumph on the recruiting trail, landing prep All-American Rodney Rogers from Hillside High in Durham. He would be everything he was hyped to be: second-team All-ACC as a freshman in 1991; first-team All-ACC as a junior; ACC player of the year as a junior in 1993.

But as good as Rogers became, Odom's second big recruiting triumph in the fall of 1990 might have been more important. Randolph Childress, a Maryland native who prepped at Oak Hill Academy in Virginia, was regarded as a good, not a great, prospect. But he averaged 14.0 points a game as a freshman, teaming with Rogers to help Wake Forest improve from 12–16 in Odom's first season to 19–11 in his second. Childress missed the 1991–92 season with a knee injury, but he returned the next year to average 19.7 points and help Rogers and the Deacs win twenty-one games and reach the NCAA Sweet 16.

Childress brought far more to Odom's team than his deadly shooting ability. "He had what we needed at the time," Odom told writer Dan Collins. "We needed confidence. If you think back, Wake was a talented team that couldn't finish. He helped change that."

When Rogers turned pro after his junior season, Childress became the unquestioned leader of a team that was expected to take a step back after its 1993 success. But Odom was exploring new recruiting avenues, looking for any way to get an edge on his more established rivals at UNC and Duke. He became one of the first coaches to go overseas in search of talent. In the fall of 1993,

Odom brought in a three-man freshman class that was all foreign. The most celebrated of the three was Makhtar Ndiaye, a powerful 6-foot-9 center from Dakar, Senegal. "He's a pro," gushed Dean Smith when asked about Ndiaye.

Odom also landed 6-foot-10 Richardo Peral, a slender wing man from Valladolid, Spain, who was regarded as one of the best junior players in Europe. Then there was a third guy that Odom expected to redshirt—a slim 6-foot-10 center from St. Croix in the Virgin Islands named Tim Duncan.

Odom had first learned of Duncan from Chris King, a forward on his first Wake teams who had toured the Virgin Islands with a U.S. junior team. After making a few phone calls, Odom decided to fly to St. Croix and see for himself. Their first meeting is the stuff of legend. Odom visited the local playground where he expected to see Duncan playing. Instead, the sixteen-year-old big man sat down beside the Deacon coach and introduced himself. "I can play the game, coach," he told Odom.

Duncan had started his athletic career as a swimmer, but Hurricane Hugo, which roared over the Virgin Islands in 1989 (continuing on through the heart of Tobacco Road), had wrecked the pool where he trained. Duncan found that he disliked training in the ocean, so he switched to basketball.

"Tim Duncan came here as the third recruit," Odom admitted to Dan Collins. "He was almost an addendum. He was the dot under the exclamation point. And it turned out, he was the statement. He ended up being the period."

Odom first suspected that he had an unexpected prize that first fall, when his veteran players came to him after pickup games and began to rave about the "addendum" from the Virgin Islands. All ideas about redshirting Duncan disappeared when the NCAA arrived to investigate the recruiting of Ndiaye.

Odom had employed the services of a Senegalese native who was a maintenance worker from Greensboro to act as interpreter for the French-speaking prospect. During the year when Ndiaye prepped at Oak Hill, learning the English language and adapting to the United States, Odom's interpreter acted as a sort of guardian for his young countryman. Without Odom's knowledge, he had provided Ndiaye with a number of illegal benefits, mostly small stuff. But, as Valvano had discovered, even the small stuff can ruin a program.

Odom got off lucky. The NCAA accepted his testimony that the interpreter had acted without authority and merely ruled that Ndiaye was ineligible to play for Wake Forest and gave the Deacons a one-year probation without a postseason ban. The Senegalese big man promptly transferred to Michigan, where he became a quite ordinary player—although he would return to make his mark on Tobacco Road. Odom, relieved to dodge further sanctions, was forced to use Duncan instead.

"The coaches told me I'd better be ready or my tropical butt was going to get cooked," Duncan said. "They weren't kidding."

Duncan started his first game as a freshman against Alaska-Anchorage in the Great Alaskan Shootout. He didn't attempt a shot in that game, but he did pull down seven rebounds in just ten minutes of action. Two nights later, he played forty minutes in an overtime victory over Wisconsin-Green Bay, and as December turned into January, Duncan was reeling off double-doubles with regularity.

Childress was still the star, as he proved when the Deacons took on No. 2 Duke in Cameron. Wake Forest trailed 68–66 with seconds remaining when Childress, who already had twenty-one points on the night, took the ball right at 6-foot-8 Grant Hill, who would later be named the national defensive player of the year. Hill took a step back to cut off the drive and Childress pulled back and launched a quick jumper over Hill's fingertips.

The shot swished and as Cameron roared, Duke pushed the ball up and got it to Hill for a fifteen-foot jumper at the buzzer. When his shot rolled off, Mike Krzyzewski gestured for his team to gather around him to prepare for the overtime.

Only there wasn't going to be an overtime. What no one had noticed in all the bedlam was that when Childress had stepped back, he had stepped back behind the three-point arch. His shot was not a game-tying two-pointer, but a game-winning three-pointer.

Childress bedeviled Duke again two weeks later in Winston-Salem, pouring in twenty-eight points as the Deacs swept the ACC regular season champions. The 6-foot-2 guard averaged 19.6 points and shot 41.5% from three-point range to finish second in the All-ACC voting to Duke's Hill. Duncan—who averaged a modest 9.8 points and 9.6 rebounds and an ACC-high 3.8 blocked shots—finished second behind Maryland's Joe Smith in the ACC rookie of the year vote.

That 21–12 season merely laid the groundwork for Odom's breakthrough season in 1994–95. Childress (20.1 points, 5.2 assists, 43.8% on three-pointers) remained an All-ACC performer, while Duncan blossomed from a promising young player into a star, averaging 16.8 points, 12.5 rebounds, and 4.2 blocked shots.

The Deacons opened the season on the fringes of the top 25, but climbed in the polls by winning nine of ten games through early January. They cracked the top 10 with successive victories in February over Duke—one on a jumper by Childress with six seconds left. Odom's team won its last seven regular season games and finished as one of four league teams deadlocked atop the regular season standings.

Wake Forest won the four-way draw as the top seed in the ACC Tournament, but that almost turned into disaster as Duke—its season in shambles after losing head coach Mike Krzyzewski—stormed out of the play-in game and quickly seized an eighteen-point first-half lead on the Deacons.

During a TV time-out, Childress began screaming at his lackadaisical teammates. He then responded to his own temper tantrum, scoring ten straight field goals to wipe out the deficit before the halftime buzzer. Childress remained hot in the second half, finishing with forty points as the Deacons pulled away for an 87–70 victory. It was Wake's sixth straight victory over Duke—and Childress was almost single-handedly responsible for three of them.

The senior guard, playing with a dislocated pinky finger, remained hot in the semifinals, pouring in thirty points and passing out seven assists in a hard-fought victory over Virginia. And he proved unstoppable in the title game against North Carolina.

The Tar Heels had been the one roadblock to Odom's rebuilding efforts. The Deacons had won just three of fourteen meetings with UNC since Odom's arrival. A year earlier, Carolina had knocked Wake out of the ACC Tournament with an overtime victory in the semifinals. With Duke's demise in 1995, UNC was the team Wake had to beat to claim superiority on Tobacco Road for the first time in over twenty years.

Duncan—with sixteen points, twenty rebounds, and three blocked shots—was magnificent for the Deacons. But it was Childress, playing forty-four minutes and scoring thirty-seven points, who made the difference. The score was tied at 80-all when he slashed into the lane and pulled up for a twelve-foot jumper—almost the exact same shot as the one he hit to beat Duke in Durham a month earlier. This one had the same result, swishing through to give Wake an 82–80 victory and its first ACC title since Chappell and Packer had cut down the nets in 1962.

Odom was hoping to use the tournament triumph to catapult his team to the Final Four, but Childress came down with the flu, leaving the Deacons below par in a Sweet 16 matchup with Oklahoma State. Duncan had twelve points, twenty-two rebounds, and eight blocked shots against Bryant "Big Country" Reeves. But even though the ailing Childress scored twenty-two points, he didn't shoot well and no one else in the lineup could pick up the slack.

THE BEST PLAYER IN COLLEGE BASKETBALL

The Golden State Warriors made Maryland's Joe Smith the number one pick in the 1995 NBA draft. But Jerry West, the widely respected general manager of the Los Angeles Lakers, told reporters that had he come out, Wake Forest's Tim Duncan would have be a clear No.1 choice.

Duncan, who was merely a third-team AP All-American in 1995, was in no hurry to become a professional. He terrorized his ACC opponents, especially in Durham, where frustrated Duke center Greg Newton fumed, "He's not that good."

Considering the fact that Duncan had just abused the Devils with twenty-four points, fourteen rebounds, and four blocked shots in a 57–54 Wake Forest victory, it was a pretty ridiculous thing for Newton to say. Duncan, apparently amused when reporters ran to him with Newton's intemperate remarks, responded, "I think Greg Newton is the greatest player I've ever seen."

Many observers were beginning to say similar things about Duncan—and their tongues weren't planted in their cheeks.

"He was as good a big man as I ever played against," Duke's Chris Collins said. "I was never in a game against him when you didn't feel his presence. Whenever you'd drive, if he didn't block you, you at least knew he was there. He changed the game."

While Duncan continued to elevate his game as a junior, Odom struggled to repair his backcourt after the departure of Childress. He ended up pairing Rusty LaRue, who was also the quarterback of the Wake football team, with Tony Rutland, a sophomore from Hampton, Virginia, who had played on the same AAU team as Allen Iverson and Joe Smith. Both guards were dangerous three-point shooters, something Odom badly needed to keep opponents from packing their defenses down low to stop Duncan. Rutland assumed the playmaking role, struggling early in the year to overcome a turnover problem.

But as he matured late, the Deacons emerged as a national championship contender. At least that's the way it looked as Wake Forest closed the regular season by beating Tobacco Road rivals UNC and N.C. State, then stormed into the ACC Tournament finals by routing Virginia and Clemson. Duncan was magnificent in the first two rounds of the tournament: nineteen points, fifteen rebounds, six blocked shots against the Cavs; twenty-two points, nineteen rebounds, two blocks against the Tigers. He was even better in the finals against Georgia Tech: twenty-seven points, twenty-one rebounds, four blocked shots.

But it was the combination of Duncan inside and Rutland on the perimeter that helped the Deacons forge an eighteen-point second-half lead on the Yellow Jackets. Wake appeared as if it would win going away, when Rutland (who had hit five of seven three-pointers at that point) slipped driving to the basket and injured his knee. The Deacons almost collapsed in Rutland's absence, barely holding on for a 75–74 victory to become the first ACC team to win back-to-back ACC titles since UNC turned the trick with James Worthy and Sam Perkins in 1981–82.

But Rutland's injury cast a pall over Wake's NCAA chances. He played twenty-one ineffective minutes in the second-round victory over Texas and just three minutes in a victory over Louisville. The Deacon point guard wasn't able to play at all in the regional finals against Kentucky. Wildcat coach Rick Pitino, an old friend of Odom's from their days as counselors at the Five-Star Camp, took advantage of Rutland's absence by employing a full-court press that forced the Deacons into twenty turnovers.

It was frustrating for Odom and the Deacs: two very realistic chances to reach the Final Four and play for the national championship were both ruined by physical problems in the backcourt. Childress's illness in 1995 and Rutland's injury in 1996 were devastating blows for a program that didn't get many chances for national success. How many more chances would Wake get?

Duncan's decision to pass up the NBA and return for his senior year gave Odom one more chance to grab the prize that had eluded the Deacons for so long—one more chance to reach the Final Four for the first time since 1962 and maybe play for the national championship.

But there were no guarantees, even with the best player in college basketball returning in the middle. Odom still had to find the right complementary players to surround his superstar. And he couldn't overlook his Tobacco Road rivals, who were not about to step aside and let Odom steal the limelight.

17

THE ELDER STATESMAN

No one knew it at the time, but Dean Smith first seriously considered retirement after the 1991 season. He later told reporters than almost every year after that, he felt so drained after the season that he was sure it would be his last. Then every fall, as preseason practice approached, he'd get excited again and start to feel energized.

"If October 15 ever comes around and I don't feel that way, that's when I'm going to retire," Smith said.

Any chance that the Tar Heel coach would step down after the 1995 season disappeared that spring when All-Americans Jerry Stackhouse and Rasheed Wallace decided to turn pro. Smith had lost underclassmen before—starting with Bob McAdoo and continuing through Worthy, Jordan, and Reid. But his previous departures had all left after their junior seasons. Stackhouse and Wallace left after their sophomore seasons, signaling a growing trend in college basketball.

The twin departures left Smith confronting another major rebuilding job. And he didn't want to dump that job on his successor. So the aging coach stayed after the 1995 Final Four run and he constructed another powerful team.

Smith's new building blocks were a trio of freshmen forwards, including prep All-Americans Antawn Jamison from Charlotte and Vince Carter from Ormond Beach, Florida. The plan was for the two young forwards to team with center Serge Zwikker and veteran guards Jeff McInnis and Dante Calabria in the starting lineup. But while Jamison stepped right in and became an immediate star, the even more highly touted Carter struggled to learn Smith's system. It was almost a replay of the Donald Williams saga: UNC fans grumbled as the obviously gifted player was relegated to a minor role, and their revered coach continued to put his system ahead of raw talent.

While Carter languished on the bench, Smith's third recruit proved to be a pleasant surprise. German native Ademola Okulaja stepped into the starting lineup and provided the defense and rebounding that Smith was looking for. Another surprise was sophomore guard Shammond Williams. When Smith signed the Greenville (S.C.) native after a year of prep school, it was widely reported that Williams was recruited merely to help recruit his first cousin, celebrated big man Kevin Garnett. That seemed credible as Williams barely played as a freshman. But such talk faded as the slim guard displayed a deft shooting touch as UNC's third guard in his second season.

Jamison would become the third freshman in ACC history to win first-team All-ACC honors. But he was not enough to carry North Carolina to its accustomed heights. The Tar Heels won twenty-one games, but the team made an embarrassingly quick exit from the ACC Tournament, being bounced in the quarterfinals by Clemson on a last-second dunk by Greg Buckner. They were then eliminated from the NCAA Tournament in the second round by Texas Tech.

Smith was again trapped by his refusal to leave his successor with a less than powerful team. And despite Jamison's obvious promise, the 1996–97 Tar Heels looked anything but powerful after losing their starting backcourt. There was another consideration that weighed on Smith as he considered his future. He had ended the 1996 season with 851 career wins, just 25 behind Adolph Rupp's all-time record of 876. "That record meant nothing to me," Smith said, joking that he'd quit when he got one win short of the record.

However, Smith was influenced by the desire of most of his former players and coaches, who believed he should stay and break the record—for them. "I received scores of letters and calls from former players who thought the record would serve as a compliment for those who had played for me," Smith said. "When put in that light, it took on a different meaning for me. They convinced me that retiring just to keep from breaking the record would be the wrong thing to do."

It didn't look like Smith would have to worry about the record as UNC opened the season slowly. The graduation of senior guard Dante Calabria and the curious decision by junior Jeff McInnis to turn pro left Smith without a returning backcourt starter. In fact, the only scholarship guards on the roster were lightly regarded junior Shammond Williams and two freshmen: Terrence Newby, who was far more coveted as a football prospect than as a basketball player; and prep All-American Ed Cota, a twenty-year-old native of Panama who had grown up in Brooklyn.

And when the Heels opened the ACC season with three straight losses, Smith's chances of catching Rupp appeared to be very slim indeed. In fact, UNC's chances of even extending Smith's string of thirty-two straight winning seasons in ACC play began to look a little shaky as the 0–3 Heels faced defeat on their home floor against N.C. State, projected to be the league's worst team.

The Wolfpack, trying to get things started for new coach Herb Sendek, owned a 56–47 lead and possession of the ball with 2:34 to play. But with the Tar Heel season teetering on the brink of extinction, Shammond Williams turned the tide. Carolina exploited the ballhandling problems of guard Ishua Benjamin, a shooting guard playing out of poisition at the point, to rally for an improbable victory. "It wasn't pretty, but it was important," Smith said.

UNC was still alive. But in a league dominated by Tim Duncan's mighty presence, how far back could the Tar Heels come? The ACC has always boasted of its balance and its competitiveness. Until the late 1960s, that meant that any of the four teams on Tobacco Road could rule the league. But with the arrival of Frank McGuire at South Carolina and Lefty Driesell at Maryland, the non-North Carolina teams became competitive too. By 1997, Rick Barnes was making national noise at Clemson, Gary Williams was building Maryland into a perennial power, Jeff Jones had enjoyed solid success at Virginia, and Bobby Cremins was a fixture at Georgia Tech. Parity had arrived.

There has never been a regular season race to match the one that unfolded that season on and off Tobacco Road in 1997. The league was supposed to be dominated by Wake Forest, which started the season No. 4 in the AP's preseason poll as 7-foot freshman Loren Woods joined Duncan to form the nation's most formidable post tandem. And the Deacons appeared to live up to the hype, opening the season with thirteen straight wins and climbing to No. 2 in the rankings. But that's when the craziness seemed to start.

It began in Winston-Salem, when Maryland visited Joel Coliseum. The Terps, using a tactic that Virginia had tried with some success in a 58–54 loss to the Deacs, elected not to double-team Duncan. Instead, the Maryland defense let the All-American big man battle center Obinna Ekezie one-on-one and concentrated on shutting down his complimentary shooters. Duncan scored twenty-six points in the slow-paced game, but the starting backcourt of Tony Rutland and Jerry Braswell combined to hit just three of twenty shots. The Terps led by seven with five minutes left—but Duncan led the Deacs back, and his two free throws tied the game at 51 with seventeen seconds left.

Maryland got the ball to Laron Profit, who launched a three-pointer as the buzzer sounded. Veteran official Dick "Froggy" Paparo raised both arms over his head to signal that the basket was good. As it turned out, replays showed that Profit's shot was late: Wake's first loss had come on a bad call.

There would be worse to come.

A month later, the Deacons were locked in a surprisingly tough game with last-place N.C. State. Rutland, who had cost Wake a win in regulation with an untimely turnover, responded with four straight points in the last minute of overtime to put the Deacs up two with 3.7 seconds left. State got the ball in-bounds to guard C.C. Harrison, who dribbled toward the top of the key and launched a shot at the buzzer. Official Mike Wood raised his arm to signal the shot a three-point attempt; when it banked in off the glass and through the basket, he raised his other arm and State celebrated its 60–59 upset.

Only it should have been double overtime. Replays showed that while this time Wood had gotten the timing right—Harrison's shot was definitely released before the buzzer sounded—he had missed the fact that the Wolfpack guard had his right foot on the three-point line when he launched the shot. For the second time in less than a month, Wake Forest was robbed—at home!

It got worse. Clemson—in the hunt for its second ACC regular season title—suffered a crucial loss to N.C. State when Frank Scagliotta, one of the best refs in the business, mistakenly called a ball out of bounds off Clemson's Terrell McIntyre. But the ball had actually been kicked out by N.C. State's Jeremy Hyatt. Those three disputed games would open the door for a surprise team to sprint through for the ACC regular season title. But even that team would need a bit of help from the ACC officials to vault past the Deacs.

THE RETURN OF THE BLUE DEVILS

Mike Krzyzewski had achieved miracles in 1996, winning eighteen games with a team that had lost two NBA lottery picks off the 13–18 team from the year before. "That was probably the best coaching job Coach K ever did," Chris Collins said.

Although Collins graduated after that season, Krzyzewski still had four starters returning in 1997, plus he was able to add two significant veterans—guard Trajan Langdon, back after missing the 1996 season with a knee injury, and 6-foot-8 Roshown McLeod, a former starter at St. John's who had practiced with the Devils for a season after transferring to Duke. In addition, Krzyzewski had added three freshmen, including McDonald's All-American Nate James, the tough son of a Marine from Maryland.

However, the key improvement in the 1997 Devils was internal: the emergence of 5-foot-10 point guard Steve Wojciechowski as a special player in his junior year. "Wojo" still wasn't a scorer, but his playmaking and defense were all that Krzyzewski could desire. The junior point guard demonstrated his new prowess in the opener against St. Joseph's when he passed out eight assists without a turnover. With Langdon returning at the top of his game (the "Alaskan Assassin" would earn first-team All-ACC honors as he hit 44% of his three-point tries), the Blue Devils would boast the ACC's best backcourt.

Problems up front would prevent Duke from taking off in the early going. Newton, the flaky Canadian who would rather get another tattoo than work on his rebounding, was ineffective in the middle. With Taymon Domzalski, the only other big man on the roster, hobbled with bad knees, Krzyzewski began to search for another solution to his weakness in the middle. Just before UNC visited Cameron for the last game of the first half of the ACC season, the Duke coach decided on a desperate gamble. He turned to 6-foot-6 freshman Chris Carrawell.

Two years before, Carrawell had been regarded as one of the best prospects in the junior class, but a series of shoulder problems had dropped him way down in the ratings. A prep teammate of Wake Forest's celebrated recruit Loren Woods, he arrived at Duke as the least heralded of Krzyzewski's three recruits, his game still limited by the brace he wore on his right shoulder.

Krzyzewski's idea was to start Carrawell ahead of Newton in an attempt to motivate his lackadaisical big man. Neither player turned out to be much of a factor against the Heels. Instead, it was Langdon and senior Jeff Capel—who actually started in a three-guard alignment—who combined for forty-seven points to help beat the Tar Heels, snapping Duke's seven-game losing streak to its hated rival.

"We wanted to win bad," Capel said. "We wanted to beat Carolina for ourselves and for our students. We felt we deserved it. We felt our students deserved it. It was huge for us. It was huge for them."

Capel would finish his Duke career with a 1–7 record against Carolina. In a strange twist to the rivalry, his younger brother Jason would sign with the Tar Heels and in his four years at Chapel Hill would compile a 1–10 record against Duke. Combined, the two Capel brothers were 2–17 in the Duke-Carolina series.

Jeff Capel's only career victory over the Tar Heels left Duke at 5–3 in the ACC and UNC at 3–5. Neither appeared to be much of a factor in the ACC race at that point as Wake Forest, Maryland, and surprising Clemson looked to be the class of the league. It wasn't until Duke visited Wake Forest on February 5 that the Blue Devils emerged as a contender for the ACC regular season title. And the key move was Krzyzewski's decision to give up on Newton and commit to a small lineup. He started three guards and two forwards: the 6-foot-8 McLeod and 6-foot-6 Carrawell against a team that was 7-foot-1, 6-foot-10, 6-foot-10 across the front line. "It was a good move," Odom said of Krzyzewski's strategy. "It was a new look, something we weren't used to. We had trouble adjusting to it."

Only Duncan was effective for the Deacs (twenty-six points) as the Blue Devils shot out to a six-point halftime lead and nursed it a through the second half. Down the stretch, Carrawell did an amazing job keeping the ball away from Duncan and forcing the Deacons to settle for perimeter shots. Duke's 73–68 victory, combined with Wake's two phantom defeats, suddenly put the Blue Devils back in the ACC title race.

It took another officiating snafu (a late-game screwup at Virginia that evoked memories of the 1972 Olympic finals in Munich) to push the Blue Devils past the slumping Deacons in the standings. But just when it appeared that Krzyzewski had done the ACC's best coaching job, he was overshadowed by the old master.

THE TAR HEEL EXPRESS
Krzyzewski saw it coming.

Moments after Duke's midseason victory over North Carolina, he told his team, "That was a great win because you beat a hell of a basketball team. I guarantee you that team isn't going to lose very often the rest of the season."

At the time, UNC was 12–6 overall, 3–5 in the ACC, and would drop to No. 20 in the next AP poll. Smith was still thirteen wins short of Rupp's record and didn't appear likely to get those wins in 1997.

But the schedule was set up to give the Heels a little momentum. Three straight homecourt wins over Middle Tennessee State, Florida State, and Virginia got the team rolling again. The surge might have ended in Raleigh; but Benjamin—the goat in Chapel Hill, when the Pack let the game slip away—committed another crucial turnover, and freshman Ed Cota hit a short jumper with seconds left to give UNC a 45–44 victory. After beating slumping Georgia Tech in Atlanta, the Tar Heels returned home and handled No. 4 Wake Forest with surprising ease. The Deacons, shaken by the bizarre officiating that plagued them and unable to find any consistent guard play, were unraveling around Duncan. "Everything is work for us right now," Odom complained. "Everything is hard."

It was starting to come easy for North Carolina. The twin keys were the emergence of Carter—finally freed from the bench and playing with the consistency that Smith demanded—and the development of Cota at the point. Carter brought explosive athleticism and a solid three-point shot to the frontcourt to balance Jamison's steady play down low. Cota, still a shaky defender and only a slightly better shooter than predecessor King Rice, was proving to be one of the most creative playmakers ever seen in the ACC.

UNC's winning streak had stretched to eight straight games when Duke visited the Smith Center for the regular season finale. The Blue Devils had already clinched the regular season title; but a victory by the Tar Heels would give UNC a second-place tie with Wake Forest and make a major statement headed into postseason play. It would also leave Smith just five wins short of breaking Rupp's record.

North Carolina, getting thirty-three points from Jamison and an amazing 49–18 advantage on the boards, withstood a blizzard of three-pointers by the Devils. Duke, hitting seventeen of thirty-four three-point tries, couldn't get any closer than four points in the final minutes, allowing the Heels to celebrate a 91–85 victory.

Smith was four wins short of Rupp.

Krzyzewski infuriated the Tar Heel nation with his postgame comments, when he downplayed the loss—suggesting that because his team had already clinched the regular season title, his players weren't emotionally "up" for the game. Not up for Duke-Carolina?

So, they wondered, what was his excuse five days later, when the top-seeded Blue Devils were upset by N.C. State in the ACC Tournament quarterfinals?

"They beat us, pure and simple," Krzyzewski told the press. "They were better than us today. Period."

The truth was that Duke had shot its bolt. The Devils, playing small and up-tempo with a very thin team, never regained their legs in March—a fatal flaw for a team that relied on quickness and jump-shooting. After being sent to Charlotte for the NCAA Tournament, the Blue Devils made a quick exit. Duke managed a lackluster opening win over Murray State but was bounced in the second round by hot-shooting Providence, coached by future Virginia coach Pete Gillen.

It was almost as if, after a season of balance and controversy, everybody was getting out of the way to clear the path for Dean Smith's triumphant march to the ultimate coaching record. Duke was gone—and Wake Forest was soon to follow.

The Deacons weren't the same team in March: they were not the same team that started the season ranked so high. Duncan was still the best player in the league—indeed, the best in all of college basketball; but the team was collapsing around him. The guards had no confidence, the self-critical Woods was on the verge of a nervous breakdown, and the talented Ricardo Peral was just a shell of the player he had once been. "I swear," Odom said. "Our perimeter guys are like gunfighters who lost a fight somewhere and can't get their confidence back."

With no support for Duncan, Wake's last chance to capitalize on Odom's great recruiting bonanza fizzled quickly. The Deacons collapsed against North Carolina in the ACC Tournament semifinals; then they couldn't cope with Stanford's physical defensive style in the second round of the NCAA Tournament. Duncan would sweep every national player of the year award and would be drafted No. 1 in the NBA draft. But he would never play in a Final Four.

Dean Smith, who had grumbled after his team's less-than-impressive victory over Virginia in the quarterfinals, was ecstatic after his team's tournament victory over the Deacons, his team's eleventh straight win. "We played awfully well," he said. "I didn't know that we could play that well."

Smith was now just two wins short of tying Rupp. He insisted that he wasn't counting—but everybody else was. "My job is to talk about this year's team," he told the media. "Your job, I guess, is to ask a distracting question. The only win I'm worried about is the next one."

Smith earned victory No. 875 on Sunday afternoon, beating surprising N.C. State, which had fought its way from the play-in game to the title game, thanks to another strong game from Shammond Williams. The once unheralded recruit scored sixty points in the three tournament games to win the Case Award as the tourney MVP.

Smith once again tried to deflect the postgame questions about Rupp's record, which was now just one game away, by talking about Williams's unexpected emergence as an ACC star.

"I haven't won a single game," he said. "Players win games, not coaches."

But the only way the Tar Heel coach could have avoided the media circus that would engulf his team as he pursued the record would have been to follow up on his joking promise the previous summer: he could have quit after winning his thirteenth ACC Tournament title (no one else had more than four).

Obviously, Smith wasn't going to bail on a team that might give him his third NCAA title. The Tar Heels, seeded No. 1 in the East, were sent to Winston-Salem's Lawrence Joel Coliseum for the two games that would vault UNC's coach past Kentucky's legend.

CBS, which now televised all of the NCAA Tournament action, looked ahead to a potential second-round matchup between North Carolina and Indiana and scheduled that game for a nationwide feed at noon on Saturday. That way, the entire college basketball world could see Smith break the record against Indiana's Bobby Knight—a good friend of Smith's who was the active coach with the best chance of eventually contending for the record himself someday.

However, the dream matchup had to survive two first-round games on Thursday night. North Carolina (as tight as top-seeded Duke had been against Mississippi Valley State eleven years earlier) trailed No. 16 seed Fairfield University by seven points at the half. UNC rallied in the final twenty minutes behind twenty-two points by Carter and ten assists by Cota—but that didn't put the Stags away until the final minute of the 82–74 victory.

Smith was at 876 wins, exactly matching Rupp's record victory total.

Indiana was not as lucky as the Tar Heels were. Knight's Hoosiers were blown out by Colorado, turning CBS's Saturday NCAA opener into a one-sided coaching affair. Maybe that was for the best. The historic moment was drama enough and a thrilling game would have detracted from it. Dozens of Smith's former players arrived to be on hand when their mentor became the winningest coach of all time.

"I don't know where they all got tickets," Smith said, genuinely touched by the outpouring of affection. "It was so much fun to see them in the hallway. That is a special time as any teacher knows when a former pupil comes back. That was special."

The Tar Heels generated some unnecessary drama with another slow start, but a 30–8 spurt early in the second half blew the game open and allowed the celebration to begin long before the buzzer sounded on UNC's 73–56 victory.

"Dean Smith is the finest coach ever, the best coach to ever coach the college game," Wake's Dave Odom said. "He should have this record. And it is a record that belongs in the ACC and in the state of North Carolina. That record ought to be resting in this state somewhere."

It would have been a Hollywood ending if the Tar Heels could have followed Smith's record-breaking moment with a run to the national title. But an old bugaboo—poor shooting at the Final Four—cropped up to kill UNC's chances in the NCAA semifinals against Arizona. Shammond Williams, so good throughout UNC's postseason run, missed twelve of thirteen shots as the Tar Heels blew an early eleven-point lead.

"I told the players they'd had a great year and I meant it," Smith said. "I would have liked to have had the year last one more game and see what happened."

The ending was disappointing. But after reviving a team that had seemed dead at midseason and driving them to the Final Four, shattering Rupp's record in the process, Smith had obviously completed one of his best coaching jobs. And, as the Tar Heels returned from Indianapolis, no one could have suspected that the winningest coach in college basketball history had coached his last game.

18

GUT VERSUS K

DEAN SMITH WENT ABOUT HIS BUSINESS IN THE SUMMER AND early fall of 1997, waiting for the approach of preseason practice to restore his energy and enthusiasm.

The off-season actually went very well for the Tar Heels. Both Antawn Jamison and Vince Carter were returning, along with classmate Ademola Oku-laja. Starters Ed Cota and Shammond Williams were back in the backcourt. To that solid core would be added a couple of premier recruits: 7-foot big man Brendan Haywood from Greensboro and Max Owens, a 6-foot-4 guard from Macon, Georgia, who was one of the first products of Mt. Zion Christian Academy, a new prep basketball factory in Durham.

As if that wasn't enough evidence to prove that Smith's program was in great shape, the Tar Heels already had verbal commitments from two prime prospects from the Class of 1998: 6-foot-9 power forward Kris Lang of Gasto-nia (N.C.) and 6-foot-8 Jason Capel of Cheseapeake (Va.), the younger brother of former Duke standout Jeff Capel.

If there was ever a time for Smith to hand over a thriving program to his suc-cessor, it was in the fall of 1997. UNC executed a perfect handoff from Smith to his successor on the afternoon of October 9, 1997. More than a hundred re-porters, including almost every top basketball writer in the country, gathered in the Skipper Bowles Room next to the Smith Center to witness the transition.

"Every year for the past eight years, I've been saying maybe it's time to do something else," Smith told the media throng. "I enjoy basketball. I enjoy coaching basketball. It's the out-of-season things that I haven't been able to handle very well."

As soon as Smith finished speaking, Athletic Director Dick Baddour turned to his left and pointed to Bill Guthridge, announcing that Smith's long-time assistant would take over the job. The sixty-two-year-old Kansas native admitted that he had long planned to retire when Smith did. "I always said my goal was to go out when he did, [but] I am not ready to go," he said.

In many ways, the scene resembled the press conference in 1961, when Frank McGuire handed the program to Smith. Once again, there was far more focus on the departing coach than on the apparently unremarkable successor.

But Guthridge was a far more interesting character than many in the audience that day had suspected. Although he would come to be portrayed as a genial, grandfatherly figure characterized by his nickname, "Coach Gut," long-time Tar Heel observers understood that he was a passionate man. That passion was best characterized by his angry confrontation with referee Pete Pavia after the 1991 Final Four loss to Kansas.

Guthridge didn't have much reason to display his wild side as North Carolina opened the 1997–98 season in spectacular fashion. The Tar Heels beat No. 7 UCLA and No. 6 Purdue to win the Great Alaskan Shootout. On the way home, they knocked off Louisville in Chicago's United Center.

Guthridge quickly developed a six-man rotation that featured his five returning regulars from Smith's last team (Jamison, Carter, Cota, Williams, and Okulaja) and senior big man Makhtar Ndiaye. The Senegalese product was the same player who had gotten Wake Forest's Dave Odom in trouble four years before. He had transferred to Michigan and played there for two years before returning to UNC. Although he played little for the Tar Heels in 1997, he was one of the six regulars for Guthridge's first team.

THE CLASH OF TITANS

While North Carolina was rolling to seventeen straight victories to open the season, eight miles away, Mike Krzyzewski was fine-tuning another Duke powerhouse.

The four returning starters off Coach K's undersized 1997 ACC regular season champs had been reinforced by a four-man recruiting class that was being heralded as the most talented group ever seen on Tobacco Road. It included three frontcourt players picked by one recruiting service or another as the nation's best prospect: 6-foot-9 New York power forward Elton Brand, 6-foot-11 California center Chris Burgess, and 6-foot-8 Michigan forward Shane Battier. The fourth member of the class was 6-foot-2 Georgia guard William Avery.

Avery, who had overcome some major academic problems to qualify, soon found a role as the team's third guard behind Wojciechowski and Langdon. But the three freshman big men were the ones who made the difference as Duke got off to a fast start, winning nine straight games to open the season—including an upset of No. 1 Arizona in Hawaii.

Duke was 10–1 when Brand, the best of the freshmen, suffered a broken foot in practice. But Roshown McLeod, who had struggled early as the freshmen had enjoyed the limelight, stepped into Brand's spot and began to play at a very high level. Duke reeled off eleven straight wins after a narrow loss at Michigan and took a 20–1 record and a No. 1 ranking into Chapel Hill on the night of February 5. With UNC at 22–1 (losing only in overtime at Maryland) and ranked No. 2, the game marked the second time on Tobacco Road the two old rivals had met as the nation's two top-ranked teams. "It's going to be the rumble in the jungle," UNC's Ndiaye proclaimed.

Actually, the game turned out to be a disappointment. UNC scored twelve straight points late in the first half and built a sixteen-point halftime lead. The margin hit twenty before Ndiaye almost single-handedly got Duke back in the game. Called for his fifth personal foul, the senior center screamed in anger at official Curtis Shaw. The referee whistled Ndiaye for a technical foul—technically his sixth foul of the game—and Duke, given four free throws and possession, were able to score six straight points. The inspired Blue Devils trimmed UNC's lead to 73–69, but the Tar Heels responded by scoring eighteen straight points to win going away, 97–73.

In a sense, No. 1 Duke was blown out twice in one game. "Once they get on a run, they're hard to stop," Wojciechowski said. "They just kept pouring it on. They beat on us."

North Carolina took over the No. 1 spot in the national standings and held it until N.C. State visited Chapel Hill and pulled off one of the most remarkable upsets in their long rivalry. Senior guard C.C. Harrison hit eight of nine three-point tries and scored thirty-one points as the unranked Pack scored an 86–72 victory.

"N.C. State played a perfect game," UNC's Jamison said. "What else can you say? Usually, an N.C. State team will get rattled and they get all turned around. This time they played with a lot of confidence."

UNC's loss to N.C. State sent Duke back into the top spot in the national rankings. The Blue Devils celebrated with a 120–84 Sunday afternoon massacre of No. 12 ranked UCLA in front of the largest media contingent ever to cover a Duke game.

Many of the reporters were there to cover the unexpected return of Elton Brand, who was back in uniform after missing two months and fifteen games. He wasn't in the starting lineup, but the young big man came off the bench to score sixteen points in fourteen minutes. Brand was expected to be a huge factor the final Saturday of the regular season, when No. 3 North Carolina came to Cameron.

It was a mild, sunny day outside, and Cameron, without air-conditioning, was sweltering even before the tipoff. The Cameron Crazies were stunned by North Carolina's performance in the first half. It was Makhtar Ndiaye's turn in the alphabetical rotation to come off the bench and the five holdovers from 1997 didn't appear to miss him. Jamison—on his way to a twenty-three-point, thirteen-rebound effort—was tearing Duke up inside as UNC took a 42–30 halftime lead. The Tar Heels stretched their advantage to 64–37 with just over eleven minutes left.

Nothing Coach K said or did changed the momentum of the game. Instead, it was Brand who brought the Devils back. "Elton was the X-factor," Duke's Chris Carrawell said. "We got the ball to him almost every time down."

Ndiaye, futilely trying to defend the freshman big man, fouled out with nearly ten minutes to play. At least this time he got to the bench without drawing a technical. Neither Jamison nor Okulaja could handle Duke's 270-pound freshman down low, and when Guthridge turned to the 7-foot, 255-pound Haywood, Brand abused his inexperienced opponent.

Cameron began to roar as Duke cut into the Carolina lead. As the Tar Heel defense sagged in to stop Brand in the post, McLeod and Langdon began to hit from outside. Carrawell, converting his only basket of the day, scored on a drive to tie the game with exactly two minutes left. After Vince Carter threw the ball away at the other end, McLeod blew past the exhausted Jamison to score the go-ahead points.

Carolina, down for the first time all day, got the ball to Cota, who drove for the basket and was fouled with 3.8 seconds left. Two free throws would tie the game. But Cota, an 82.4% free throw shooter that season, missed the first free throw. With UNC still down two, he had to miss the second on purpose.

Amazingly, Haywood stole the rebound from a flatfooted Brand. As the freshman tried to follow, he was fouled by Duke's weary freshman big man. Once again a Tar Heel was going to the line with a chance to tie the game. However, Haywood also clanked his first try and had to attempt the same intentional miss as Cota had tried. This time, the buzzer sounded while the two teams were scrambling for the ball, giving Duke a 77–75 victory.

The TV cameras caught Steve Wojciechowski as he raced across the floor to hug Krzyzewski. The senior guard had scored just one point against the Tar Heels; but he had passed out eleven assists and committed just one turnover, while limiting Cota, his opposite number, to six points and five turnovers.

"I'll take my point guard through any alley, any dark street," Krzyzewski said. "I'm not saying he's the most talented guy out there, but he's remarkable. He wouldn't let us lose."

Guthridge might have been more inclined to credit the victory to Brand, who had fourteen of his sixteen points in the second half, or McLeod, who had twenty-three points and hit three of four three-pointers. It was just the third loss of Guthridge's short coaching career.

But there's one advantage to losing the final game of the season: there's always a chance for redemption. Eight days after the bitter loss in Cameron, Carolina took its revenge in the ACC title game at the Greensboro Coliseum. For thirty minutes, the title game followed a familiar path: UNC scored twelve straight points late in the first half to take command, but Duke fought back and forged a 57-all tie with eleven minutes to play. At that point, UNC wrote a new script, scoring thirteen straight points to seize command again. Jamison, who was considered questionable at gametime due to a pulled groin muscle, went thirty-six minutes and led the Heels with twenty-two points and eighteen rebounds.

"This is still Dean's team," Guthridge told the media after the net-cutting ceremonies. "He recruited them all and taught them all how to play basketball as a team. It's his system."

One of his players disagreed.

"We know this is Coach Gut's team," Cota told reporters. "He doesn't want to take any of the credit, but this is his team."

Guthridge joined Duke's Vic Bubas as the only two coaches to claim league titles in their first seasons as an ACC head coach. He would finish his first season with more wins than any first-year coach in the history of Tobacco Road.

He was 2–1 in his duel with Krzyzewski, but the season was not over and there was still a chance for his Duke rival to claim the ultimate trump card in postseason play.

OUR NATURAL REGION

Mike Krzyzewski was not a happy man as he met with the media on Monday, following the ACC championship game and the announcement that night of the NCAA Tournament pairings.

In the first place, he was angry about the behavior of several Carolina players in the wake of their title game victory the day before. Krzyzewski, meeting with the media after the game, didn't see what happened; but his wife and three daughters, seated just behind press row, let him know how the Tar Heels celebrated. The worst offender was Ndiaye, who hopped on the scorer's table right in front of the Krzyzewski women and began taunting them by pounding his chest, as if he were stabbing himself with a dagger.

"Certainly people should celebrate," Krzyzewski told reporters. "You should do it with your own fans. I don't think you should jump up on the scorer's table and yell at opposing fans. I don't think you can put a dagger in the heart of opposing fans. I don't think those things are healthy. They can incite a riot."

Krzyzewski was also angry about the pairings. Duke was seeded No. 1 in the Southeast Regional, needing to win two games in Lexington (Ky.) and two games in St. Petersburg (Fla.) to reach the Final Four in San Antonio. Krzyzewski thought Duke deserved the No. 1 seed in the East Region. His words evoked eerie echoes of Dean Smith's whining about the NCAA pairings in the late 1980s. The Tar Heel coach had been the first to bring up the term "our natural region" after being sent to the Southeast instead of the East after beating Duke in the 1989 ACC Tournament.

As it turned out, Duke did indeed face a hostile reception in Lexington, although it's hard tell how much of that was generated by Krzyzewski's well-publicized words and how much was due to the simple fact that hometown Kentucky was the No. 2 seed in the Southeast and would need to get past Duke to reach the Final Four. For whatever reason, thousands of Wildcat fans turned out for the open practices before Friday's first round and showered the Blue Devils with a mixture of boos and profanity.

The hostility didn't impact the games as Duke easily disposed of Radford in the first round, then held off Oklahoma State on Sunday to earn a trip to the Sweet 16. The Blue Devils seemed on their way to San Antonio when they opened with an easy victory over Syracuse in the regional semifinals, then built a seventeen-point second-half lead on Kentucky in the finals. But Kentucky rallied as Duke went cold from the floor and the foul line. The Wildcats erased the Blue Devil lead and pulled out an 86–84 victory.

"This was a great basketball game," Krzyzewski said. "It was a game that was won—like the '92 game—not one that was lost. I don't think we did things bad. They just did things great."

North Carolina's path through the East Regionals didn't turn out to be a breeze either. After the Tar Heels took care of Navy in the first round, they found themselves fighting for their lives before pulling out an overtime victory over UNC Charlotte. North Carolina returned to Greensboro after the narrow victory and, backed by the loud, partisan fans at the familiar coliseum on Battleground Avenue, knocked off Michigan State and Connecticut—two young teams that were a year away from the Final Four.

For Williams, the memory of his 1-for-13 nightmare from the 1997 Final Four still haunting him, the return ticket to the Final Four was a chance at redemption.

"I felt bad that I did not help my team last year, that I didn't come through for them," the senior guard said. "I basically made a vow to myself that I was going to try and do the best I could to help us get in this position again. Lo and behold, and by the grace of God, here we are. Hopefully, we can make the best out of it this time."

North Carolina arrived in San Antonio as the prohibitive favorite to not only knock off West champion Utah in the semifinals, but to claim its second national title in the decade. And when Kentucky edged Stanford in overtime to win Saturday's first semifinal, media and fans began drooling at the potential championship game matchup between college basketball's two winningest programs.

Only it didn't happen. North Carolina, bitten by the shooting bug for the fourth time in five Final Four appearances in the 1990s, hit just three of twenty-three three-pointers and trailed the Utes all the way in a 65–59 loss. Williams followed his 1-for-13 Final Four effort in 1997 with a 2-for-12 game against Utah.

"Every shot I shot, I thought was on the mark," Williams said. "Every shot I hit dead center on the rim or the back of the rim and came out."

Questions about North Carolina's shooting woes took a backseat to the postgame uproar caused by Makhtar Ndiaye. Utah freshman Britton Johnsen had complained that Ndiaye had spit on him during the game. When confronted by the accusation, the well-traveled Senegalese center told reporters that Johnson had called him "a nigger."

Utah coach Rick Majerus went ballistic. At a press conference the next day, he not only denied that his player had used the racial epithet, he offered to fly Johnson to North Carolina to take a lie detector test. "If he's lying, I'll resign on the spot," Majerus said.

Back in Chapel Hill, Guthridge met with Ndiaye and afterward, the school issued a statement from Ndiaye in which he apologized and admitted that his accusation was false. That was bad enough. But two months later, Ndiaye was charged with assault for an altercation after a minor traffic accident; on the stand in that trial, he testified he had nothing to do with that statement and said it had been put out without consulting him! The ugly incident wrote a nasty end to a great season for the Tar Heels and their sixty-two-year-old rookie head coach.

K BACK ON TOP

At least Bill Guthridge didn't have worry about Ndiaye's antics the next season. The well-traveled big man, who managed to alienate three of the four Tobacco Road schools during his tenure (making him the anti-Bones McKinney in our story?), was gone—along with Shammond Williams, the gutsy little guard who had given UNC so much, except in Final Four play.

The early departures of Antawn Jamison and Vince Carter made Guthridge's second season even more difficult. Their decision to turn pro was hardly a surprise. Jamison, the unanimous national player of the year as a junior, was the fourth player taken in the NBA draft, while Carter, a second-team All-American as a junior, was taken fifth. But even with three starters gone from UNC's 32–4 team, the talent still appeared to be flowing into Chapel Hill.

The Heels would spend the entire season ranked in the top fifteen, would win twenty-four games, reach the ACC Tournament finals, and sweep rivals N.C. State and Wake Forest. Anywhere else, that would be a great season—but not on Tobacco Road, not in a year when neighboring Duke was enjoying one of the great seasons in ACC basketball history. Krzyzewski's post-1995 rebuilding effort came to fruition as Duke achieved a dominance over the ACC that had never been seen before, and has not been seen since.

The Blue Devils actually started fairly slowly as Krzyzewski moved to replace graduated starters Steve Wojciechowski and Roshown McLeod. But he had William Avery prepared to take over Wojo's point guard duties and junior Chris Carrawell, his bum shoulder corrected by surgery, slid into McLeod's forward spot alongside Brand and Battier. Fifth-year senior Trajan Langdon provided the outside firepower, while 6-foot-6 freshman Corey Maggette, a Chicago native whose athleticism evoked comparisons with Michael Jordan, fit right in as the sixth man. Former starters Nate James, Chris Burgess, and Taymon Domzalski made Duke's depth the envy of the league.

"Domzalski can't even get off the bench for them," Virginia coach Pete Gillen complained. "If he was at Virginia, we'd build a statue to him, right beside Thomas Jefferson."

As ACC play started, there was no stopping Duke's express. The Blue Devils didn't just beat their opponents, they annihilated them, usually by halftime. The stampede started in College Park, where the No. 4 ranked Terps were lying in wait, convinced that super guard Stevie Francis and company had the firepower to dismantle the Devils.

"Duke has never seen a team as quick as this Maryland team," a Baltimore radio man told his audience just before tipoff.

Two hours later, he was describing Duke's 82–64 victory in somber terms. The rematch in Durham was decided by the same margin as Battier, inspired by a documentary on the Shaolin monks, exploded for a career high twenty-seven points.

Duke turned the ACC regular season race into a joke, winning fifteen of sixteen games by double figures. North Carolina put up as good a battle as anybody before losing 89–77 in Durham. But when the two teams met again in Chapel Hill, it was ugly. Duke, playing without injured starter Shane Battier, broke open a close game at the half and hammered the Tar Heels 81–61, which was UNC's worst loss ever in the Smith Center and the worst at home since a 1975 loss to Maryland in Carmichael.

Of course, many times in the Duke-Carolina rivalry, one team would suffer a bad beat in the regular season finale and redeem it with a win in the tournament. North Carolina, playing its best basketball of the season, put itself in position to do that by upsetting No. 5 Maryland in the ACC semifinals. Duke had to play without guard Trajan Langdon, who was nursing an ankle injury. But even with that edge, the Tar Heels lost even worse than in Chapel Hill, 96–73 this time.

Afterward, Ed Cota gave reporters a laugh when he shrugged off William Avery's twenty-nine-point performance in the championship game. "He's not that hard to guard," Cota insisted.

Guthridge, in his second year, had clearly fallen behind in his competition with Krzyzewski. That didn't sit too well with Tar Heel fans spoiled by Dean Smith's decades of consistent excellence. The mood in Chapel Hill grew even more somber when UNC traveled to Seattle and bombed against Weber State, the school's first-ever loss in the NCAA round of 64. Harold "The Show" Arceneaux poured in thirty-six points, while UNC's Haywood managed one point and no rebounds against 6-foot-7 Andy Jensen, who was described by the Carolina big man as, "like the dirty old man at the YMCA."

The Tar Heel humiliation delighted Blue Devil fans, who were enjoying their own cakewalk through the East Regionals. Duke blew through two opponents in Charlotte, leaving dazzled Tulsa coach Bill Self raving about the team that had routed his 97–56. "They wanted to send a message," Self said. "The message is, There's a runaway freight train coming—get out of the way!"

Southwest Missouri State and Temple were standing on the tracks in the Meadowlands. The Blue Devils ran both teams over with relative ease. In fact, the only trouble Duke encountered in the familiar New Jersey arena was the growing media speculation about the future of Krzyzewski's star-studded team.

In an era when top college programs were routinely ravaged by early defections to the NBA, Krzyzewski's Duke dynasty had remained strangely untouched. Danny Ferry, the son of an NBA general manager, had come very close to turning pro after winning ACC Player of the Year honors as a junior in 1988; but his NBA deliberations received almost no attention at the time. Christian Laettner squelched all speculation very early when he had a chance to jump after leading Duke to the 1991 national title. Grant Hill turned down the chance to leave early after his injury-plagued 1993 season.

How much longer could Krzyzewski remain unscathed by the NBA plague?

Most of the speculation in New Jersey centered around Brand, who handled the situation with poise, answering the inevitable questions about his future by explaining that he'd make that decision after the season. But there was another pro intrusion into Duke's title drive that weekend. On the morning of the Temple game, Chicago columnist Sam Smith wrote an article suggesting that if every college player in the country was available in the draft, Duke freshman Corey Maggette would be the first player taken. Maggette, who wasn't even starting for Duke at the time, laughed the article off when asked about it by reporters. But it later became clear that Smith's article had a huge influence on his thinking.

In fact, Brand and Maggette weren't the only Duke players thinking about the NBA, which may have had something to do with what happened the next weekend in St. Petersburg, Florida. The 1999 Final Four was played in the same Tropicana Arena that had proved such bad luck for the Blue Devils in the 1998 Southeast Regional title game. It would once again bedevil the Devils.

Duke, which had won its first two NCAA games by an average of forty-one points and its second two NCAA games by an average of nineteen points, barely squeaked by Michigan State, 68–62, in the semifinals, thanks to eighteen points and fifteen rebounds by Elton Brand.

The championship game matched Duke against a strong team from Connecticut, which had battled the Blue Devils for the No.1 ranking all season. In fact, the Huskies had spent more weeks atop the poll than Duke, although the Blue Devils were a solid favorite in the pregame betting line.

"Clearly what they've done—not only the quantity of their wins, but also the quality of their wins—they've established themselves as the dominant team," UConn coach Jim Calhoun said. "They've proven beyond a reasonable doubt that they're the best team. They've had the best season."

But Duke sophomore Shane Battier was uncomfortable with all the accolades. "We can't even start to talk about our place until we win the national championship," he said.

He was right to be cautious. UConn dueled Duke on even terms throughout the first half of the title game, collapsing its defense to keep Brand under control. The Blue Devil star managed to score fifteen points on the night, but he didn't do a good job of passing out of the double team. Langdon, the one senior in the Duke lineup, was the team's only consistent offensive threat. The inability of Duke's other offensive weapons to catch fire explains why, with the game on the line, Krzyzewski asked Langdon to try and create the winning play one-on-one.

"Absolutely, positively, absolutely—I want Trajan Langdon to take that shot," Krzyzewski said. "Win or lose with Trajan Langdon. It's a set we've run a number of times and most of the time it's successful. Tonight it wasn't."

Duke was trailing 75–74 when Langdon brought the ball up against UConn defensive ace Ricky Moore. But when the Alaskan Assassin tried to make his move, he was whistled for traveling. It was the end of Duke's hopes as UConn hit two free throws to clinch a 77–74 victory.

Afterwards, Krzyzewski wrapped his arms around a distraught Will Avery, who was in tears having lost his head-to-head matchup with former prep teammate Ricky Moore.

"I have a hard time being sad," Krzyzewski said in the postgame press conference. "I'm sorry, I don't coach for winning. I coach for relationships. I've got the best. These kids have been an amazing group of kids and they've had a sensational year."

There are not many years when a 37–2 record—the best in Duke history—and a runner-up finish in the NCAA Tournament would be considered a disappointment. But the 1999 Blue Devils were so good, so dominant, that the title game loss to a very good UConn team left the Duke nation feeling curiously unfulfilled. And their disappointment was not unreasonable: one more win and Duke's 1999 team would have been ranked as one of the best teams, maybe *the* best team, ever seen on Tobacco Road. No team, neither UNC in 1957 nor N.C. State in 1973–74, ever dominated the ACC the way Duke did in 1999. The only difference is those great teams won the national title. Duke's most talented team came up one game—one play—short.

The disappointment got even worse after the season as Duke was suddenly struck by the NBA plague. After years of immunity to early defections, that spring the Blue Devils suffered the worst single-season early-entry losses in NCAA history. It started, as expected, with Brand, who had swept the national player of the year awards. He sat on a podium with Krzyzewski two weeks after the UConn loss and, with his the blessing of his coaches, announced he was entering the draft.

"It's obvious that Elton is making the right decision for everybody involved," Krzyzewski said. "I could not be more happy about this."

The Duke coach wasn't quite as happy a week later, when sophomore William Avery announced that he was also turning pro. There was no press conference this time, no kind words from Krzyzewski for the player he had comforted in the wake of the title game loss. Duke was still reeling from Avery's decision when sophomore center Chris Burgess announced that he was transferring to Utah. Once regarded as a surefire pro, the gifted but erratic big man could never find a role to play at Duke. He was more notable around the league for his horrific free throw shooting (43.5%) than for his scoring or rebounding.

That wasn't the end of Duke's spring misery. Maggette—influenced by Smith's column and angry over his lack of playing time in the title game—elected to jump to the NBA, despite the advice of his hero Michael Jordan, who told the young Blue Devil standout to stay in school.

Draft night at the MCI Center in Washington, D.C. turned out to be a Duke-fest. The Bulls used the first pick in the draft to take Brand. Cleveland took senior guard Trajan Langdon at No. 11. Maggette finally went to Seattle at No. 13 (he was promptly traded to Orlando) and Avery was picked No. 14 by Minnesota. No college team had ever had four players taken in the top fourteen picks of the draft.

Duke's lineup was officially devastated. Only three of the 1999 team's top nine players would return the next season: two role players and a little-used sub.

The ABD Club could breathe a sigh of relief. Not only had the most talented Blue Devil team in the Krzyzewski era failed to win it all, the NBA had finally brought Krzyzewski's program back to the pack. For Carolina fans unhappy with Guthridge's performance against Duke, the opportunity was there to reclaim control of Tobacco Road.

19

REBUILDING A CHAMPION

Mike Krzyzewski was flat on his back in the spring of 1999 when he received three visitors to his home. The Duke coach was laid up after hip replacement surgery, left alone to contemplate the apparent ruin of his program, when Shane Battier, Chris Carrawell, and Nate James—the only returning players from Duke's 1999 team—stopped by to cheer up the depressed coach.

"We decided to go over to Coach while he was recuperating, just to give him our vote of confidence—to tell him the kingdom was not falling," Battier said. "We told him, 'You have three pillars who are going to be warriors and will fight to the end to maintain Duke basketball.'"

Krzyzewski liked what he heard from his veterans. He knew they were a talented trio, even if that didn't show up in the stats. Battier was a two-year starter who had concentrated on defense and rebounding in his first two seasons. Coach K loved Carrawell's toughness and his willingness to do whatever the team needed most—be it defense, rebounding, playmaking, or occasionally scoring. James, a powerfully built 6-foot-5 swing man, had struggled with injuries in his first three seasons at Duke. In fact, he had missed almost all of the 1998 season, receiving a medical hardship year after playing in just six games.

That was the foundation. Luckily, Krzyzewski had recruited another monster class to fill in the gaps—his second No. 1 rated recruiting class in three years. The prize was 6-foot-2 Jason Williams, a muscular point guard from Plainfield, New Jersey, who had grown up hoping to play for North Carolina.

"I was a big Dean Smith fan," Williams told Dick Weiss. "I loved North Carolina. I had North Carolina shorts, the jersey, everything. I had a picture of Michael Jordan on the wall in my bedroom. But there was no real interest from North Carolina. I went there on an unofficial visit and met Bill Guthridge. I was excited. Then Guthridge told me, 'We think you're a really good player but we don't think you can fit into the North Carolina system.'"

That proved to be a huge recruiting mistake for the Tar Heels—as big as Smith's mistake in holding off Bobby Hurley in an attempt to get Kenny Anderson. Williams would team with fellow freshmen Carlos Boozer, a big man from Alaska, and Mike Dunleavy, the 6-foot-9 son of NBA coach Mike Dunleavey, Sr., to form the nucleus of Duke's 2001 national championship team.

The 2000 season didn't get off to a great start for the rebuilt Blue Devils. Boozer, who was expected to start in the middle, broke his foot in a preseason pickup game. He was just returning to action when Duke opened the season in New York, losing two heartbreaking games to Stanford and Connecticut. Duke had not started 0–2 since the 1958–59 season. But the twin defeats didn't deflate the young Devils. Instead, an emotional outburst by Carrawell sparked the remarkable run that was to follow.

"The reason we're so tough is that we lost those two games in New York," Carrawell said. "The feeling we had coming back from New York, I've never had that feeling before. We had to question ourselves and the question I asked was, 'Do we want to be a mediocre team or like past Duke teams? Remember New York'—that's been my motto."

Duke took Carrawell's words to heart, winning eighteen straight games after its return from New York. Williams emerged as an electric scorer and a dangerous, if erratic, playmaker, several times flirting with double-figure assists and turnovers in the same game. Dunleavy, whose father had played for Frank McGuire at South Carolina, was developing into a versatile all-around player. And as Boozer worked his way back into shape, he began to mimic Brand's powerful presence down low.

Still, the key to Duke's surprising surge were the three holdovers, especially Carrawell and Battier, who had transformed themselves from role players into stars. The 6-foot-6 Carrawell emerged as a special player: he simply would not let Duke lose. He would be content to score thirteen points in a romp over Davidson, but when the team was struggling in its ACC opener at Virginia, the senior swing man poured in twenty-five points and added three blocked shots as the Devils pulled out a 109–100 victory in overtime.

"He's a great player . . . he's a competitor," Virginia coach Pete Gillen said of Carrawell. "He gives them toughness and he's helped their young players come along quickly."

Unlike the year before, when Duke overpowered the league, the new Blue Devils were barely winning game after game. When N.C. State came to Durham, it took a controversial palming call on Justin Gainey and an overtime to produce a four-point win. It took an improbable banked three-pointer from freshman Nick Horvath to force an overtime against DePaul and save another narrow win.

Somehow, Duke had won sixteen straight games when the Blue Devils traveled to Chapel Hill for the matchup with their biggest rivals. They found a dispirited Carolina team, just coming off a four-game losing streak that had seen the team roundly booed by its own fans during a loss to UCLA.

The Tar Heels should have been better in 2000 with a veteran team missing only Okulaja from Guthridge's twenty-four-win team in 1999. Freshman Joe Forte, an explosive offensive wing player from Greenbelt (Md.), filled that gap nicely and was averaging almost seventeen points a game for the Tar Heels. UNC still had Haywood, Kris Lang, and slender 6-foot-10 forward Brian Bersticker down low, plus an addition from the Tar Heel football team: All-American defensive end Julius Peppers, a 6-foot-7, 260-pound monster who played with surprising grace on the court.

Still, it was the backcourt of Cota and Forte who combined for forty-one points and helped UNC erase a nineteen-point second-half deficit to force overtime when Duke visited the Smith Center. The Blue Devils answered with forty-eight points from Carrawell and Battier. But in overtime, freshman Jason Williams made the decisive plays—putting the Devils up with a driving layup, feeding Boozer for a dunk, then hitting a wide-open Battier for a three-pointer that clinched the 90–86 victory.

"We all look at overtime like, 'Now it's time to go,'" Williams said. "When you look in Shane's eyes or Chris's eyes, you can see they have an urgency to win. I think their leadership pulled us through."

The UNC win marked the emerging strength of Jason Williams. It was becoming clear that even on nights when he was not playing well, the freshman guard displayed the ability to step up late and make big plays. He did it at Virginia, when he missed thirteen of his first seventeen shots, then hit the clinching three-pointer. He did it at UNC, where he shot poorly but still made the game-winning plays in overtime. It was a quality that he would display in even more spectacular fashion later in his career.

"I think Jason willed more games late than any player since Christian Laettner," Duke assistant coach Johnny Dawkins said. "He had the uncanny ability to go on to the next thing."

Was North Carolina ready to go on to the next thing? Guthridge, so popular in his first season as head coach, was hearing the rumbles from a fan base that thought basketball success was its birthright. The overtime loss to Duke dropped UNC to 13–9 and unlike 1997, there would be no dramatic February turnaround. As the hated Blue Devils were rolling toward a fourth straight ACC regular season title, the Tar Heels were scrambling to qualify for the NCAA Tournament. It wasn't a sure thing when UNC finished 18–12, then fell flat in the ACC Tournament opener against Wake Forest. "We're on the bubble and that's really strange," guard Max Owens said.

There was some controversy when UNC got an at-large bid, while Virginia was left out of the field. The Cavs had a better overall record and had beaten UNC twice head-to-head. But the committee decided that the Tar Heels were a more dangerous team. They gave Guthridge's team the No. 8 seed in the Southeast.

At the time, it appeared to be a daunting path: a first-round game against Missouri, coached by former Duke assistant Quin Snyder, then a potential second-round matchup with top-seeded Stanford. There wasn't a lot of optimism in Chapel Hill as the Heels left for their regional site in Birmingham, Alabama.

Instead, most of the eyes on Tobacco Road were focused on Duke, back in its familiar role as the No. 1 seed in the East Regional. After an easy first-round victory over Lamar in Winston-Salem's Joel Coliseum, the Blue Devils were put to the test by a familiar rival in a game that would serve as a preview of things to come on Tobacco Road.

Roy Williams had emerged as one of college basketball's biggest names at Kansas, compiling the best winning percentage of any active coach. But despite two Final Four appearances, he was haunted by postseason failures—especially in 1997, when his No. 1 ranked Kansas team was upset in the regional finals by Arizona. The former Tar Heel assistant said he almost quit the game after dealing with some unsavory recruiting practices, but he found himself revitalized when he brought in a new bunch of players whose character was as strong as their talent.

That young group—featuring big men Nick Collison and Drew Gooden and guards Kirk Hinrich and Jeff Boschee—took on top-seeded Duke in a memorable second-round game in Joel Coliseum. Duke got nothing from the ailing Dunleavy, and Jason Williams was thoroughly outplayed by Hinrich. Only Battier, playing one of the great defensive games ever seen on Tobacco Road, kept Duke in it.

"They have maybe the most alert, most aware defensive player that I can ever remember in college basketball—Shane Battier," Williams said.

The tension mounted as the two teams dueled in a tight, physical game. Emotions overflowed on the sidelines as Krzyzewski and Williams engaged in a face-to-face shouting matchup during a first-half confrontation.

In the end, Battier's play (twenty-one points, eight blocked shots, eight rebounds, two steals) and two late defensive plays by Carlos Boozer made the difference as Duke pulled out a 69–64 victory and advanced to the Sweet 16 in Syracuse. But that proved the last hurrah for an overachieving young team. Duke, weakened when freshman Mike Dunleavy was struck with mononucleosis, ran out of gas against Florida in the Sweet 16, missing five straight three-point tries in the final ninety seconds to turn a four-point lead into an 87–78 loss.

"These kids, I think, were worn out," Krzyzewski said. "We played with our hearts the whole year and they won two championships and finished number one in the [final AP poll]. So if we're going to wear out, I'd rather try to wear out trying to win."

Compared to the expectations after the talent exodus the previous spring, Duke's 29–5 record—including a 15–1 ACC mark and another ACC Tournament title—could only be considered an amazing success story. And with only Carrawell graduating and nobody turning pro, the Blue Devils were well positioned to make a serious national title run in 2001.

It would have been a glorious spring for the Duke nation—except for one thing. Eight miles away, North Carolina's Tar Heels had come back from the dead.

In the old days, meaning when Dean Smith was at the helm, nobody would have been surprised when a less-than-successful UNC team salvaged the season with a couple of postseason wins. Smith's underachieving 1990 team had avoided embarrassment by beating Southwest Missouri State and upsetting top-seeded Oklahoma in the NCAA Tournament.

In a way, Carolina's mild first-round upset of Missouri seemed to be that kind of achievement. By beating the ex-Dukie Snyder and his team, the Tar Heels washed out the bad taste left in their mouths by the Wake Forest loss and somewhat atoned for the previous year's ignominious first-round loss to Weber State. It wasn't until UNC stunned top-seeded Stanford in the second round (thanks to a strong offensive performance by freshman Joe Forte and a rugged twenty-four-minute stint by football star Julius Peppers) that bewildered Tar Heel fans realized that their underachieving team was on an amazing postseason roll.

Everything seemed to be opening up for Guthridge and the Heels as they traveled to Austin, Texas, for the Southeast Regionals. The No. 2 seed in the region, Cincinnati, was upset in the second round by Tulsa and third-seeded Ohio State was dumped by Miami of Florida. The path to the Final Four in Indianapolis was suddenly free of obstacles.

"Coach kept telling us, 'We're just a step away,'" Haywood said. "We believed it, but no one else did. We had a rough season. Wouldn't it be something if we could be there [in the Final Four] again?"

Forte was on fire again as UNC got past Tennessee in the semifinals, scoring twenty-two points to lead all scorers. He was even hotter in the regional title game as his twenty-eight-point explosion was just enough to carry the Heels past Tulsa and into the Final Four.

"This win shows that we're still here," sophomore Kris Long told the press. "People were saying that we were history. We were old news. Now we're showing that we're still alive and kicking. The tradition at Carolina will never die."

UNC's wild run ended in the Final Four against the same Florida team that had knocked off Duke. Forte, so hot in the regionals, hit just five of sixteen shots in the national semifinals in Indianapolis, succumbing to the same Final Four shooting disease that had plagued Rick Fox, Dante Calabria, and Shammond Williams (twice) in the previous decade.

The unexpected Final Four appearance left Tar Heel fans in a quandary. Did the magical March run make up for their frustrating season? And how did they feel about Guthridge? Just weeks earlier, a majority of Tar Heel fans wanted to put him out to pasture, but now he had turned in two Final Four seasons in three years. His three-season record of 80–28 matched the most wins for any coach in NCAA history over his three years, tying former N.C. State coach Everett Case for that honor.

THE AWKWARD EXCHANGE

Dean Smith had it planned perfectly. He would hand the North Carolina coaching job to his loyal assistant Bill Guthridge for a year or two so that "Gut" could enjoy a taste of success and a couple of big paychecks to carry him through retirement. Then Guthridge would hand the post off to Roy Williams, who would carry the Tar Heel program into the twenty-first century.

It was such a beautiful plan. And if Guthridge had been satisfied with one or even two seasons at the helm, Williams would have come running when UNC called.

But Guthridge did not call it quits after the 1998 season. And he did not call after 1999. And when he finally did decide to step down after the 2000 season, Williams's situation at Kansas had changed with the arrival of the kids who had restored his enthusiasm for college basketball. The result was a two-week nightmare for the Carolina program and the carefully crafted empire that Smith had built in Chapel Hill.

Instead of coming running, Williams very publicly agonized over his decision for almost a week. At one point, UNC Athletic Director Dick Baddour thought he had an agreement for Williams to come, and he even sent a proposed contract to the university's trustees for their approval. But when Williams returned to Kansas to tell his players that he was leaving, he couldn't make himself do it.

Instead, he held a press conference in Allen Fieldhouse where Williams announced, "I'm staying." The reporters on hand could hear the cheers from outside—the proceedings were being televised live to a crowd of more than 16,000 rabid Kansas fans who had packed the adjacent football stadium to watch Williams's press conference on the scoreboard. After meeting with reporters, Williams walked outside and addressed the fans, promising that now that he had turned UNC down, "I plan to coach at Kansas for the rest of my career."

It was a promise that would come back to haunt him.

Dean Smith was upset by his protégé's decision, but he was sure that Larry Brown would take the job. Unfortunately, new UNC president James Moeser didn't like the idea that both UCLA and Kansas had drawn NCAA probation for rule violations committed during Brown's tenure. The end result of Moeser's reservations was an awkward interview in which Brown later claimed that Baddour spent most of his time trying to convince him that he shouldn't take the job. Gauging the prevailing wind, Brown withdrew his name from consideration.

UNC's dilemma was now spinning out of control. Successful South Carolina coach Eddie Fogler had just announced his retirement from coaching. Former UNC standout George Karl was a successful NBA coach and he wanted the job, but the Milwaukee Bucks refused him permission to interview for the Carolina opening. UNC assistant coach Phil Ford would have been a popular choice, but his very public battle with alcoholism, including two recently revealed drunk driving convictions, cost the former Tar Heel All-American any chance for consideration.

Finally, a desperate Baddour turned to thirty-eight-year-old Matt Doherty, who had just completed his first season at Notre Dame with a loss to Wake Forest in the NIT Finals. He brought youth, enthusiasm, and the proper pedigree: not only did he play for Smith, but he had served seven years as an assistant to Williams at Kansas.

He also brought three assistant coaches with him from Notre Dame, meaning that there would be no place on his staff for veteran aides Phil Ford, Dave Hanners, or Pat Sullivan. That appeared to alienate Smith. The Hall of Fame coach—who had sat on the podium with Guthridge when Guthridge was hired and again when he had announced his retirement—this time stood in the back of the Skipper Bowles Room when Doherty was introduced, surprising reporters with a curiously negative view of the proceedings: "This is both a happy and sad day for the program," he said, explaining that the sadness stemmed from his concern about the treatment of Ford, Hanners, and Sullivan—three former UNC players who were being cast off by Doherty.

Smith's black mood would be an ominous omen for Matt Doherty's tenure at UNC. But it didn't appear to faze the new Tar Heel coach, who began rebuilding the program in his own image. He moved Smith out of his office in the basketball suite and into the basement of the building named for him. Guthridge was given a cubbyhole right beside him. Doherty also replaced the secretaries in the basketball office with new faces—a move that alienated several former players who had been nurtured in Smith's family atmosphere.

But the Tar Heel fan base, especially the student body, loved the energy and enthusiasm that Doherty brought to the program. The tall, prematurely graying coach whipped the fans into a frenzy by throwing T-shirts to the students before each game. Wearing shirts that proclaimed their status as "Doherty's Disciples," they cheered when he drew a technical foul in his very first game. Most of all, they loved that after five straight losses to hated Duke, Doherty took his team to Cameron Indoor Stadium and knocked off the Blue Devils.

Duke was still the team to beat on Tobacco Road in 2001. Carrawell was gone, but Krzyzewski had added prep All-American point guard Chris Duhon to his roster. Krzyzewski did not start his freshman star, using him as a sixth man instead as he went with the veteran lineup of Boozer, Battier, Dunleavy, James, and Williams. That rotation carried Duke to a 19–1 start and a No. 2 ranking in the national polls when UNC came to Durham on the night of February 1, 2001.

The Tar Heels were big underdogs, despite a 17–2 record and a No. 4 national ranking of their own. Doherty seemed to have the veteran Tar Heels playing with the cohesion they had lacked the year before. The team had really taken off when two-sport star Ron Curry, who joined the team after football season, moved into the starting lineup and finally began to display the talent that had made him such a heralded recruit. He was not a big scorer (Forte and the big frontline of Haywood, Lang, and Capel generated the points), but Curry was providing the same kind of defense and floor leadership that Jimmy Black provided in 1982 when Doherty rode the coattails of James Worthy and Michael Jordan to the national title.

"A lot of people forgot about me as a basketball player," Curry said. "I know other guys will get the headlines. Scorers get the headlines. I'm just on a good team, playing defense and handling the ball, and I think guys feed off that."

When UNC visited Cameron, its newfound cohesion was put to the supreme test. Like so many UNC-Duke games, this one was decided in the final seconds. Mike Dunleavy hit an amazing off-balance three-point shot with nine seconds left to tie the game and apparently force overtime. But with just 1.2 seconds remaining, Shane Battier—one of the smartest players in college basketball—committed the dumbest foul of his career, bumping UNC center Brendan Haywood thirty feet from the basket.

The Tar Heel center was only a 48% free throw shooter at that point in the season. But as he stepped to the line, he thought about three years earlier, when he had gone to the same free throw line at Cameron with a chance to tie the 1998 Duke-Carolina game with one second left and missed. This time, he swished both shots, giving the Tar Heels an 85–83 victory.

Duke would spend the next month chasing a North Carolina team that seemed to be getting better and better. The victory in Durham pushed UNC's winning streak to fifteen straight games. The streak hit eighteen straight as Carolina—installed as the nation's new No. 1 team—rolled over Georgia Tech, Wake Forest, and Maryland.

Then came a break in the schedule: these eight days would later stand as a sharp divide between the great Carolina team of January/early February and the erratic, disjointed team that finished out the season.

UNC resumed action at Clemson against the ACC's last-place team, expecting another easy win. Instead, the nationally televised Sunday game turned into a horror show as the Tar Heels were outhustled, outshot, and mainly outfought by the outmanned Tigers. Carolina bounced back after the Clemson loss to rout Florida State. Exactly one week after the Clemson debacle, the Tar Heels traveled to Virginia for another Sunday game—where they were not only beaten, but humiliated in an 86–66 loss to the Cavaliers.

There was one more Sunday left in the regular season: Duke's March 4 visit to the Smith Center. The Tar Heels clinched at least a share of the ACC regular season title with a midweek victory over N.C. State, but they would have to beat Duke on Sunday to claim the title outright. And after what had happened to Duke earlier that week, that appeared to be a game the Tar Heels could win—even on a Sunday.

DISASTER AND TRIUMPH

Duke won six of seven games after its loss to North Carolina and headed into its home finale with Maryland, still thinking of catching the suddenly erratic Tar Heels in the regular season race.

The Blue Devils expected to beat Maryland on Shane Battier's Senior Night, especially after what happened a month earlier in College Park. The inspired Terps had manhandled Duke for thirty-nine minutes and five seconds that night in Cole Field House. But with Maryland leading by ten points with fifty-five seconds left, the resilient Williams had sparked a Duke comeback that was already labeled an instant classic by ESPN.

The defeat would send the Terps into a tailspin that they were just coming out of as they traveled to Durham for the rematch with the Devils. Gary Williams's talented team trailed 60–55 when disaster struck the Blue Devils. Boozer, who was having a great game against Maryland's Lonnie Baxter, came down awkwardly after going up for a rebound. Hearing something pop in his foot, the sophomore big man headed to the locker room.

Krzyzewski soon got the worst possible news: Boozer had broken the fifth metatarsal bone in his right foot. It was exactly the same injury that Bobby Hurley had suffered in Duke's 1992 loss at North Carolina. "It's a tragic event for us," senior Nate James said.

Boozer's injury appeared to be a devastating blow to the Blue Devils' post-season hopes. Already criticized as too small and too thin to go all the way, Duke was now smaller and thinner after losing its only proven post performer. And as bad as the injury was, Krzyzewski was even more disheartened by the way his team reacted to the loss. Instead of rallying together in Boozer's absence, they came apart.

"The players were working hard, but they were working as individuals, not as a team," Krzyzewski said. "By the end of the game, our guys didn't even want the ball."

He was despondent when he met with the press following Maryland's 91–80 victory. The Duke coach retired to his office, supposedly trying to figure out a way to save the season. In reality, he later admitted, he was simply feeling sorry for himself.

"Okay, Carlos is out and it's not going to happen this year," Krzyzewski later wrote of his blackest hour. "We're not going to win the national championship . . . It's over. It's over."

Sometime during that dark night, his military training kicked in and Krzyzewski began to attack the problem rather than wallow in self-pity. Over the years, he had put two words at the heart of his coaching philosophy: next play. It was his way of saying to forget the past and move on. Now it was time for him to take his own words to heart.

As he watched video of North Carolina, Duke's next opponent, he started to formulate a plan. "We have to transform to a more uptempo style, I thought," Krzyzewski later wrote, describing his thought process. "Duhon . . . Duhon is the key. He's fast. He's a great defender. He can shoot. He'll free up Jason to do more."

The next morning, Krzyzewski stunned his staff by telling them his plan: he would replace Boozer in the middle with a committee of three little-used big men, Casey Sanders, Matt Christensen, and football player Reggie Love. And he'd replace fifth-year senior Nate James, one of the team's leaders and key contributors, with Duhon.

"Nate is going to be the key in making this work," Krzyzewski told his assistants. "He's got to accept his new role without reservations. Having him come off the bench will give us a big punch."

When Krzyzewski met with the team, he had to do two things: convince them that the season was not over and sell them on his new scheme. Because of the NCAA rules that mandate a day off each week, he had not talked to his players on the day after the Maryland loss. But he called them in for an unusual 6 a.m. practice the next day.

"I remember the next morning we walk in there to meet the team and he's like, 'Hey, guys, we're going to win the national championship and here's how we're going to do it,'" assistant coach Johnny Dawkins recalled.

Krzyzewski actually promised that if his players did exactly what he asked, they would win the national title. Dawkins, who had himself been despondent a few minutes earlier, couldn't believe the impact of Coach K's words on his team.

"When you sat in that room and looked at Battier in the eyes . . . Jason Williams in the eyes . . . Chris Duhon, Nate James," he said. "I looked in those eyes and the thing I saw more than anything was belief."

Krzyzewski was planning to unveil his team's new attacking style in Chapel Hill on the last Sunday of the regular season. The Blue Devils could still tie for the ACC regular season title with a victory, but without Boozer, what chance was there of that?

"I'll never forget the look on the face of Brendan Haywood when Casey [Sanders] stepped into the jump-ball circle," Battier told writer Donald Phillips. "He got this sarcastic smile on his face and started shaking his head. He was thinking, 'You've got to be kidding, you're starting this guy?' I looked over at Mike [Dunleavy] and we just smiled at each other. I could read his mind. We were both thinking, 'Haywood, you just don't know what's coming. You just don't know.'"

Sanders, who up to that point in his career had been little more than an afterthought at the end of the Duke bench, made two huge plays in the early minutes, beating Haywood down the court for a layup and blocking an inside shot by the Tar Heel center. He helped Duke seize an early lead and nurse it into the early minutes of the second half. It was still close when, with seventeen minutes to play, Battier made the play that broke Carolina's back. As Forte raced in for a breakaway layup, the Duke senior caught him from behind and blocked away his layup. Dunleavy got the rebound, pushed it ahead, and Duhon hit a three-pointer. Six minutes later, Duke was up 72–57 and a desperate Matt Doherty pulled his big men, Haywood and Lang—going small in an attempt to match Duke's quickness.

It didn't work and Duke almost coasted to the 95–85 victory. Battier was magnificent: twenty-five points, eleven rebounds, five blocks, and four steals. Jason Williams added thirty-three points and nine assists. Krzyzewski's new three-headed center monster limited Haywood to just twelve points on 5-of-12 shooting.

"We could have easily come out and folded and hid behind the excuse that, 'Well, we didn't have Carlos Boozer,'" Battier told reporters. "But now we have new life at a time when a lot of teams become very stagnant and very conservative."

Any doubts that the Duke players may have had about their new style of play were put to rest as they headed for Atlanta and the ACC Tournament. The Tar Heels won the draw for the top seed in the three-day event. That was a huge advantage with powerful Maryland waiting in the semifinals for the team that drew the second seed.

The 2001 ACC Tournament was played for the first time in the Georgia Dome in front of incredible crowds. The 28,000 who attended Thursday night's play-in game were a larger crowd than any that watched another conference championship game. More than 40,000 fans attended each of the next four sessions, giving the venerable tournament a Final Four atmosphere.

The Blue Devils manhandled slumping N.C. State in the first round but came out cold against Maryland in the semifinals, falling behind 10–0.

Instead of calling a time-out to settle his team down, Krzyzewski sent James into the game and the tough-minded senior promptly hit a three-pointer to stop the rout. Duke fought back as the two teams waged their third memorable battle in a six-week period. The Blue Devils used a 19–2 spurt to go up 61–47 midway through the second half; but the Terps fought back to take a 78–77 lead with 2:22 left. From that point on, the game almost resembled the Duke-Kentucky classic as each team traded magnificent plays: Dunleavy hit a driving shot to put Duke back on top; Sanders blocked a Terrence Morris layup and Dunleavy hit two free throws to give the Devils a three-point lead; Maryland's

Steve Blake drove to the top of the key and, with exactly eight seconds left, drilled a game-tying three-pointer.

At that point, Duke eschewed the time-out. Jason Williams took the in-bounds pass and pushed the ball up the court. He threw up a short shot in traffic that hit the rim and bounced off. But both Sanders and James were there to tip it in. It looked like both touched it, but James was credited with the basket that gave Duke the 82–80 victory.

"I think Casey was in the area," James said with a smile. "If he wants a little piece of the pie, that's okay with me."

As soon as the buzzer sounded, Shane Battier raced toward Juan Dixon, a painfully skinny guard who had made himself into an unlikely ACC star, and grabbed him by the shoulders. "You're a great player," Battier said. "I'll see you at the Final Four."

He didn't know how right he was. The Duke-Maryland rivalry, which has been growing in intensity ever since the Terps won in Durham in the 2000 season, would briefly overshadow the historic Duke-Carolina rivalry as the best in the ACC.

However, that wasn't evident as the two Tobacco Road neighbors took the court for the ACC championship game in Atlanta. Again, the Tar Heels, untested in victories over Clemson and Georgia Tech, seemed to have the upper hand on a Duke team that was drained—physically and emotionally— by its semifinal victory over Maryland. In addition, Doherty had had a week to study Duke's new "little-ball" strategy and should have been prepared for it.

It was close for ten minutes. But midway through the first half, Duke exploded for a 19–1 run and the Tar Heels quit. Plain and simple, they quit.

"There was just a point where they didn't want to play any more," Duke's Nate James said. "I just looked in their eyes. They were bickering with one another and just waiting for the time to expire so they could go home and regroup or whatever they wanted to do."

Duke's 79–53 victory was a bigger shocker than the Blue Devils' ten-point win in the Smith Center a week earlier. It was evidence that Krzyzewski's new gameplan was not just a fluke, but a formula for success. His promise that Duke would win the national championship didn't seem so farfetched any more.

"You can't play them like this," Forte said. "They're a team. They're a true team."

And North Carolina was a dead team. Even opening the NCAA Tournament in the familiar New Orleans Superdome, where the Tar Heels had twice won national championships, could not revive the shattered team. UNC, its month-long stay as the nation's No. 1 team a distant memory, managed a lackluster victory over Princeton in the opener but bowed out two days later against a very mediocre Penn State team. It was the team's fifth straight Sunday loss: Clemson, Virginia, Duke, Duke, and the Nittany Lions.

Afterward, Doherty cried in frustration as he tried to explain the loss. "It's a twenty-four-hour job, seven days a week," he said. "When you come up short, it hurts."

THE DRIVE TO THE TITLE

Duke's victory in the ACC title game didn't come without cost. Seven minutes into the second half of the Blue Devils' victory over UNC, Jason Williams hurt his ankle and lay on the Georgia Dome court crying in pain. Much of his distress was the fear that he had suffered a season-ending injury.

Instead, it was merely a simple sprain and the sophomore All-American was back in the lineup, his ankle heavily taped, as Duke routed Monmouth to open NCAA play. He was magnificent in victories over Missouri, UCLA, and Southern Cal, as the Blue Devils rolled to the Final Four, which was back in the Minneapolis Metrodome, where Bobby Hurley and Grant Hill had humbled the Fab Five in 1992.

It would be Krzyzewski's ninth trip to the national semifinals—the third highest total in college basketball history, trailing only John Wooden (who had twelve Final Four appearances at UCLA) and Dean Smith (who finished with eleven at UNC). And when Coach K got to Minneapolis, he found that Shane Battier's prediction in Atlanta had come true: Duke was facing Maryland for the fourth time.

The Duke-Maryland rivalry had exploded almost without warning. For almost a decade, Krzyzewski had dominated the Terrapins so thoroughly that it drove Gary Williams to distraction. The Maryland coach won his first head-to-head matchup with Coach K when he guided Boston College past the Blue Devils in the 1985 NCAA Tournament. But at Maryland, Williams lost twenty of his first twenty-one matchups with Krzyzewski—and most were not even close.

But something changed when Maryland visited Cameron in 2000 and handed Duke its only ACC loss that season. The Terps boasted a sophomore-laden team, headed by emerging star Juan Dixon in the backcourt and strongman Lonnie Baxter in the post. Williams also had heady freshman point guard Steve Blake from Miami, a player Herb Sendek had tried very hard to recruit at N.C. State. For some reason, Jason Williams always seemed to struggle in his matchups with Blake. And Dixon, a player Krzyzewski came to admire as much as any opponent he ever faced, always used to be at his best against the Blue Devils. "I love Juan Dixon," Krzyzewski said.

The Terps certainly had the Blue Devils' attention. "It seems like every time we step on the court against each other, it's a masterpiece in progress," Jason Williams said. "This will probably be a masterpiece again."

Indeed, that's just what it would be, although it didn't start that way. Just as in Atlanta, Maryland came out hot, going up 7–0 this time. Only this time, Duke didn't answer the fast start and the Terps continued to build their lead. It grew to 23–10 after eight minutes and to 34–17 at the TV time-out with 7:55 to go in the half.

"What are you afraid of—that we'll lose by forty?" Krzyzewski screamed at his shaken team. "Just settle down and do the things that got us here."

Krzyzewski's tirade had little immediate effect as Blake stretched the Maryland lead to twenty-two points with a long three-pointer to make it 39–17. No team in Final Four history had ever come back from a twenty-two-point deficit, but a three-pointer by Nate James (who else?) started the Devils on their long comeback trail. "The biggest spark we had was Nate," Krzyzewski said.

Krzyzewski had one extra weapon in his arsenal for this game. Boozer, who had returned to make a brief appearance in the two East Regional games, came off the bench against the Terps and picked up where he had left off at the moment of his injury: pounding Baxter in the paint. His play down low helped the Devils cut Maryland's lead to eight points, just before Dixon hit a long three-pointer at the buzzer to send the Terps into the locker room with an eleven-point lead.

Krzyzewski was an angry man at the break, thinking that Dixon's shot had regained the momentum for the Terps. He was frustrated by his team's inability to stop the slender junior guard and asked if anybody thought he could defend their nemesis.

"I got him," James said.

Dixon, who had scored sixteen first-half points against a variety of defenders, would score just three in the second twenty minutes. That would be the key as Duke surged closer and closer as the minutes ticked off. The Devils got it down to two points with twelve minutes left, but Maryland pushed it back to seven. A Battier three-pointer reversed the momentum, and with 6:52 left, Jason Williams (0-for-9 from behind the three-point arch at that point) did what he'd done so often in his career: he hit the three-pointer that gave Duke its first lead.

The Blue Devils slowly strangled the Terps. The final straw for the Terps came with 2:48 left, when Baxter, battling Boozer for position, was whistled for his fifth foul. CBS commentator Billy Packer, who had spent the entire game ripping the officials, lost his composure, screaming, "What are they calling here? Can you believe this?"

Duke, up five at that point, pulled away in the final seconds for a 95–84 victory as Battier (twenty-five points), Williams (twenty-three points), and Boozer (nineteen points) shared the scoring honors. But Krzyzewski singled out James as the hero of the comeback victory for the second-half defensive job he did on Dixon.

"He fought Dixon in the second half," the Duke coach said. "Maryland—and Dixon especially—dominated us in the first half. His defense on Dixon was the key."

Duke was still one game away from the national title. The Monday night opponent, Arizona, had started the season ranked No. 1. After a brief midseason swoon, they started to play like that.

"It's fitting that the two best teams are meeting to play for the national championship," Battier said. "That's the way it should be."

Starting at center for the Wildcats was a familiar face: Loren Woods, the former Wake Forest big man who had transferred to Arizona and had finally matured into an effective player under Lute Olson. Woods gave the smaller Blue Devils fits early, until the 6-foot-8 Shane Battier switched to the 7-foot-1 Arizona center. Jason Williams picked up two fouls in the first five minutes and then narrowly avoided a third when he ended up draped atop Jason Gardner after a scramble for a loose ball.

CBS commentator Billy Packer was screaming for a foul, but NCAA director of officials Hank Nichols later pointed out that the Williams-Gardner collision was covered by Rule 4, Section 38, Article 2, which essentially says that contact in pursuit of a loose ball, "should be permitted, even though the contact should be severe." By making a bridge of his body and allowing Gardner to dribble out from under him, Williams had not gained an advantage due to the contact. So despite Packer's hysterics, the non-call was the correct interpretation of the rule.

Still, even without the third foul, Williams couldn't seem to do anything right and Krzyzewski had to find another offensive threat.

Two years earlier, the Duke coach had made a tough choice on the recruiting trail and elected to pass on celebrated prospect Casey Jacobsen to take Mike Dunleavy instead. Jacobsen blossomed into an All-American at Stanford, but on the night of April 2, 2001, Krzyzewski's confidence in Dunleavy would be rewarded. Early in the second half, the slender sophomore took a feed from Duhon and dropped in a three-point shot. Just twenty-four seconds later, Battier found Dunleavy open in the corner and set him up for another three-point try: swish. Moments later, Battier made a spectacular block and save on a driving shot by Arizona's Richard Jefferson—slapping the ball back to Duhon who fed Williams and found Dunleavy for another three-pointer. His third three-pointer in forty-six seconds stretched Duke's lead to 49–39. After a brief surge by the Wildcats cut Duke's lead to one, Dunleavy scored another seven points in a 12–3 Duke run to push the margin back to ten points.

"The biggest turning point was when Dunleavy hit those threes, back to back to back," Arizona guard Jason Gardner said. "Other than that, it was even."

Battier, playing the final game of his career, made that lead stand up. He converted an old-fashioned three-point play. He slam dunked a follow shot of a Boozer miss. With the lead down to three points, he made an incredible backhanded tip-in of a Dunleavy miss. He took a feed from Williams and emphatically slammed it home. With Duke up five and just under two minutes to play, Battier set a screen and Jason Williams (1-of-10 from the three-point line for the game) stepped behind it and did what he always seemed to do: he swished the three-pointer that clinched Duke's third national championship.

Krzyzewski's promise, made just a month before in Duke's darkest hour, was redeemed on the court of the Metrodome in Minneapolis. Instead of collapsing after Boozer's injury, Duke had regrouped and won ten straight games—picking up a share of the ACC regular season championship, the ACC Tournament championship, and a national title along the way.

"I just had the most amazing year I've ever had with a group of kids," Krzyzewski said. "I've had a smile on my face since about the last thirty seconds of the game. We did play like champions."

The national title was Krzyzewski's third, tying him with his mentor Bob Knight on the all-time list. Only John Wooden (ten titles) and Adolph Rupp (four) had won more. For the deliriously happy Duke fans, only one comparison was important: K once again had one more national title than Dean Smith.

20

THE NEW DEAN OF TOBACCO ROAD

A MONTH AFTER WINNING HIS THIRD NATIONAL TITLE, MIKE Krzyzewski was voted into the Basketball Hall of Fame on the first ballot. It symbolized the status he had achieved on Tobacco Road: he was now as much an icon—to be loved and hated—as Dean Smith had been.

And just as Krzyzewski had had to fight to build his program from beneath the shadow of Smith's empire, now his Tobacco Road rivals faced the daunting task of challenging Coach K's juggernaut. That situation created tremendous pressure on the coaches trying to live up to impossible standards.

In Winston-Salem, Dave Odom gave up the fight. The years since Tim Duncan's departure had been tough on the Tobacco Road native. He had dominated Duke and challenged for national honors in the mid-1990s, but three straight NIT trips, followed by a first-round NCAA Tournament flameout against Butler in 2001, left Deacon fans grumbling. Odom tried to negotiate a new long-term contract with the school, but when that was not forthcoming, he jumped at an offer from South Carolina rather that risk his career on the 2002 season.

The Deacons turned to Skip Prosser, who had averaged over twenty-one wins a season since replacing Pete Gillen at Xavier. The fifty-two-year-old Pittsburgh native brought new energy to a program that had started to stagnate. Even more exciting for fans frustrated by Odom's carefully controlled and patient style was the fact that Prosser promised a team that would run and press and play uptempo basketball.

"The thing is, the older I get, the faster I want to play," Prosser said when introduced to the North Carolina media.

He told the reporters that he knew what he was getting into. "I went to the Final Four in Minneapolis," he said. "I noticed that two of those teams were ACC teams. I know how difficult it's going to be. That's one of the things that excites me. It's a daunting challenge, but if our players are willing to accept that challenge, I'm not going to shy away."

In Raleigh, Herb Sendek very nearly followed Odom out of the league. The bright promise of his first season at N.C. State, when he had guided a last-place team to the ACC Tournament title game, had faded after four trips to the NIT and a horrific 13–16 season in 2001. By the time N.C. State limped into the ACC Tournament in Atlanta, a group of wealthy boosters were ready to buy up Sendek's contract. But new Wolfpack Athletic Director Lee Fowler was a basketball man who had played at Vanderbilt and coached under Dana Kirk at Memphis. He knew how respected Sendek was in the coaching profession and he also saw that the embattled coach had just signed the top-rated recruiting class in the ACC. Fowler never quite said he was giving Sendek one more year to prove himself, but it was clear that 2001–02 would be his make-or-break season.

"I really felt comfortable with these freshmen coming in," Fowler said, explaining his decision. "So, long story short, I was going more on fact than emotion. I think most of the fans who wanted him out were going on eleven years of emotion."

There were also rumblings in Chapel Hill, where the late-season meltdown in 2001 had shaken some of the Tar Heel nation's confidence in Matt Doherty. Whispers of player discontent became to percolate along Tobacco Road, fueled by a stampede of players leaving the program. Forte, who had shared ACC player of the year honors with Battier, jumped to the NBA after his sophomore season, barely slipping into the first round of the NBA draft. And football/ basketball standouts Ronald Curry and Julius Peppers, who were both so vital to UNC's success the previous year, each decided to concentrate on football and not return to the basketball team.

Despite the unease about the direction of the program, there was no sense of impending disaster in Chapel Hill. The Tar Heels still had three-year starters Kris Lang and Jason Capel back to provide leadership. Sophomore guards Adam Boone and Brian Morrison appeared ready to step into the starting lineup after playing reserve roles the year before. And everybody was excited about Doherty's first recruiting class—which included McDonald's All-American Jawad Williams from Cleveland at forward, athletic wing man Jackie Manuel from Florida, and highly rated sharpshooter Melvin Scott from Maryland.

North Carolina was picked fourth in the ACC media's preseason poll and was ranked No. 19 nationally in the preseason AP poll. That ranking didn't survive to the first weekly poll. On the same night that Sendek's freshmen were beating East Carolina to go 3–0 on the new season, North Carolina was stunned by Hampton Institute in its home opener. And just to prove that that loss was no fluke, four nights later, the Heels were beaten at home by Davidson.

"We've got to stop the bleeding," senior Jason Capel said. "The biggest thing now is confidence. We have to keep our heads up and stick together."

North Carolina would battle back to even its record at 5–5 with three straight wins over the Christmas break. But an 84–62 loss to Skip Prosser's new Deacons squelched any thoughts of salvaging the season. The defeat broke Duke's record for the most lopsided win for a visitor in the Smith Center, but the Blue Devils got the record back three weeks later with an 87–58 thrashing of UNC in front of a stunned Tar Heel crowd. "I think we just wore them out," Duke's Duhon said.

At least one Carolina player was in denial. "Actually, I have to say I think we have more talent than Duke," senior Kris Lang said. "We have more depth. It's just a matter of experience for us."

Carolina would get a lot more experience in the coming weeks—and all of it bad. But there was one bright spot for Tar Heel fans as their team lost eleven of twelve games in January and early February. Doherty was proving as adroit as a recruiter as he was proving inept as a sideline coach.

During the summer and fall of 2001, Doherty and Duke's Krzyzewski were engaged in a recruiting conflict that was at such a high level that it almost defied belief. Duke and UNC had both brought in great recruiting classes in the past, but never before in the same season.

Krzyzewski started the duel by landing an early commitment from J.J. Redick, a 6-foot-4 shooting star from Roanoke, Virginia, who was proclaimed by recruiting guru Howard Garfinkel as, "the best shooter I've seen since Chris Mullins." Doherty answered by getting a verbal from Raymond Felton, a dazzling point guard from little Latta, South Carolina. He added a commitment from Rashad McCants, a cocky 6-foot-3 scorer from Asheville (N.C.) who was prepping in New Hampshire.

Krzyzewski ventured into Chicago and landed point guard Sean Dockery, that state's all-time leader in assists and steals, and highly regarded center Michael Thompson. Coach K beat Doherty head-to-head for Oklahoma power forward Shelden Williams, rated the best prospect in the country at his position. His biggest success was beating UNC for Raleigh prep star Shavlik Randolph, the grandson of former N.C. State star Ronnie Shavlik and the first clear-cut in-state recruiting loss for the Heels since David Thompson in 1971.

Doherty had better luck with Sean May, the son of former Indiana star Scott May. The heavily built 6-foot-9 forward grew up in Bloomington, in the shadow of the University of Indiana, and always assumed he'd play for Bob Knight there, just as his father did. But when Knight was abruptly dismissed by President Myles Brand in the fall of 2000, May was suddenly looking for a new place to play.

May didn't want to follow his father's coach to the basketball hinterlands of Lubbock, Texas, but he also didn't want to play for Indiana after its ill treatment of Knight. North Carolina turned out to be the perfect compromise, thanks to a major assist by Phil Ford. After being denied a spot on Doherty's staff, Ford joined the school's fund-raising organization. He used his friendship with Scott May—forged during the 1976 Olympic Games—to help Doherty land the young May in Chapel Hill.

The two competing six-man classes, which combined to produce eight prep All-Americans, would be at the center of Tobacco Road's basketball fortunes in the coming years. For Carolina fans enduring the worst season in school history, the recruits were seen as the salvation of their program; in fact, Felton was dubbed "The Savior" by fans who saw his game during an off-season AAU Tournament in the Smith Center.

For the Duke faithful, Krzyzewski's "Super Six" promised the continuation of his success after the heavy losses the team was to suffer after the 2001–02 season.

CLOSING THE GAP

The 2001–02 season turned out to be a nightmare in Chapel Hill and ultimately a disappointment in Durham, where No. 1 Duke was upset by Indiana in the regional semifinals in Lexington.

But the season was a pleasant surprise elsewhere on Tobacco Road. In Winston-Salem, Skip Prosser guided his first Wake Forest team to twenty-one wins, a third-place tie in the ACC regular season, and a first-round NCAA

Tournament victory. Amazingly, the team Wake Forest tied for third in the standings was N.C. State, back in the ACC race after ten straight second-division finishes.

Sendek, his job on the line, had taken the gutsy move of pushing Damien Wilkins out of his program after the controversial swing man had first entered and then withdrawn from the NBA draft. The graduation of Damon Thornton and Kenny Inge, two players troubled by off-court problems in their careers, also cleared the way for the Wolfpack coach to give his program a fresh start with a new group of players.

The key to the Pack's revival was colorful 6-foot-6 newcomer Julius Hodge, who labeled himself as "The Jules of Harlem on his way 2 Stardom." Hodge's talent was no surprise: he was a McDonald's All-American heavily courted by North Carolina, Syracuse, and a number of other schools before casting his lot with Sendek. He was the gem of the class that also included highly touted Georgia forward Josh Powell, DeMatha center Jordan Collins, and Maryland swing man Levi Watkins. Sendek had hoped to add foreign big man Uche Ukafor to his class, but when he lost his target to Missouri, he gambled his last scholarship on Bulgarian forward Ilian Evtimov.

The 6-foot-9 Evtimov, who had actually grown up in France, was the younger brother of former UNC recruit Vasco Evtimov, a McDonald's All-American who had flopped big time after signing with the Tar Heels in 1995. The younger Evtimov had played prep basketball in Winston-Salem but was so lightly regarded that he didn't make the top 200 list of any major recruiting service. State was his only major scholarship offer.

He would become the player his brother was supposed to be.

Hodge and Evtimov helped N.C. State to its best season since 1991. Hodge proved to be a wonderfully versatile player with the ability to contribute as a scorer, a rebounder, and as a playmaker. He also brought an infectious confidence to a team that had never known success. Evtimov demonstrated amazing ballhandling skills for a big man and a deft shooting touch. He proved to be the perfect player to plug into the high post of the new Princeton-style offense that Sendek had installed in the off-season.

That offense sputtered a bit early, but on a snowy December night in Syracuse, the Pack started to click, stunning the ninth-ranked Orangemen in the Carrier Dome. During a holiday trip to Houston, forward Marcus Melvin, a slender Fayetteville native, picked up a loose ball and threw in a three-pointer at the buzzer to give the Pack a dramatic victory over the Cougars. Less than two weeks later, N.C. State traveled to Charlottesville and shocked No. 4 ranked Virginia 81–74 as Hodge hit 7-of-8 shots and scored twenty-one points and Evtimov added fifteen points and hit four three-pointers.

Hodge spent most of the game woofing at the Cavs and their fans.

"Archie [Miller] has been telling me to keep my composure and don't play to the crowd," Hodge said. "But I'm from New York where the crowd's almost always against you and I draw energy from the crowd."

There were still bumps on the road for the Pack, including two lopsided losses to Duke and an ugly incident at College Park, where Hodge, responding to an earlier elbow in the gut from Maryland's Steve Blake, threw a forearm to the back of Blake's head. That earned the Wolfpack freshman (later the victim of an even more vicious blow from Wake Forest's Chris Paul) a one-game suspension and probably cost him the ACC Rookie of Year award.

N.C. State took advantage of North Carolina's slump to pound the Tar Heels twice, including a victory in Chapel Hill that ended with the visiting Wolfpack fans taking over the Smith Center and chanting "Red . . . White" as their team completed a 77–59 victory and disappointed UNC fans fled the building.

"I've never seen that much red in this building," said Miller, a fifth-year senior. "I thought we were in the ESA [the Entertainment and Sports Arena, where N.C. State played in Raleigh] for a little bit."

The Pack's very best moments came at the end of the season, starting in the ACC Tournament. Sendek's squad routed Virginia for the third time in a row, then upset top-seeded Maryland 86–82 in the semifinals. Hodge got his revenge on Blake, sticking the game-clinching three-pointer right in the face of his nemesis.

"When I saw him standing there, I had it in my mind that I had to make the shot," Hodge said. "I knew I wanted to come in here and have a good game because of the incident and because I have a lot of pride in my game."

Although the spotlight, as usual, was on Hodge, it was Anthony Grundy's twenty-four points that made the real difference as State became the last team to beat the NCAA title-bound Terps. Duke knocked out the Wolfack in the title game the next day, but that night State learned that it was going to the NCAA Tournament for the first time after a ten-year absence. Sendek and his team were watching the NCAA selection show at a Charlotte hotel when N.C. State's name was called in the opening minutes.

"Our name popped up so early, it was kind of a relief," Archie Miller said. "It wasn't like you see on TV where 500 people explode when their name is called. There was satisfaction and some bid smiles. It was like, 'Now we can make our noise in the tournament.'"

N.C. State drew the No. 7 seed in the East and was matched against 2000 NCAA champion Michigan State in the first round at the MCI Center in Washington, D.C. The Spartans had been to three straight Final Fours, but it was the young Pack—without a single player with NCAA experience—that showed poise down the stretch. Freshman Julius Hodge sparked a 22–3 spurt midway through the second half that helped convert a 30–18 deficit into a 68–59 victory.

"I kept saying, 'I'm not going home early . . . I'm not going home early . . . I'm not going home early,'" Hodge said.

Hodge's heroics earned the Wolfpack a second-round matchup with Connecticut, the 1999 NCAA champion. And for more than thirty-nine minutes, the young Wolfpack gave Jim Calhoun's favored Huskies all they could handle. It took a somewhat controversial ending to finally kill State's hopes. UConn was protecting a one-point lead when Caron Butler launched a desperation three-point try just as, or perhaps just after, the shot clock expired. His shot didn't come close, but State's Hodge was whistled for the barest touch of a foul.

"I don't even think I touched him and even if I did, I know it wasn't hard enough to make that call," Hodge complained,

Butler's three free throws ended the Pack's season, but there was no denying that Sendek's program had turned the corner in 2002. With twenty-three wins, a third-place finish in the ACC standings, a spot in the ACC Tournament title game, a return to the NCAA Tournament, and—best of all—the promise of the 2002 freshman class, State was a player on Tobacco Road again.

THE KIDS ARE ALRIGHT

For Tar Heel fans, the 2002–03 season opener against Penn State was as eagerly awaited as any epic matchup with Duke or N.C. State. For more than eight months since the Tar Heels had completed their disastrous 8–20 campaign with a loss to Duke in the first round of the ACC Tournament, the school's fans had been counting the days to the first game of the new season.

Nobody had been looking forward to the new season more anxiously than Matt Doherty, who in the midst of the previous season's misery had told a friend, "The hammer will fall" when the new kids arrived.

Well, they arrived and were on display the night of November 18 when UNC faced the Nittany Lions in the Smith Center in the first round of the preseason NIT. Three freshmen—Raymond Felton, Rashad McCants, and Sean May—were in the starting lineup along with sophomore players Jawad Williams and Jackie Manuel. And the hammer did indeed fall on the team that had knocked UNC out of the 2001 NCAA Tournament.

Carolina roared to a 54–29 halftime lead and coasted to a 85–55 victory as McCants poured in twenty-eight points (the most ever for a UNC freshman in his first game), Felton added ten assists, and May put up a double-double with seventeen points and ten rebounds.

"There's a lot of pressure to erase the memory of last season," May said. "People don't understand that even though we weren't here yet, we were still a part of that and it still hurt us. We have a chip on our shoulder."

It was a bit closer two nights later, when UNC beat Rutgers in the second round of the preseason tournament. But the Tar Heels still won and a week later, the team returned to the national stage with a mind-boggling 67–56 upset of No. 2 Kansas in Madison Square Garden.

"Some people said we just needed to get to New York and that would be a great statement for our team," Doherty said. "We didn't want to just get to New York, we wanted a good showing."

Two nights after bumping off Kansas, UNC's kids dumped Stanford in the NIT title game. In Chapel Hill, it was as if Carolina had won the national title. The Tar Heels vaulted from unranked to No. 12 in the AP ranking in one week, which was the fastest climb in that poll's history.

But UNC's youngsters weren't the only kids stirring up excitement on Tobacco Road. In Durham, Krzyzewski's Super Six made their debut by winning twelve straight games, although the heralded Randolph was hobbled and soon sidelined by a hip problem (the first of many physical woes that would turn his college career into a major disappointment).

Physical problems also plagued Duke's Tobacco Road neighbors. In Raleigh, Evtimov tore an ACL in a preseason scrimmage and was lost for the season. N.C. State won seven of eight against a weak nonconference schedule; but even with Josh Powell developing as a productive player down low, the Pack couldn't build on its 2002 success.

And North Carolina's bright hopes were tarnished when May went down with a broken foot during a post-Christmas return to New York's

Madison Square Garden for the Holiday Festival. The Tar Heels lost to Iona after losing May late in the first half. Losing the talented young big man hurt badly because Doherty simply didn't have a replacement. At times—as when UNC upset No. 6 UConn or No. 10 Duke in Chapel Hill—the Tar Heels would get enough from the team's talented young perimeter players to pull an upset. But this was no longer the team that had looked so good in the preseason NIT.

Surprisingly, the one Tobacco Road team expected to battle physical problems all season turned out to be the most healthy—and the most successful. During the preseason media day in Greensboro, Wake Forest's Prosser had complained his senior star Josh Howard was hobbled by bad knees and might not be able to play. He cited back problems that threatened to sideline Lithuanian big man Vytas Danelius. "Some guys are day to day," Prosser told reporters. "Josh is almost minute to minute."

But when the season opened, both players were not only in the lineup—both were playing well, along with a pair of freshmen who were every bit as good as any of the kids at Duke or Carolina: Eric Williams, a 6-foot-9, 270-pound monster from Wake Forest, the original site of the school he now played for; and Justin Gray, a guard from Charlotte, who had refined his game at Oak Hill Academy in Virginia.

The two pickups indicated that Prosser was following the strategy that Carl Tacy and Dave Odom had used to challenge their more prominent rivals on Tobacco Road. He was beating them to the punch for unheralded Tobacco Road products.

For example, early in the recruiting process, Williams, like most in-state players, was very interested in North Carolina. But Doherty was focused on more prominent national targets and didn't have time for the big kid from rural Wake County. When he did finally make a belated bid to lure Williams, it was too late: Prosser already had him locked up. State was the only other Tobacco Road team to offer Gray. And Chris Paul, a tiny jet of a guard from Winston-Salem, committed to Wake in the fall of 2002 while Doherty was trying to convince him to come to UNC as a walk-on. "Skip had recruited him longer than anybody," Paul's prep coach, David Laton, said.

Although Prosser inherited Josh Howard from Dave Odom, the 6-foot-6 forward from Winston-Salem fit the profile of the prototypical Wake recruit perfectly: an unheralded prospect from Tobacco Road without an offer from

UNC, Duke, or N.C. State. Howard had been a good player for three seasons at Wake; but as a senior, he blossomed into a star—averaging 19.5 points and 8.3 rebounds while playing the best defense in the league. He led Wake Forest, picked sixth in the preseason media poll, to the ACC regular season title and a final No. 8 national ranking.

Unfortunately, the Deacons surprising season fizzled in postseason when Wake Forest was upset in the ACC Tournament semifinals by N.C. State. It was the second season in a row that the Wolfpack had beaten the ACC regular season champ in the ACC semifinals and the third time in Sendek's tenure that he had taken a team to the ACC Tournament championship game.

And for thirty minutes against Duke that Sunday afternoon in Greensboro, it looked like the Wolfpack coach was going to claim his first conference title. The driving force for the Pack's title run was the tandem of Hodge and Josh Powell. It was Powell, a 6-foot-8 Georgia native, who neutralized ACC rookie of the year Chris Bosh in the opening round as State slipped past Georgia Tech. It was Hodge, with thirty-one points and nine rebounds, who rallied the Pack in an 87–83 victory over Wake Forest in the semifinals.

Duke had stumbled into the tournament after losing two of its last three regular season games, including a contentious 82–79 loss to North Carolina in Chapel Hill that featured a shouting match between Doherty and Duke assistant Chris Collins.

When the two rivals squared off again six days later in the ACC Tournament semifinals, Blue Devils assistant coach Johnny Dawkins very clearly refused to shake hands with Doherty during a pregame meeting. The game marked Sean May's first attempt to return from his foot injury, but he was ineffective in ten minutes of action and his presence seemed to disrupt a Tar Heel team that had been playing well. Duke raced to a 54–33 halftime lead and was never threatened en route to a 75–63 victory that pretty well killed UNC's chances of earning an NCAA Tournament bid.

"There is a lot of talk about how good they are going to be and all that," Duke's Casey Sanders said of the Heels. "But we came out and showed we're good now and we just took it to them."

But Duke dropped fifteen points behind N.C. State in the tournament championship game. Along press row, ACC officials were picking up ballots for the all-tournament team. Writers were allowed to vote either/or on the tournament MVP winner, picking the star of each team so that a player for the championship team could be honored as the Case Award winner. With Powell en route to a twenty-six-point game in the finals, he was listed on most ballots as the MVP should State win the title. Daniel Ewing, coming off big games in the first two rounds, was the only Duke player most writers could think of to list in the unlikely event the Blue Devils rallied.

That created a bit of a problem when Duke did rally—solely because freshman J.J. Redick went nuts. The freshman guard scored twenty of his game-high thirty points in the final 10:05 of the championship game, leading Duke from a 55–40 deficit to an 84–77 victory.

"I looked up one time and we were up," State's Marcus Melvin said. "Then I turned around and looked up again after Redick hit about four 3s and went to the free throw line three or four times and 'woosh'—we're down."

Because of the early voting, it was too late to name Redick as the tournament MVP. In fact, so many ballots were turned in before his explosion that the Duke freshman didn't even make the all-tournament team!

The championship was Duke's fifth conference title in a row, and nobody else had ever won more than three in a row. It was also the high point of a season that ended two weeks later with a lackluster loss to Kansas in the NCAA West Regional semifinals.

Nobody on Tobacco Road had much postseason success. Not only did the Deacons flame out in the second round of the NCAA Tournament against Auburn, but N.C. State lost a heartbreaker to California in the first round in Oklahoma City. North Carolina, trying to become the first team to win the preseason NIT and the postseason NIT in the same season, saw that dream end with a quarterfinal loss to Georgetown in the Smith Center.

At least UNC's 19–16 season was a huge improvement on the 8–20 mark the previous year. And with every scholarship player due to return, the embattled Doherty appeared to be secure in his job.

21

THE PRODIGAL SON FINALLY RETURNS

Roy Williams, his tie loosened and his expensive suit soaked with sweat, was sipping a soft drink outside the Kansas dressing room in the New Orleans Superdome when Bonnie Bernstein stuck the microphone in his face.

Just minutes earlier, Syracuse had edged Kansas in the 2003 NCAA championship game. It was the second straight year, and the fourth time in his career, that Williams's Jayhawks had come up short in the Final Four. The disappointed Kansas coach had just met with his team and was now preparing for his obligatory interview with the attractive CBS reporter. Her first questions were about the brilliance of Syracuse freshman Carmelo Anthony and Williams's frustration over his own team's uncharacteristically bad free throw shooting.

When Bernstein asked the Kansas coach the inevitable question about the vacant North Carolina coaching job, Williams gave a vague, diplomatic answer. It was when she followed up by essentially repeating the same question that all the pain and frustration of the night came bubbling up. "I could give a shit about North Carolina right now," Williams announced to a national TV audience.

It was an unfortunate moment. It was also evidence that for the second time in three years, the most successful program on Tobacco Road was stumbling through another awkward coaching transition. As it turned out, North Carolina's 19–16 record with what turned out to be the third youngest team in ACC history was not enough to save Matt Doherty's job. The record may have indicated progress in his third season, but there were issues behind the scenes that doomed the third-year coach.

Dean Smith, exiled to his cubbyhole in the Smith Center basement, re-mained curiously unsupportive. It's not that Smith ever publicly criticized Do-herty, but given several chances to defend the embattled coach, the UNC icon—perhaps still embittered by the fate of his former assistant coaches and Doherty's dismissal of his office staff—pointedly refused to speak on behalf of his former player.

Hints of Doherty's difficulties in dealing with his players had long been a staple of Internet rumors and sports talk radio gossip. Specific instances of Do-herty's behavior occasionally reached the mainstream media, as when the father of UNC transfer Adam Boone blasted the coach for verbally abusing his son. Even more damaging was a comment by Jawad Williams after his freshman sea-son, when he told the student newspaper, "If things don't change around here, I'm leaving."

Doherty vowed to make changes, but as his third season came to a close, rumors began to swirl that his players were threatening to leave en masse. On the very night that Kansas beat Duke in the West Regional semifinals, Baddour met with the UNC players as a group, then began a series of one-on-one inter-views to hear their grievances. That led to a meeting two days later—at the same time as Kansas was upsetting top-seeded Arizona in the West Regional title game—between Baddour and Doherty. Afterward, the UNC athletic di-rector would claim that Doherty offered to resign, while Doherty would tell re-porters that he was told he had two choices: resign or be fired.

"The issue here is not about basketball . . . It's leadership," UNC chancel-lor James Moeser told reporters on Tuesday night, April 1 at a press conference called to announce Doherty's resignation.

The new ex-coach was not present at the Smith Center, but most of the Tar Heel players were. A picture of the team slumped in their chairs and dressed as if about to appear in a rap video, wearing bandanas and turned-around baseball caps and baggy jeans, appeared in most of the newspapers across the state, reinforcing the perception that Doherty was the victim of a re-volt by a group of selfish, vindictive players.

"We get the image of thugs," Jawad Williams complained. "A lot of peo-ple were on the outside looking in. If you were here, you'd understand what a lot of people went through. Not just the players, but a lot of other people too."

The timing could have been better for Williams, who was trying to prepare his Kansas team for the Final Four in New Orleans. He got almost as many questions about the Carolina job as he did about his team's semifinal matchup with Marquette. As the week went on and Baddour remained in Chapel Hill, it became obvious that the Tar Heels were waiting on Williams to complete his season before making a second run at the former UNC assistant coach.

Carolina's interest put Williams in a most awkward position, especially after his promise three years earlier that he would finish his career in Kansas.

But when the Jayhawks returned to Lawrence from New Orleans, Williams admitted to waiting reporters that he had a decision to make. It was a very different decision in many ways than the one he had made three years earlier. The group of players that he loved so much—Gooden, Hinrich, and Collison—had completed their eligibility and were leaving. His good friend Bob Frederick, the man who had taken a chance on the unknown UNC assistant coach fifteen years earlier, had retired as Athletic Director and was replaced by Al Bohl, who had publicly clashed with Williams on a number of occasions.

There was one other thing. "I turned Dean down once," Williams later said. "I couldn't do it again." Instead, he hopped a private plane for the trip halfway across the country, back to Tobacco Road, where he was born and raised.

"I came back because it was the right thing to do," Williams said on the night of April 14, when he was finally introduced as the Tar Heel coach. "Last time, I stayed at Kansas because it was the right thing to do."

UNC's long struggle to bring Williams home was just the latest twist in the battle for supremacy on Tobacco Road. But he still had to prove that he could restore the Carolina program to the greatness that Dean Smith had made the birthright of every member of the Tar Heel nation. And he had to do it with the players recruited by Doherty—the "babies," the "whiners," the "thugs" (terms used in newspaper reports to describe the unhappy Tar Heel players) who had gotten their previous coach fired.

"I will respect you," Williams told his new team at their first meeting. "I expect you to play unbelievably hard and I expect you to be unbelievably unselfish."

Perhaps symbolically, the Carolina players who had shown up at Doherty's dismissal dressed as punks all wore coats and ties and looked like choirboys when Williams was introduced. "This is how we are," point guard Raymond Felton said, pointing to his dark, pin-striped suit. "We have respect for Carolina."

The players expected Williams to teach them how to win. "I feel like we've got the best coach in the world right now and he's going to take us to some pretty high places," center Sean May said. But how long would it take?

Carolina fans were looking for immediate success as the 2003–04 season opened with six straight victories, including an impressive 88–81 win over Illinois in Greensboro. Few listened as Williams complained that his new players were still novices at the defensive end, a message that may have begun to register when the Tar Heels gave up 119 points in a triple overtime loss to Wake Forest in Chapel Hill.

"You don't need to be a nuclear physicist to figure out we need to guard people better," Williams said. "Our kids want to guard, but it's hard work. It takes time to develop the habit of doing that every time."

Prosser had similar complaints about his defense after a game where thirteen players scored in double figures. A year before, the Deacons had been the ACC's best defensive team. But the graduation of Josh Howard, the league's best one-on-one defender, and a back injury that sidelined Vytas Danelius had unhinged the Wake defense. Freshman Chris Paul and sophomore Justin Gray would challenge UNC's Raymond Felton and Rashad McCants as the nation's best backcourt, but defensive problems would limit both teams in one of the strongest, most balanced seasons in ACC history.

"We had so much success early on that I think subconsciously we got into this mindset that we could just outscore guys," Prosser said. "In this league, that's tough to do."

Both UNC and Wake ended up trailing their Tobacco Road rivals in the ACC standings.

Herb Sendek survived the off-season departure of Josh Powell, who unwisely entered the NBA draft and went undrafted. The return of Evtimov, back after missing the 2003 season with a knee injury, and the addition of Turkish guard Engin Atsur gave the Pack a deep, versatile lineup that frustrated ACC foes with a unique, patient offense. The loquacious Hodge continued to amuse fans and provoke opponents with his nonstop repartee. But he also emerged as the league's most complete player and claimed ACC player of the year honors after finishing second in the league in scoring, first in field goal percentage, fourth in free throw percentage, seventh in assists, and ninth in rebounding.

"He is just that one great player who lifts you up a level," Manhattan coach Bobby Gonzales said after losing to Hodge and the Pack. "I think they have some very good pieces, but Julius is what makes them a good team—like Danny Manning at Kansas."

Only Duke managed to finish ahead of N.C. State in the ACC regular season standings, thanks to the best defense in the league. With senior Chris Duhon applying on-the-ball pressure at the point, sophomore Shelden Williams leading the league in blocked shots down low, and junior Daniel Ewing and freshman Luol Deng emerging as two of the best wing defenders in the league, the Blue Devils opened 21–1 and climbed to No. 1 in the nation.

"We want to be a great defensive team," Duke's Duhon said. "Last year our main focus was trying to outscore the other team. This year, we've seen that even when we struggle at the offensive end, our defense has helped us win games."

The Blue Devils temporarily squelched the new challenge coming from Chapel Hill with two memorable victories over the Tar Heels. In the first game at the Smith Center, Rashad McCants hit a three-pointer to tie the game with thirteen seconds left in overtime. But the Tar Heels failed to pick up Duhon on the ensuing inbounds play and the senior playmaker drove the length of the court to score the game-winner on a reverse layup. A month later in Durham, Duke was nursing a three-point lead as McCants drove for a potential game-tying shot. But double-teamed by Duhon and J.J. Redick, the Tar Heel guard lost the ball, then lost the race with Redick to the floor to secure the loose ball. Redick's two free throws gave Duke a 70–65 victory and a sweep of the new Tar Heel coach. "It hurts to lose, but it hurts more because it's Duke," Sean May said. "You're bleeding and you can't stop."

Carolina would make a quick exit from both the ACC and NCAA tournaments, ending the season at 19–11, only slightly better than Doherty's last season. Williams had warned optimistic Tar Heel fans not to expect miracles: "Ol' Roy ain't that good," he said.

The postseason proved equally frustrating at Wake Forest, where the Deacons reached the Sweet 16 before losing to once-beaten St. Joseph's, and at N.C. State, where the Pack collapsed in the final four minutes of a 75–73 loss to Vanderbilt.

Duke came within a couple of plays of greatness but, like N.C. State, couldn't hold a lead. The Blue Devils blew a twelve-point lead over Maryland with five minutes left in the ACC title game, and they lost in overtime. And Krzyzewski's team led UConn most of the way in the NCAA semifinals in San Antonio before watching an eight-point lead disappear in the final three minutes of a 79–78 loss. "We were so close . . . It just kind of slipped out of our fingers," Shavlik Randolph said.

The Blue Devils could only watch in frustration as UConn defeated Georgia Tech (a team Duke had beaten in two of three matchups) in the title game. Still, Krzyzewski left San Antonio convinced that he would have one of his best teams in 2005. His Super Six, down to five after the transfer of Michael Thompson, would be juniors. The reliable Ewing would be back to provide senior leadership. Deng had the potential to become the best player in college basketball as a sophomore. And Shaun Livingston, a bona fide 6-foot-7 playmaking prospect from Illinois, was coming to replace Duhon at the point.

Unfortunately for the Blue Devils, both Deng and Livingston surprised him by deciding to turn pro. It was hard to argue with their decisions (both went in the top seven in the NBA draft). But the unexpected departure of two key players put Krzyzewski in an awkward position heading into the 2004–05 season.

Coach K almost left the problem for someone else to solve.

His temptation stemmed from events in the NBA. After losing to the Detroit Pistons in the 2004 NBA finals, Phil Jackson resigned as head coach of the Los Angeles Lakers. General manager Mitch Kupchak, the former Carolina center, was scouring the basketball world, looking for a replacement. He first asked UNC head coach Roy Williams if he'd be interested in talking about the job. Williams, who had seriously considered the Lakers almost a decade earlier, told Kupchak that he was committed to rebuilding the Carolina program.

Kupchak, who had called Krzyzewski to discuss draft prospects, casually asked the Duke coach if he'd be interested in talking about the Laker job. Coach K—who had given the NBA serious consideration when the Boston Celtics called in 1990, and again when the Portland Trail Blazers offered big money in 1994—had told local reporters he was no longer interested in the NBA. But in June of 2004, the Duke coach surprised Kupchak by telling him that he would like to talk about replacing Jackson.

"Usually, somewhere along the end of the season, you take inventory of who you are, where you're at, and what you're going to do," Krzyzewski explained. "I talked to Mitch Kupchak and he started talking about this. It came at a time when I was taking inventory. I said, 'I'm fifty-seven, maybe I should just look.' As it went on, I took a closer and closer look."

When the news that Krzyzewski was meeting with Laker officials leaked over the Fourth of July weekend, the fireworks that exploded over Tobacco Road had nothing to do with Independence Day. Cynics noted that Duke had a new president and that ten years earlier, Krzyzewski had used his flirtation with the Trail Blazers to bring Duke President Nan Keohane to heel. Was he doing the same to new president Richard Brodhead?

Krzyzewski made the Lakers—and the Duke basketball nation—sweat over the holiday weekend before calling a press conference to announce his decision to stay at Duke. "The allure of coaching in college has no price . . . it's just one of those priceless things," Krzyzewski said. "I've never made a decision based on what was going to make me the most money. To me, it's what's going to give me the most happiness. And I've been really happy at Duke and fulfilled at Duke."

Members of the ABD Club were quick to label the entire episode as a grandstand play, designed to enhance the stature of the Blue Devil coach. Not coincidentally, Krzyzewski used the summer and the early fall that followed to line up the nation's top-rated recruiting class—the fourth time since getting Brand, Battier, and company in 1997 that his class was rated the best in the country.

But the newcomers wouldn't help the undermanned Blue Devils in 2004–05. Without Deng and Livingston, Duke appeared to be a step behind Tobacco Road rivals UNC and Wake Forest in the talent department—not to mention Georgia Tech, which returned six seniors off its 2004 NCAA runner-up team. The ACC was so loaded that at one point early in the season, four league teams were ranked in the top 10—including three of the four members of Tobacco Road—and N.C. State peaked at No. 12 in the nation.

"We could have as many teams that could vie for the national title as we've ever had," Duke's Krzyzewski said. "Talent-wise, our league is the most talented league in the country. There's no question about that."

And the preseason consensus was that North Carolina owned the most talent in the powerful league. For Roy Williams, his second season would be the real test of just how good "Ol' Roy" was. He returned a group of juniors and seniors that could match anybody in college basketball at the offensive end. Could he teach them the defense and cohesiveness that had characterized his teams at Kansas?

The Tar Heel coach, like Krzyzewski, had his off-season disappointments. Prize recruit JamesOn Curry, a slender guard from Burlington, North Carolina, was caught selling narcotics in a police drug sting. When Curry pled guilty to a felony, UNC refused him admission. Another heralded recruit, New Jersey swing man J.R. Smith, elected to jump straight to the NBA and was picked No. 18 in the first round by the New Orleans Jazz.

Pro scouts suggested that Marvin Williams, a versatile 6-foot-8 forward from Bremerton, Washington, would have gone in the top 10, but unlike Smith and Duke's Livingston, Williams elected to delay the NBA and attend college. His addition to the UNC roster was very good news—but not the best news Roy Williams received in the off-season. Even better were the reports that the Tar Heel coach was hearing about how Sean May was remaking his body. The gifted big man had long been limited by his bulk and his lack of stamina. Heading into his junior season, May was determined to change that.

"I never had to work that hard in high school," May said. "I really didn't understand what it took. After my [sophomore] season, I went to my strength coach and talked about a plan. I'd come in at 7 and go run and work out for about forty-five minutes on the track. Then I'd go to class and come back and lift with the team. I was only playing pickup once or twice a week. I was concentrating on my diet and running on the track."

May's dedication to his off-season workout regimen was a sign that UNC's players were listening to what Williams was trying so hard to teach them. But as the new season approached, there were also signs that they still had lessons to learn. Point guard Raymond Felton played in a summer league game that he thought was sanctioned. But he was wrong, and by not checking with UNC's compliance officer, as Williams had warned his players to do, Felton drew a one-game suspension from the NCAA.

Even worse from Williams's point of view were the words Rashad McCants used to describe his Carolina experience in a TV interview he gave at the opening of practice. "It's like being in jail," he said. "You're not allowed to do certain things. You're not allowed to say certain things, but once you get out of jail, you're free. I'm in my sentence and I'm doing my time."

Roy Williams was incensed at McCants's comment, which was the latest in a series of awkward encounters between the outspoken guard and the media. Earlier in the summer, during trials for a U.S. international team, McCants shared the backcourt with Wake Forest's Chris Paul. After one session, he told reporters that Paul was the best point guard he'd ever played with—a clear slap at teammate Raymond Felton.

The ABC brigade got even more reason to laugh at the Tar Heels when the season opened. North Carolina, headed for Hawaii and an appearance in the Maui Invitational Tournament, actually opened the season en route, stopping off in Oakland to face Santa Clara. Playing without Felton, the debut was a disaster. The Tar Heels fell apart in a 77–66 loss to the unranked Broncos.

"I've got to do a heck of a lot better job than this," UNC's Williams said. "Ticked off is what I am, but I'm ticked off at myself, not the kids."

But the questions that suddenly swirled around the Carolina program were blown away as Felton returned to the lineup in Hawaii and the Tar Heels routed Brigham Young, Tennessee, and Iowa on successive nights. The big three of Felton at the point, May in the middle, and McCants on the wing were getting strong support from freshman Marvin Williams off the bench and from veterans Jackie Manuel, Jawad Williams, and David Noel, who were content to sacrifice their offensive games to become role players on a team that looked increasingly like a real national championship contender.

For once, the big challenge to the Tar Heels didn't come from Durham, where a succession of injuries and illness and complicated Mike Krzyzewski's rebuilding efforts, but from Wake Forest, where the Deacons had climbed to No. 1 in the national rankings for the first time in the school's history. Despite an early loss to unbeaten Illinois, Prosser's talented team opened 15–1 and won the first big showdown on Tobacco Road, knocking off the Tar Heels 95–82 in Winston-Salem as Paul (twenty-six points, eight assists) outplayed Felton (sixteen points, five assists).

The loss at Wake didn't hurt the Tar Heels nearly as much as their visit to Durham three weeks later. Krzyzewski had worked miracles with a team staggered by a long list of physical problems and guided the crippled Blue Devils to fifteen straight wins to open the season. However, that success came against a fairly weak nonconference schedule, so even though the records were similar when No. 2 ranked North Carolina (19–2) took on No. 7 ranked Duke (17–2) in Cameron, the game was considered anything but an even match. This was a game the Tar Heel nation expected to win after enduring six seasons of Blue Devil domination.

"Whoa, whoa, whoa!" Roy Williams responded when asked about such expectations. "Nobody is a favorite going into Cameron Indoor Stadium. Give me a break. Nobody will ever be a favorite going to play Duke at Duke."

For Williams, it was a game he needed to win to get over the same hump that Frank McGuire once faced against Everett Case, that Vic Bubas faced against McGuire, that Dean Smith faced against Bubas, and that Norm Sloan, Jim Valvano, Mike Kzyzewski, and so many other coaches faced against Smith.

But the victory didn't come, despite a superb game by May, who had twenty-three points and eighteen rebounds against the nation's best post defender. Unfortunately, he was the only player effective against Duke's Shelden Williams, who had five blocked shots and five steals, while altering or intimidating at least another half-dozen Tar Heel shots. Duke forced twenty-three Carolina turnovers—including one on the last play of the game as the Tar Heels tried to get up a game-winning shot. Down 71–70, Felton appeared to have a lane to the basket when Duke's Daniel Ewing gambled on a steal. Instead of driving, the Tar Heel point guard elected to run the play Williams had called in the huddle. Duke's J.J. Redick, anticipating the Tar Heel design, denied the crucial pass to McCants on the wing—for the second year in a row making a key defensive play against the Tar Heels. Felton, who had picked up his dribble prematurely, tried to feed David Noel on the other wing, but the defensive specialist fumbled the ball and kicked it out of bounds.

As the Cameron Crazies celebrated around them, Felton and McCants stood inches apart, their faces a mask of rage and frustration. "We played so bad," McCants said. "It's gotta be the worst game we've ever played . . . even worse than Santa Clara. And we almost won."

But "almost" doesn't count on Tobacco Road. The defeat in Durham hung like a dark cloud over what was shaping up to be a great season for the Tar Heels. That's why it was so important for North Carolina when Duke came to Chapel Hill for the final day of the regular season. The Tar Heels had won six straight games since the loss in Cameron to clinch a share of the regular season title. But it would be an empty championship if Carolina couldn't break through against the Blue Devils.

"It's crazy how much people get into it," UNC's May said before the Duke game. "Just walking around town this week, this is some people's national championship."

The outcome of the regular season's two dramatic Sunday games, related earlier in the Prologue, was not the end of the season's story. As always, the triumphs and tragedies of the regular season would be overshadowed by postseason play. The four Tobacco Road rivals had driven each other to such heights that the definitive test of any team was not a fast start in November and December or even a head-to-head matchup in January or February. Now superiority was determined in March—when the "official" ACC championship was decided by the league's postseason tournament, and beyond that, in NCAA play, where a national championship was the ultimate trump card.

For instance, N.C. State—so disappointed to lose that regular season finale to Wake Forest—got its revenge five days later, when the Pack knocked the Deacons out of the ACC Tournament at the MCI Center in Washington, D.C. Chris Paul sat on the bench in street clothes, serving a one-game suspension for his low blow against Julius Hodge.

Wake Forest, missing the talented playmaker, had more turnovers than assists. "We had players in there capable of winning the game, so I'm not going to sit here and talk about who didn't play," Prosser said.

Hodge had little to say about his absent assailant, for once refusing to engage in a verbal sparring match. "This was all about focusing on trying to win, not about anyone else," he said. "I'm a motivated person and my teammates feed off that. We wanted to play this one the right way, the classy way."

Duke, forced to watch UNC cut down the nets that Sunday night in the Smith Center, watched the Tar Heels fizzle a week later in the MCI Center. Williams's top-seeded team barely survived a quarterfinal matchup with Clemson, then fell in the semifinals to Georgia Tech.

"There are three parts to our season and I think we forgot about the middle part—the ACC Tournament," Roy Williams said. "Maybe some guys were looking ahead."

While the Tar Heels were already turning their attention to the NCAA Tournament, Duke took advantage of its good fortune to claim its sixth ACC championship in seven years. It wasn't easy. The Blue Devils needed thirty-five points from Redick to edge N.C. State in the semifinals. Krzyzewski's team couldn't celebrate a title-game victory over Georgia Tech until Shelden Williams tipped in freshman David McClure's missed free throw with one second left to give Krzyzewski his ninth ACC title.

"I am astounded that we're ACC champions," the Duke coach said. "We needed a lot of heart to win. I'm so proud of my team, not just for this game, but for the entire season. They have found ways to win."

Duke's ACC Tournament victory put the onus of the rivalry back on North Carolina. If the Tar Heels wanted to end the Blue Devil reign as the king of Tobacco Road, they would have to go further than the Blue Devils in NCAA play—something that hadn't happened since Guthridge's 2000 team had gone on its wild postseason ride.

Adding to the drama, the NCAA selection committee made both Duke and UNC No. 1 seeds. Under the tournament's new pod system, the committee sent both to Charlotte for two games. Wake Forest, which had been expecting a No. 1 seed and a spot in Charlotte, found itself sent to Cleveland as a No. 2 seed. N.C. State, just happy to get a bid, was not complaining about its trip to dreary Worcester, Massachusetts, even if it did present the daunting prospect of matchups there with UNC Charlotte and potentially powerful Connecticut. "Just playing in the NCAAs four straight years—that hasn't happened for awhile," State's Ilian Evtimov said.

The real show was in Charlotte, where Duke and North Carolina found themselves sharing the familiar Charlotte Coliseum. Tar Heel fans, long expecting to land in the Queen City, had bought up most of the tickets, leaving the outnumbered Blue Devils feeling like aliens in their own state.

"There were not as many Duke people here as we would have thought," Duke's Shavlik Randolph said after hearing the hostile reception during the open pregame practices. "It was a little surprising when we came out. I was expecting to hear more cheers. When I walked in and saw all the Carolina Blue . . . there are a lot of people out there who want us to lose."

Krzyzewski tried to make light of the hostile crowd. "I've been in places where every person in the place was booing me," he said, "then I walked out of my house."

It wasn't just the crowd at the Coliseum. Charlotte, the largest city on Tobacco Road, has always been a Tar Heel town at heart. The Blue Devils found that out the night before their opening game, when they were heckled as they entered a ritzy restaurant for dinner. The next morning, a waitress serving the team breakfast also expressed anti-Duke sentiments. The Blue Devils might have been better off in Nashville or Cleveland or even Boise, Idaho. The hostile crowds at the Coliseum gave Delaware State loud moral support as the No. 16 seed led the Blue Devils early. That was in sharp contrast to the overwhelming support that the crowds gave UNC as the Tar Heels rolled to an easy victory over Oakland (Mich.).

Tobacco Road's two most prominent programs were favored to win second-round NCAA games in the same building. Sound familiar? The situation evoked memories of Black Sunday in 1979, when Penn upset UNC and St. John's knocked off favored Duke in Reynolds Coliseum.

But there was no such nightmare in Charlotte. North Carolina absolutely destroyed Iowa State to advance to the Sweet 16, while Duke overcame Mississippi State after a much tougher battle. Shelden Williams had thirteen points and fifteen rebounds in the 63–55 win and contributed two key blocked shots in the closing minute.

"I'm telling you, I feel honored to win this game," Krzyzewski said. "I've been in a number of second-round games, but this was as tough as any. Boy, we feel fortunate to win."

By winning, Krzyzewski passed former UNC coach Dean Smith as the winningest coach in NCAA Tournament history. The Mississippi State victory was his sixty-sixth NCAA win, one more than Smith's sixty-five. It also propelled Duke into the Sweet 16 for the eighth straight time. North Carolina was back in the regional semifinals for the first time since 2000. The two powers were joined in the Sweet 16 by N.C. State—which fought off UNC Charlotte in the opener in Worcester, then overcame defending national champion Connecticut in the second round.

"This game is about pride, respect, and a little payback," Hodge said.

The Wolfpack star not only got a chance to pay Connecticut back for that controversial 2002 loss: he also got to make the winning play against Ed Nelson, the player who beat him out for the ACC rookie of the year award that season. Nelson, who started his college career at Georgia Tech, tried to cut off Hodge after Charlie Villanueva tied the game with fifteen seconds left.

"I saw Ed Nelson and he thought I was going to kick it back out," Hodge said. "He hesitated and I just tried to draw contact and make a big time play."

The result was a moment that looked very much like the Rosenbluth–Wendell Carr collision in 1957: Hodge's shot went in and Nelson was called for the foul. His free throw sent N.C. State into the Sweet 16 for the first time since 1989.

"Oh man, oh man," Hodge told reporters. "I've been trying to cry for the last couple of minutes but I can't. I want some tears or something."

Surprisingly, the one Tobacco Road team that didn't survive the first weekend of the NCAA Tournament was Wake Forest, which beat Chattanooga in the first round to equal the school record with twenty-seven victories. But defensive shortcomings again doomed the Deacons in a 111–105 double overtime loss to West Virginia. Despite the surprising elimination of the Deacons, three Tobacco Road teams were left in the tournament—creating an eye-opening moment at the Raleigh-Durham Airport.

"When we were leaving to come to Austin [Texas], there were three chartered jets all waiting at the Raleigh-Durham Airport with three teams all leaving at the same time," Duke's Krzyzewski said. "It was like we were all deploying to our areas of competition. All of a sudden I'm looking and I'm thinking, 'This probably hasn't happened before.'"

Only one of the three Triangle teams would survive Friday night's regional semifinals. Duke and N.C. State were eliminated at almost the same moment: the Blue Devils were losing to Michigan State in Austin, Texas, while the Wolfpack was falling to Wisconsin in Syracuse, New York. North Carolina played the second game in the Carrier Dome, barely surviving a late rally by Villanova to avoid creating a "Black Friday" on Tobacco Road. Two days later, the Tar Heels pulled away from Wisconsin in the second half to earn a trip to the Final Four in St. Louis. It marked the eighteenth time in the twenty-five years since the NCAA expanded its field that at least one team from Tobacco Road had reached the NCAA semifinals. UNC was looking to give the region its ninth national title.

When North Carolina checked into their hotel in St. Louis, the Tar Heels were surprised to find a contingent of Blue Devils waiting for them. J.J. Redick, in town for the Rupp Award ceremonies, and Daniel Ewing, on hand to play in the NABC All-Star Game, were waiting in the lobby along with Duke Sports Information Director Jon Jackson. Roy Williams was surprised—and a little skeptical—when Redick shook his hand and said, "I'll be pulling for you guys."

A lot of coaches were pulling for the popular Williams in St. Louis, hoping he would escape the title of the Best Coach to Never Win a National Title. This was his fifth trip to the Final Four—putting him in a class with his mentor Dean Smith, who came up empty six times before finally winning his first title in New Orleans, and with his rival Mike Krzyzewski, who missed four times before winning in his fifth try Indianapolis.

Smith tried to watch UNC's semifinal game against Michigan State from the stands at the Edward R. Jones Dome, but the familiar coach was so besieged by autograph seekers that he had to retire to a private box. He watched as UNC started with another frigid Final Four shooting performance. Senior Jawad Williams, a former prep All-American who had been overshadowed for the last three years by his younger teammates, ignited a dramatic turnaround to open the second half as UNC hit sixteen of its first twenty-three shots to blow the game open. Williams, easily the most obscure of the three UNC Williamses (after Coach Roy and freshman phenom Marvin) finished with twenty points as the Heels coasted to an 87–71 victory.

Dean Smith tried to visit the Carolina locker room to congratulate his protégé on his victory, but he found his way blocked by a security guard who refused to let the Tar Heel legend past. Smith would be better prepared on Monday night.

The championship game between once-beaten No. 1 Illinois and No. 2 North Carolina appeared to match the nation's two best teams (and it was the first No. 1 vs. No. 2 matchup in the title game since No. 1 UCLA beat No. 2 Kentucky in 1975). But there was another view of the title game: that it matched the nation's most *talented* team (North Carolina) against the nation's best *team* (Illinois).

"Hearing that really makes me upset," UNC's Felton said. "They have a talented team; we have a talented team. But to have someone say they play together better as a team, that makes me upset because we haven't won thirty-two games on talent alone."

Perhaps the most inspired player on either team was UNC big man Sean May, who was hoping to duplicate his father's title game performance from 1976. The former Indiana All-American scored twenty-six points and pulled down eight rebounds to help Indiana knock off Michigan in Philadelphia. On the night before the younger May took on Illinois, he showed his teammates a videotape of his father's championship game.

"It was a Christmas present," Sean May said. "It was hilarious, just watching [my father] after the game, talking and jumping around and wearing those tight little shorts. I had never seen it before. I didn't know there was a copy. I didn't know they had TV back then."

May celebrated his twenty-first birthday that Monday night by almost exactly duplicating his father's stat line with twenty-six points and ten rebounds against Illinois. He helped UNC build a fifteen-point second-half lead in the title game—but it took a dramatic tip-in of a McCants miss by freshman Marvin Williams to squelch a late rally by the Illini and help the Tar Heels hold on for a 75–70 victory. "We did it together and we got it done for Coach Williams," May said.

This time, Dean Smith had no problem joining the Tar Heel celebration. Not only did he have the proper pass, but he was accompanied by Michael Jordan, whose celebrity opened all doors. The former Tar Heel star hugged the assistant who had befriended him almost a quarter century before. It was the first of many heartfelt congratulations that Roy Williams would receive in the coming days. He and his triumphant team were greeted by 13,000 fans when they returned to Chapel Hill. The Tar Heel faithful cheered their fourth national title (their fifth if you count the 1924 Helms championship, which all true Carolina fans do).

Even more than the NCAA trophy, Carolina's fans cheered UNC's return to the top of Tobacco Road. After six years of Duke dominance, the Tar Heels were once again the best program in the best college basketball state in the country.

At least until the next season.

AFTERWORD

LIFE GOES ON, ESPECIALLY ON TOBACCO ROAD.

Less than a month after UNC's triumphant return from St. Louis, Roy Williams sat on a podium at the Smith Center and watched three of his star underclassmen announce their decision to turn pro. It was really four: the always mercurial Rashad McCants had staged his own announcement a week earlier. Later in the summer, the four UNC underclassmen would all go in the top fourteen picks of the NBA draft, precisely matching the draft record Duke set after the 1999 season.

The Blue Devils had recovered from that exodus to win a national championship two years later. Would Roy Williams be able to rebuild his program so quickly? Or would his Tobacco Road neighbors feast on the carcass of Carolina's suddenly depleted roster?

As the 2005–06 season approached, Duke appeared to be positioned to regain supremacy on Tobacco Road. All-Americans J.J. Redick and Shelden Williams resisted the urge to join the Carolina quartet in the NBA draft. In fact, Williams—projected as a potential lottery pick if he had come out—cited UNC's 2005 success as a reason to stay at Duke: "We have a good chance of doing some of the same things that Carolina did," the Duke standout said. "I think we have a chance to do something special."

Wake Forest's Skip Prosser lost Chris Paul to the draft, but the Deacons got lucky when big man Eric Williams withdrew his name from the NBA draft list. The combination of Williams down low and senior Justin Gray on the perimeter left Wake Forest with enough weapons to be formidable again. N.C. State lost senior Julius Hodge, but Herb Sendek still retained one of the most experienced teams in the ACC, including fifth-year senior Ilian Evtimov.

The rivalries will continue, as white-hot as ever. Duke and Carolina, Wake and State, Wake and Carolina, State and Duke: every Tobacco Road matchup, in any combination, echoes the drama of ancient heroes—from the Gray Fox to McGuire, from the Hoosier Hotshots to "Four Catholics and a Jew," from Bones and Chappell to Bubas and Heyman, from Smith and Charlie "Charles" Scott to Stormin' Norman and David, from Jimmy V and his 1983 Cardiac Pack to Coach K and his back-to-back triumphs to Ol' Roy and yesterday's championship.

It's Tobacco Road, where basketball is king and the battle for supremacy never ends.

BIBLIOGRAPHY

Books

Feinstein, John, *Forever's Team,* Villard Books, New York, 1989

Golenbock, Peter, *Personal Fouls,* Carroll & Graf Publishers, New York, 1989

Jacobs, Barry, *Three Paths to Glory,* MacMillan Publishing Company, New York, 1993

Krzyzewski, Mike (with Donald Phillips), *Five-Point Play,* Warner Books, New York, 2001

Menzer, Joe, *Four Corners,* Simon and Schuster, New York, 1999

Morris, Ron, *ACC Basketball, An Illustrated History,* Four Corners Press, Chapel Hill, 1988

Peeler, Tim, *The Legends of N.C. State Basketball,* Sports Publishing LLC, Champaign, Ill., 2004

Sloan, Norman (with Larry Guest), *Confessions of a Coach,* Rutledge Hill Press, Nashville, Tn., 1991

Smith, Dean (with John Kilgo and Sally Jenkins), *A Coach's Life,* Random House, New York, 2000

Thompson, David (with Sean Stormes and Marshall Terrill), *Skywalker,* Sports Publishing LLC, Champaign, Ill., 2003

Valvano, Jim (with Curry Kirkpatrick), *Valvano: They Gave Me a Lifetime Contract and Then They Declared Me Dead,* Pocket Books, New York, 1991

Weiss, Dick, *True Blue,* Sports Publishing LLC, Champaign, Ill., 2005

Newspapers

Atlanta Journal-Constitution
Charlotte Observer
Charlotte News
Durham *Herald-Sun*
Durham Morning Herald
Durham Sun
Greensboro Daily News
Greensboro *News-Record*
Raleigh *News & Observer*
Raleigh Times
Richmond News-Leader
Winston-Salem Journal

ABOUT THE AUTHOR

ALWYN FEATHERSTON is a Durham native and a 1973 graduate of Duke University, and he has covered ACC basketball since 1970. He joined the *Durham Sun* in 1974 and he served as the UNC, Duke, and N.C. State beat writer for the *Herald-Sun* until 2005. He now works as a freelance writer in the Durham area. He has won a number of awards for his writing, including the 2001 National Association of Sports Writers first-place award for game coverage and four North Carolina Press Association Awards. Featherston is the author of *Saving the Breakout: The 30th Division's Heroic Stand at Mortain, August 7–12, 1944* (Presidio Press, 1993).

INDEX